D0151578

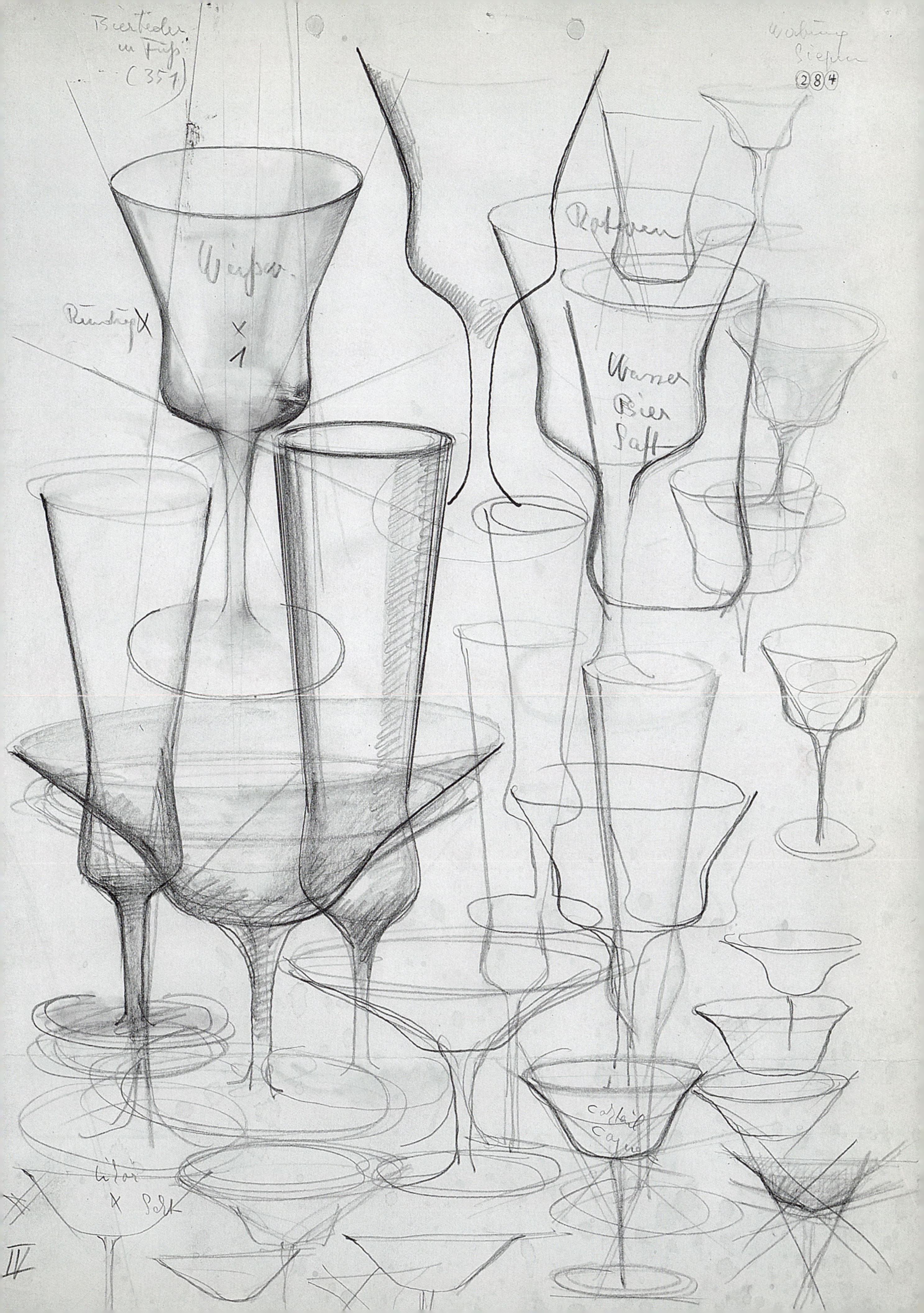

(351)
284
Rotwein
Warmes
Bier
Saft
IV

Wilhelm Wagenfeld (1900–1990)

Wilhelm Wagenfeld (1900–1990)

Edited by Beate Manske
on behalf of The Wilhelm Wagenfeld Stiftung,
Bremen

Hatje Cantz Publishers

Thanks for kind support, to

Erika Wagenfeld

Securitas Versicherungen

Catalogue to accompany the exhibition
"100 Years of Wilhelm Wagenfeld"
at Wilhelm Wagenfeld Haus, Bremen
31 May to 31 October 2000

Editor: Beate Manske on behalf of Wilhelm Wagenfeld Stiftung, Bremen
Idea and Editing: Beate Manske
Assistance: Kathrin Hager
Translations and Copy Editing: Janet Brümmer, Helen Nurse, Stephen Reader
Design: Büro Brückner + Partner, Bremen
Layout: Christine Müller

Typesetting: Weyhing digital, Ostfildern-Ruit
Set in Berthold Akzidenz Grotesk
Reproductions: Repromayer, Reutlingen
Production:
Dr. Cantz'sche Druckerei, Ostfildern-Ruit

The translators wish to thank Dr. Helmut Ricke, Director of the Kunstmuseum Düsseldorf and Glasmuseum Hentrich for his kind and speedy help on the glassmaking terms; and Ute Barba of Hatje Cantz Publishers for her encouragement, cheer and co-ordinating resilience; and Leo. J. B., H. N., S. R.; and Charlie

Front cover illustration: *Max* salt shaker, WMF/Geislingen, 1952/54, photo: Fliegner, Bremen
Back cover illustration: *Max* + *Moritz* salt/pepper shakers, pepper mill, WMF/Geislingen, 1952/54
Front end paper: *Camillo* glass service, drawing for WMF/Geislingen, 4 April 1951
Glasses with cut stem, drawing for WMF/Geislingen, 1951
Frontispiece: Wilhelm Wagenfeld at the Hochschule für bildende Künste, Hamburg, 1961, photo: Ulrich Mack
Back end paper: Spirits bottle, drawing for Bado/Säckingen, 7 May 1967
Form 3600 cutlery, drawing for WMF/Geislingen, February 1951

Published by
Hatje Cantz Publishers
Senefelderstraße 12
D-73760 Ostfildern-Ruit
T. 00 49 / (0) 7 11 / 4 40 50
F. 00 49 / (0) 7 11 / 4 40 52 20
Internet: www.hatjecantz.de

Distribution in the US
DAP, Distributed Art Publishers
155 Avenue of the Americas, Second Floor
New York, NY 10013
T. 001-212-6271999
F. 001-212-6279484

ISBN 3-7757-0885-5 (German edition)
ISBN 3-7757-0886-3 (English edition)
Printed in Germany

Contents

"Redefining the Weight of Things"
The Hundredth Anniversary of Wilhelm Wagenfeld's Birth

Tilmann Buddensieg

The centenary of the birth of a great artistic designer personality of the extraordinary stature of Wilhelm Wagenfeld – he was born in 1900 at the height of the "Jugendstil" period – is a good opportunity to look back upon his life's work. His immortal, timeless creations of simple objects for everyday use played a dominating role in the product culture of the middle fifty years of the twentieth century. We are thus confronted by the fundamental achievement of the objects and appliances he designed, not to mention the even vaster œuvre of "projects, projects, designs and designs for every imaginable thing".[1]

It is therefore easy to understand why the idea of retaining the influence of these works for the future concerns us. We are confronted by the "question of the relevance of Wilhelm Wagenfeld's work to modern product design", as posed by Kurt Nemitz.[2] The still "contemporary and timeless designs", the major role Wagenfeld has played in product design of the modern era since the Werkbund, the Bauhaus and the new beginning after 1945 represent for most of his admirers an obvious legacy for the future – despite the general consciousness of a "fundamental change of values", an often deplored "lack of innovation" and "short-lived sensationalism".[3] Can we really proceed on the assumption of the continuing timelessness of Wilhelm Wagenfeld's work? And will this optimistic hope for continuity do justice to the high historical status of Wilhelm Wagenfeld? Ultimately, it is doubtless the longevity and the timelessness of Wagenfeld's products that places them worlds away from today's zeitgeist-kowtowing products. Should his work not be liberated from strict pigeon-holing as design history only, and our perception rather be opened up to include Wagenfeld's admiration of the pitchers, teapots, bottles and bowls of East Asian cultures, of vessels of Greek and Roman origin, and of cups and tankards from the middle ages and the baroque period? We should, like Klaus Lehmann, inquire into the wealth of "potential in terms of the history of ideas"[4] contained in his works and also in his as yet unpublished and uncollected writings; but that implies a project far larger than this brief introduction.

My doubts about the continuum prevail and are corroborated by the artist's own manifest awareness, having been appointed to the WMF (Württembergische Metallwarenfabrik) since the 1950s, of the many difficulties then obstructing his work. His notes from these years speak an eloquent language: "[...] more drawings [...]. Nothing implemented, constant 'ifs and buts'. Everything that appears important to me is rejected."[5] In a letter to the sympathetic American sales representative Gordon F. Fraser on 14 January 1952, he wrote: "You cannot believe, could scarcely believe, how lonely my work in Geislingen often is, when everything I do is criticised, and nothing or almost nothing is carried out, while the folders are full to bursting with objects finalised to the last detail [...]."[6]

"One of Wagenfeld's most painful experiences came when WMF [...] terminated his contract at the end of the year [1966]. [...] an almost entirely new board of directors [had] introduced radical changes to the product line. The collaboration between the WMF and Wagenfeld was practically at an end."[7] It must have been particularly galling for him that the company should then have sought to reach a supposedly larger target group of consumers with Wagenfeld design in the shape of "more instantly appealing and cheaper look-alikes".[8] Thus all his attempts to replace "the conventional and disappointing" aspects of production in a manufacturing company bit by bit with "something better",[9] had failed. "The design and utilitarian quality" of his "designs which were the result of a series of developmental processes"[10] were exposed to the cheap competition of "surreptitious variations of my work" in keeping with the "'public taste' of the retailers and sales representatives"[11] In 1970 the trade journal of the WMF printed the phrase: "An end to the mustiness of the fifties!" As a result, a large number of

Wagenfeld's designs were removed from the programme – a great disappointment for him, which he sarcastically shook off, renouncing the company as a "pack of mean-spirited fellows".[12]

These very personal memories of a working relationship at once successful and full of conflict, with a major industrial concern, make for some highly revealing art history. Even the fainthearted and unsuccessful attempts to re-issue some "classical" designs of Wagenfeld's in very limited production runs merely reaffirmed the ruthless assertion of the end of an era. Wilhelm Wagenfeld left behind him the vacuum a great talent leaves in the midst of a sophisticated and economical world of products for everyday use. The forsaking only shows the special merits of an achievement the dimensions of which – especially with respect to the simple creations – no longer fit into today's value system. The problem is not that they are submerged in it, unrecognised, but rather that they go beyond its scope.

It was Hegel who discerned the departure from the arts, in particular literature, and its irrevocable demise in the "romantic genre": "The praise sung [...] of these subjects, divers ways of contemplating and comprehending [...] has been sung to exhaustion."[13] But according to Hegel, this was also the prerequisite for bringing back the great creations of the past "into the hearts of the people" "to the living present" – the only "fresh" medium there was.

It is only once the end of the continuum of Wagenfeld's influence on today's debate on design has been reached that his works can be elevated into the patrimony of history. His "ways of contemplating and comprehending" things were always pronounced; now they are explicit in a double sense: said, and done.

The cheap adaptations of Wagenfeld's profoundly considered designs that he observed coming from his workplace in the 1950s[14] were just the prelude to today's almost completely market-controlling process of slurring and slightly modifying artistically superior designs for mass consumption. IKEA, the major Scandinavian concern which has been selling its products on the German market since 1974, has cleverly made billions on this concept, subtly erasing the demarcation between good and not only bad design and copies, but also better, original and new products. Rather than wasting money, brains and time to achieve Wagenfeld's utopia of unmistakability for the brand, consumers' middle-class desire for durability, fine materials, originality of design and visible value is undermined, cheated and given back to them tongue-in-cheek via the dumping-brew of price, material and processing. In this way, the vast potential of industrially produced consumer goods has been diluted into a vaster insipidness, and abandoned to stylish, ever new and inconsequential adaptation by talented designers. This mass market avoids too close a proximity to kitsch and to "cold" metal, keeps its distance from expensive and authentic materials – with the exception of knotted pine. The trend has yet to strike upon the historicism of the lion's paw.

The only niche for good design, for those willing to pay the price and apart from genuine antiques and exacting reproductions of modern classics, is for exclusive, locally exalted Milanese creations. For Wilhelm Wagenfeld it was already obvious in the 1960s and 1970s whence the real threat to the minimalism of good and cheap products would come – from what was to be the considerable market sector of the new rich.

Wagenfeld opposed the hollow totality of mass production, geared to satisfy any and every taste, with the universality of good design for the satisfying and civilising use of the right objects. His bowls and vases, glasses and containers, his cutlery and dishes all communicate their power, even across an inherited oak table or a commonplace ambience. This universality aimed at the "most far-reaching effect possible on the overall production" of a large company such as WMF. Wagenfeld, according to WMF's managing director Arthur Burkhardt[15] "goes all out and to the end" – in fond memory of the all-embracing design brief he had received from Karl Mey, a former pupil of Emil Rathenau's and supervisory board chairman of the Lausitzer Glassworks at Weisswasser. For, Wilhelm Wagenfeld was never really concerned with the individual product, finished to perfection of whatever kind, but rather its complementary utility and design in a series of products.

How very many extraordinary sets of glasses he succeeded in producing between the *Oberweimar* service dating from the year 1935 in Weisswasser, and the year 1963 at WMF! How short-lived their production, and how persistent the desire to use them! – Since the 1960s I have drunk from no other glasses than those of Wilhelm Wagenfeld, preferably from the *Lobenstein* service from the Lausitzer Glassworks, of 1937. Drinking from the red wine goblet, 150 millimetres high with an infinite opening of 125 millimetres across, is almost a cult experience. Today, with production ceased, their increasing scarcity and irreplaceability make their daily use – which was what they were made for – an impossibility.

Like the works of many other great designers of our century, with Carl-Wolfgang Schümann's Cologne catalogue from 1973 as a guiding hand it has been possible to collect the entire works from flea markets. I use the Wagenfeld cutlery from WMF on a daily basis and as well to serve my guests, accompanied by my *Urbino* service from the Königliche Porzellan-Manufaktur, designed by Trude Petri, whom Wagenfeld greatly admired.

Never before did the luxury of sophisticated design and simple utility form such an affordable unit, never before had the resigned utopia of Ernst Bloch – who dreamed, like all moralists, of a "luxury for everyone" product design – been so real. An unavoidable by-product of such legitimate luxury of well-balanced and enjoyable design is a disregard for commercial strategies to exploit consumer wishes, marketing concepts, fashion trends and nostalgic escape routes.

Wagenfeld recognised that there was no place for his creative imagination in areas where the main aim was the seasonal styling of trends and fashionable emotions, for example in car design. Even in the external and arbitrary casings and packaging for electrical appliances, however aesthetic and elegant they might be – for electric shavers, washing machines, televisions or computers – he saw no room for artistic intervention. As he said, the "frill-makers of yesterday have become the smooth-makers of today".[16]

This universalism of Wagenfeld's always remained indebted, in its own way, to that of the Bauhaus. It differed subtly and radically from the provincialism of the simple life and the nostalgia for local origins for the archetype, in which, during the reign of National Socialism, "good form" found a survival niche; yet it is precisely in the superficial proximity to the remarkable creations of Hermann Gretsch that the superior, at once more intelligent, "inspired" and individual object world of Wilhelm Wagenfeld is manifest.

Naturally the continuum of usable glasses and cutlery in the style of a timeless modernism still exists. However, only Milan product designer Enzo Mari is in a position to link the Italian minimalism and purism of the 1950s to Wagenfeld's rigorism of research into utility and the material production process. Both men had, and still have, in view of today's merchandise output, an awareness of being up to their ears in "merda".[17]

His whole life long Wilhelm Wagenfeld read the works of Friedrich Nietzsche, a fact he emphatically confirmed in conversations. There is no space here for any extensive foray into that interest; but Nietzsche's entirely unnoticed contemplations on "the smallest and most everyday of objects in daily use in everyday life"[18] could easily have been familiar to Wagenfeld. This also applies to Nietzsche's prophetic thoughts about a new age of industrial goods production, in which "the value of a thing would be [...] determined by the law of supply and demand". This would become "moulded upon an entire culture [...] and every desire and ability."[19] Already in *Human, All-Too Human* he saw "in the competition of labour and vendors [...] the public made [...] the judge," albeit a public that, lacking in expertise, bought these products "for their seeming quality;" that "the quality of the merchandise must therefore deteriorate" and the "durability" of the products suffer. For the layman, then, the "cheapness of the goods" was "sham and fraud".[20]

Subsequently we find Nietzsche pondering the effect that material objects and their usage have on people, thoughts very similar to Wagenfeld's life-long preoccupation.[21] Nietzsche wanted "to become again a good neighbour to familiar things".[22] Zarathustra cried out: "How rich is this earth in small perfect things, in well-turned out objects! Surround yourselves with small, good, perfect things, you superior people! Their golden maturity heals the heart. Perfection teaches us to hope".[23]

It was Wagenfeld's conviction that "objects must do us good, and make us take notice and think about them".[24] The use of an object, for Wagenfeld, always had to do with the question "of being able to live with it". Its value, he believed, was not simply there, but rather "constantly changing in its relationship to us". The artist was to lead "the buyer to a consciousness [...] of everything necessary for survival," and make him "more demanding and at the same time less pretentious".[25]

This leads to one of Nietzsche's most central thoughts concerning the relationship of beauty and utility in the way a thing was made: "I want to learn more and more to see the necessary in things as their beauty, and thereby become one of those who make things beautiful."[26]

This became one of the fundamental tenets for the design of objects and buildings for the avant-garde of the 20th century. It applied to the exposed water pipes and gas lines of Henry van de Velde's Haby hairdresser's salon in Berlin (1901), for the iron girders of the AEG turbine plant by Peter Behrens (1909), for the steel supports of the Neue Nationalgalerie by Mies van der Rohe (1962) and for Wagenfeld's egg cups for WMF. Wilhelm Wagenfeld – in a literal analogy to Nietzsche's ideas – made simple objects of utility, in their "necessity" for living, objects of beauty.

Notes

The title of this essay was taken from Friedrich Nietzsche's *The Gay Science (Fröhliche Wissenschaft)*. See Kritische Studienausgabe, eds. Giorgio Colli and Mazzino Montinari, Munich 1988 (hereafter referred to as KSA), vol. 2, p. 519; see also the rejected versions of KSA, vol. 14, p. 261, and also *Unfashionable Observations (Unzeitgemässe Betrachtungen III),* KSA, vol. 1, p. 360.

The text owes much to the conversations with Andrea Buddensieg and could not have been written without the assistance of Anja Schmalfuss.

1 Wilhelm Wagenfeld, "Notizen", in: *Zeitgemäss und zeitbeständig. Industrieformen von Wilhelm Wagenfeld,* ed. Carlo Burschel and Beate Manske, Bremen 1997, p. 30 (hereafter referred to as *Zeitgemäss und zeitbeständig).*
2 Kurt Nemitz, "Grusswort", in: *Zeitgemäss und zeitbeständig,* p. 7.
3 Nemitz, p.7.
4 Klaus Lehmann, "Was ich Wilhelm Wagenfeld hätte sagen wollen", in: *Zeitgemäss und zeitbeständig,* p. 11.
5 Wilhelm Wagenfeld 1997 (see note 1), p. 31.
6 Beate Manske, "'Fünfzehn Jahre waren nicht vergeblich'. Wilhelm Wagenfelds Mitarbeit in der WMF", in: *Zeitgemäss und zeitbeständig,* p. 39.
7 Manske p. 47.
8 Manske p. 43.
9 Manske p. 31.
10 Manske p. 43.
11 Manske p. 39.
12 Letter from Erika Wagenfeld to the author, 7 January 2000.
13 Georg Wilhelm Friedrich Hegel, *Vorlesungen über die Ästhetik,* ed. Rüdiger Bubner, Stuttgart 1971, pp. 677 f.
14 Beate Manske 1997 (see note 6), p. 43.
15 Arthur Burkhardt, "Über die Verkäuflichkeit des Guten", in: *Zeitgemäss und zeitbeständig,* p. 49.
16 Lisa Hockemeyer, "Hässlichkeit verkauft sich schlecht", in: *Zeitgemäss und zeitbeständig,* p. 22.
17 See François Burkhardt with Juli Capella and Francesca Picchi, *Perché un libro su Enzo Mari,* Italian/English, Milan 1997; Antonio d'Avossa and Francesca Picchi, *Enzo Mari,* Catalan/Italian, Milan 1999. For comments on the *Berlin* dishes by Enzo Mari for the Königliche Porzellan-Manufaktur Berlin (KPM), see Tilmann Buddensieg's essay, "Am Ende ein neues Geschirr", in: *Arbeiten in Berlin. Ausstellung eines Porzellanservices entworfen für die KPM,* ed. Enzo Mari, exh. cat. Schloss Charlottenburg, Berlin, etc.; Milan 1996, pp. 36 ff.
18 Friedrich Nietzsche, *The Gay Science (Die fröhliche Wissenschaft),* KSA, vol. 3, p. 538.
19 Nietzsche, *Daybreak (Morgenröthe),* KSA, vol. 3, p. 156.
20 Nietzsche, *Human, All-Too Human (Menschliches, Allzumenschliches),* KSA, vol. 2, p. 675, and *Daybreak (Morgenröthe),* KSA, vol. 3, pp. 145 f.
21 See also Wagenfeld's wonderful book *Wesen and Gestalt der Dinge um uns,* Potsdam 1948, unaltered reprint, Worpsweder Verlag 1990, and Lisa Hockemeyer 1997 (see note 16), pp. 26 f.
22 Friedrich Nietzsche, *Human, All-Too Human (Menschliches, Allzumenschliches),* KSA, vol. 2, pp. 542 f.
23 Friedrich Nietzsche, *Thus Spoke Zarathustra (Also sprach Zarathustra),* KSA, vol. 3, p. 364.
24 Wilhelm Wagenfeld 1948 (see note 21), p. 124.
25 Wagenfeld (1948) p. 136.
26 Friedrich Nietzsche, *The Gay Science (Die fröhliche Wissenschaft),* KSA, vol. 3, p. 521.

From Material to Model
Wagenfeld and the Metal Workshops at the Bauhaus and at the Bauhochschule in Weimar

Siegfried Gronert

1 The living-room, *Haus am Horn*, Weimar. Furniture by Marcel Breuer, carpet by Marta Erps-Breuer, wall lamp by László Moholy-Nagy, standard lamp by Gyula Pap; summer 1923

Wilhelm Wagenfeld's work during his time at Weimar, from 1923 to 1930 – consisting wholly of objects in metal and lighting appliances – has been amply documented in recent years by the Bauhaus Archive in Berlin.[1] To every extant document on the two Bauhaus lamps of 1923/24 there is a history of several legal hearings.[2] What is there still to say about Wagenfeld's works at Weimar? This article aims to highlight some highly specific points and concerns an aspect of central importance for design activities at the Weimar Bauhaus and its successor there, the Bauhochschule – the development of prototype models for industrial manufacture.

By November of 1923, when Wagenfeld arrived at the "Staatliches Bauhaus Weimar", crucial decisions for the time ahead had already been made. Following the turbulent years upon its foundation by Walter Gropius in 1919, Johannes Itten, initiator of the preliminary "Vorkurs" at the Bauhaus, had already left Weimar and László Moholy-Nagy, the Hungarian Constructivist, had taken the course over and was in charge of the metal workshop. Equally decisive for the new phase in progress had been the recent Bauhaus Exhibition, from July to September 1923. The experimental "Versuchshaus", largely furnished by the school's workshops, and other, concurrent exhibitions, had made manifest the departure of the Bauhaus from its Expressionist beginnings in favour of a Constructivist approach.

The changes of 1923 were linked with one fundamental to the structure of the workshops. It concerned the part of skilled craft in the "Lehrwerkstätten" (teaching workshops) and their status within a comprehensive integrated school of art for architecture and art.[3] In the initial phase of the Bauhaus, craft as "the wellspring of creative production" (founding manifesto, 1919) was a mainstay in the dual training structure of the workshops, which were supervised respectively by a Master of Form and a Master of Craft. The exhibition had not yet closed when, in September 1923, Gropius delivered a speech at the annual convention of the Deutscher Werkbund, also at Weimar. The speech bore the seminal title, "Art and Technology – a New Unity". Although no copy of the speech survives, the change of direction comes through clearly enough in subsequent essays by Gropius and in his Bauhaus prospectus of 1925. It defines the Bauhaus workshops as "essentially, *laboratories* in which appliances perfected to a reproducible state and typical for the present age, are carefully developed in model form and continually improved upon."[4] This gave the teaching workshops a new, additional and outward-looking function as experimental workshops for industrial production.

In that same period, from 1923 to 1925, Wagenfeld, owing to the knowledge, skills and experience he had brought with him, was far less a student than part of the staff of the Bauhaus metal workshop. In Thuringia, of which Weimar was the capital, political attacks on the Bauhaus were increasing; in 1925, when its teaching contracts were annulled, the institution moved to Dessau, which was under a Social Democratic administration. But Wagenfeld remained in Weimar, working at first as an assistant at the "Staatliche Bauhochschule Weimar" that Otto Bartning founded in 1926 and then, from 1928 to the closure of the Bauhochschule in 1930, as the head of the metal workshop. In these seven years at Weimar, Wagenfeld was increasingly the definitive impulse behind the school's experimental models in the metalworking domain.

Upon his apprenticeship at the drawing office of silverware manufacturers Koch & Bergfeld, during which he had also attended the school of arts and crafts at Bremen, Wagenfeld obtained a grant that enabled him to enter courses in design, modelling, silversmithing and metal engraving at the drawing academy at Hanau.[5] A photograph taken in June 1922 conveys the concept underlying academic training there. Craft skills are highlighted explicitly in several balls of putty, a box containing the same material, some punches and other metal-chasing tools; the academic artistic nature of the syllabus is manifest in plaster casts hanging serried on the wall behind. The fundamental concept consisted in introducing the artist-craftsmen to acknowledged works of art as a means of empowering them to design their own works. This was an advance on the notion prevalent in the middle of the previous century, that an artistic design should form the blueprint for the craftsman; but it was still firmly rooted in the academicism of the late 19th century.

This was the climate in which the academic art-and-craft objects came about with which Wagenfeld applied to the Bauhaus at Weimar in 1923. Six years later, one of these pieces, a casket with architectural and figurative ornamentation, figured in a piece of Bauhochschule publicity – crossed out and accompanied by a passage that reads like an extension of Gropius' laboratory image. "The aim is not a beautiful picture, but to work out clear, practical working and construction drawings as a consequence of sound design and experiment. For the workshop's task, besides making individual pieces, is to create models capable of industrial reproduction."[6] Exemplary models by Wagenfeld in this sense illustrate the caption. They are of one of his "fat/lean" sauce boats, door knobs and lamps.

2 Wilhelm Wagenfeld (sixth from left) in the drawing studio of the Zeichenakademie at Hanau, June 1922

3 Monstrance, hand-embossed silver, Zeichenakademie Hanau, 1921/22

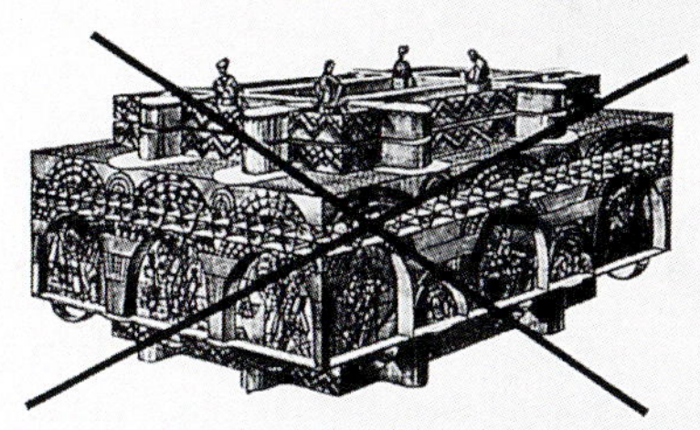

Nicht auf das schöne Bild kommt es an,

4 Casket, hand-embossed metal, Zeichenakademie Hanau, 1922, illustrated in: *Staatliche Bauhochschule Weimar 1929,* Weimar 1929

Wagenfeld, now head of the metal workshop at the Bauhochschule, was not only renouncing his early work with that gesture (there was the time he had given away the prints he had completed to date and destroyed the blocks and plates with the same radicality before setting out for Weimar).[7] In the spheres of art and craft, the new orientation toward industrial production meant that, in relation to craft training as it had been, traditional techniques had to be abandoned or changed; it also implied the far greater challenge of defying the persistent received ethos of the craft trades that derived their sense of identity from historical and highly specific questions of both material and form. Thus the gesture marked a break with Wagenfeld's own origins in the art of silversmithing, and his unreserved acknowledgement of model-based experimental work for serial production. It was a principle to which Wagenfeld was to remain indebted in both theory and practice, his later experiences in the glassmaking industry giving him a preference for close collaboration with an industrial plant.[8]

Were the metal workshops capable of manufacturing experimental models for industrial production at all? Technically, the change of raw material in the production of models, from precious silver to the base materials of brass, copper and above all, nickel silver (a silver-coloured alloy of nickel, copper and zinc) – realistic enough if items of everyday use were to be the aim – presented no problems; most jobs could be done with the same tools as were used for silver. With the exception of a silver teapot in 1929, Wagenfeld worked only with base materials during his entire period at Weimar. A photograph taken in the summer of 1923 for the Bauhaus exhibition reveals the modest level to which the metal workshop, accommodated on the first floor of the former school of arts and crafts, was fitted out. Two workbenches of the kind traditional in the goldsmith and silversmiths' trade can be seen, each with three work spaces. On the bench in the foreground are a flat dapping die for beating sheet metal into hemispheres and segments, a bench brush and other tools. A knee vice, a hand-operated drilling machine and, in the background, a grinder, complete the stock. By the window, a hand drill of a kind in use since medieval times was conceivably included as a pointer to the workshop's craft tradition. Wagenfeld was later to write, "In our metal workshop stood just one antiquated grinder and buffer, no mechanical tools but this, only makeshift manual ones for our training."[9] Contrary to usual workshop practice, the benches conspicuously sport finished pieces. These were completed in the few months previous by Gyula Pap, Richard Winkelmayer and Martin Jahn. The current state of serial production as applied to a traditional artefact type is demonstrated by a seven-armed candelabrum by Pap (on the left, in front of the partition wall). This work was represented in the Bauhaus exhibition by a total of five examples. The publication, *Staatliches Bauhaus Weimar* (1923) featured the candelabrum as a "standard job for mechanical reproduction". Its foot had been spun at the Weimar silversmithing factory of Theodor Müller.[10]

5 Fat/lean sauce boat, 1928, illustrated in: *Staatliche Bauhochschule Weimar 1929*, Weimar 1929

Converting from traditional types to serial production might be done, as it was in the case of the candelabrum, by simplifying the forms so that they could be spun on a lathe – a route Wagenfeld once called "extracting the fancy bits";[11] but this was just one aspect of the conversion. Writing in retrospect, Wagenfeld was to elaborate, "Around 1920, factories were still to a large extent manual workshops in which machines had only begun to take over from the manual work to a very limited degree. Manufacture of 'mass goods' consisted primarily of manual labour organised by way of division and mechanisation."[12] Wagenfeld's own test models, largely made by hand, likewise came about along this principle of division and mechanised production of component elements. The concept of the model, articulated in theory in 1923, only now acquired practical, physical shape.

Wagenfeld's very first piece of work at the metal workshop, a mocha machine, reflected the current state of debate at the Bauhaus. The boiler and stand have been raised or embossed in copper and assembled as a unified apparatus. In the following, I refer to such composite entities of originally separated parts as an assembly.

Wagenfeld employed another assembly technique by no means uncommon amongst silversmiths for his tea caddies of 1924. Nickel silver sheet, possibly beaten, has been bent to form a tube and soldered

6 The rooms at the metal workshop in the workshop building of the Bauhaus, summer 1923

7 Members of the metal workshop, (left to right) front: Josef Knau, Wilhelm Wagenfeld, Otto Rittweger; back: Max Krajewsky, Marianne Brandt, Christian Dell, László Moholy-Nagy. Photograph: Hans Przyrembl, 1924/25

along the lateral seam. The base has been soldered in or on. The differences between a piece of traditional beaten work and the assembly technique as outlined emerge clearly in the two fat/lean sauce boats completed in 1924. The vessel's basic shape, with two different spouts to enable the separate pouring of fatty and lean fluids, is derived from an earlier work by Christian Dell, the Master of Form at the metal workshop from 1922 to 1925.[13] The type only became widely known through Wagenfeld's models, however. The first, crater-shaped version, raised in nickel silver, was a prentice piece. The next, contrasting version consists

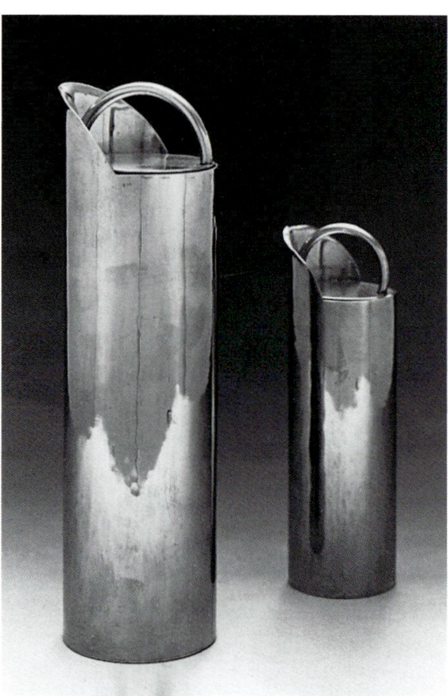

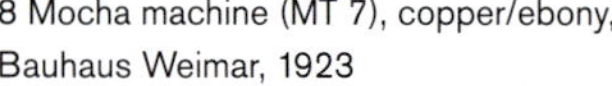

8 Mocha machine (MT 7), copper/ebony, Bauhaus Weimar, 1923

9 Tea caddies (MT 38–39), nickel silver, Bauhaus Weimar, 1924

of a cylindrical body bent out of sheet, with a soldered-on base and hoop foot. The crater version would have necessitated a complicated sequence of operations, which made it less suited as a model for mass production.[14]

From today's vantage point, Wagenfeld's consistent use of the assembly technique from his first works on seems surprising; yet the techniques he was using were all known – though largely by-passed in the gold and silversmithing crafts. In the mental order of things, the form embossed into shape by hand was to the turned or spun form as silver was to nickel silver. Thus a publication issued by the Deutscher Werkbund ("Crafts Association") in 1926 opines about gold and silver, quite in keeping with the conventional view, "The machine product increasingly separates the form from the material; skilled workmanship has the living form grow out of the material."[15]

Apart from the lamps made from late in 1923 on, which, incorporating semi-fabricated, partly machine-made components, once again made the assembly form a dynamic issue (see the contributions to this volume by Beate Manske and Klaus Struve), Wagenfeld did not deviate from the tried and tested options of the assembly principle, at least for the time being. He was still true to them when he made the coffee and tea set of nickel silver, one of his last works at the Weimar Bauhaus. The body of these vessels is made of a (probably beaten) piece of sheet metal, bent and soldered together with its base and hoop foot. The constructivist vocabulary of the cylindrical body of the vessel and the handles with their stereometric shape, set off from the body, is enhanced in the eccentric positioning of the lid, and, though hardly discernible in the photograph, by the knob on the lid as well as the hinge being set in a line at right angles to the axis of handle and spout. At the time, Wagenfeld justified the arrangement, which Marianne Brandt was also then applying, on functional grounds. – "The eccentric arrangement of lid and knob was a functional necessity, preventing any spilling-over of the liquid inside."[16]

Fourteen years later, Wagenfeld was saying the exact opposite. "In the metal workshop at the Bauhaus my last piece of work was a service of cylindrical shapes with handles on it that resembled the grab handles on a tram. On theoretical considerations the lids were off-centre and the spouts rigidly tailored to the whole. Once the set was finished, I knew that nothing was right about it except at best the realisation of theoretical intentions."[17] In comparison to his later models in their functional sophistica-

10 Fat/lean sauce boat (MT 15), nickel silver/ebony, glass cover, Bauhaus Weimar, 1924

11 Fat/lean sauce boat (MT 50), nickel silver/ebony, Bauhaus Weimar, 1924

12 Coffee and tea set (MT 40–43, 45), nickel silver/ebony, Bauhaus Weimar, 1924

tion, Wagenfeld's early works from his time at Weimar do, in fact, suffer from the birth-pangs of nascent utility.[18]

In the early days of the metal workshop of the Bauhochschule, it had to rely upon the modest technical equipment it had inherited from the Weimar Bauhaus. But when Wagenfeld took charge of the workshop in 1928 and a spinning lathe was acquired, a number of models were constructed of spun parts – bowls and saucers, a tea caddy, another fat/lean sauce boat and a kettle. The hint of conical tapering in the bodies of the tea caddy and the fat/lean sauce boat in particular betray their origins at the lathe. The top of the caddy is an assembly constructed on that basis. Likewise the kettle of 1930, the last vessel Wagenfeld made at Weimar, consists of a spun hemispherical body with a brazed-on base. With the exception of the sauce boat, the spun models were then manufactured by Walther & Wagner, the metal goods factory in Schleiz, under conditions comparable to those at the Bauhochshule.[19] Now there was no discernible distinction between the model from the experimental workshop for an industrial plant and the model as a prototype in industrial production.

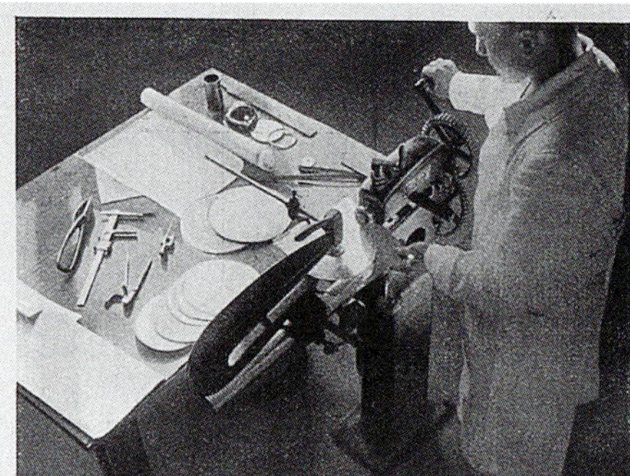
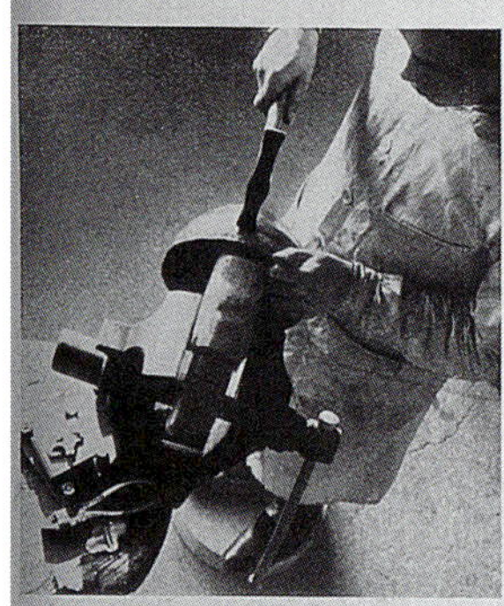

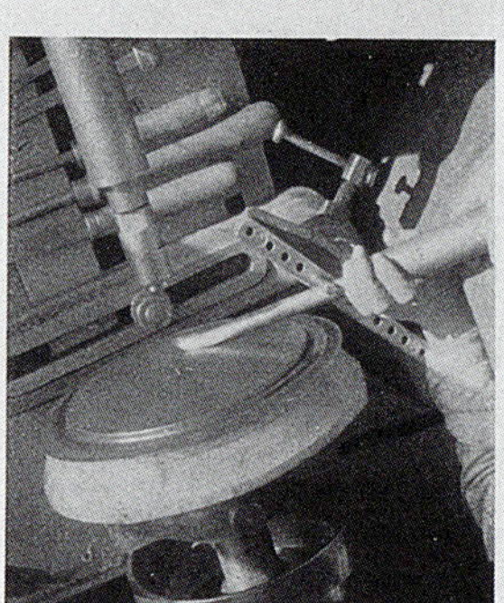

13 The metal workshop at the Bauhochschule, Weimar; room with storage shelves, circular shears, work with the embossing hammer, making a spinning mould at the turning-lathe, spinning lathe, 1928/29

14 Metal workshop at the Bauhochschule, Weimar, workbench, 1928/29

15 Tea caddy, silver-plated brass, Walther & Wagner/Schleiz, 1927/29

16 Fat/lean sauce boat, nickel silver/Trolit, Walther & Wagner/Schleiz, 1929

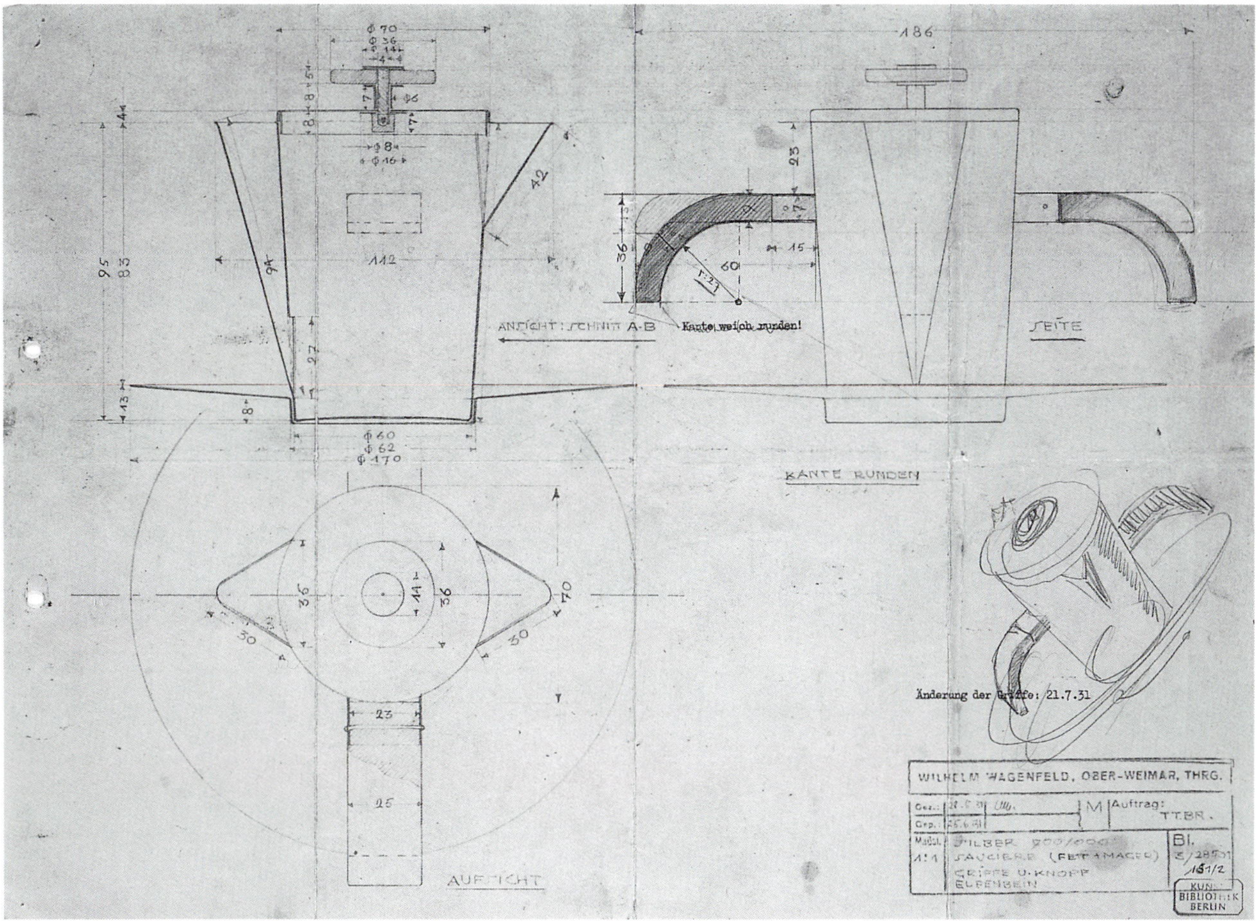

17 Workshop drawing for a fat/lean sauce boat with ivory handles, one-off piece, 1931

Of all the models, the fittings and mountings made by Loevy in Berlin best illustrate the concept of a model from the School's experimental workshop. At the Bauhochschule workshop, Wagenfeld experimented with different handles and shapes until, in 1928, he had a usable model. The caption to a display panel of the whole series through its development in the journal, *Die Form* of 1931, says, tersely, "Gradual improvement and elaboration of the models. Course of development. Above the earlier models, below the latest model."[20] Through the "course of development", form and material were reduced to a minimum; with good reason, since, in the casting process, every ounce counts. In 1930 the room-door handle weighing 285 grammes cost 7 Reichsmark the pair; the smaller jib-door knob 6.80 M and the larger front door model no less than 15 M.[21] By comparison, the somewhat larger and more ornate room door handle by Rachlis weighed in at 370 grammes and cost 15 M the pair. The Wagenfeld handle (see pl. 19, 20, p. 21), enjoyed great success, as the coat rack accessories of the same date appear to have done, until the firm, renowned for its architect models (Gropius, Behrens and others), was closed down in 1933. As Wagenfeld recalled, "Sales must have been extremely high, my income out of it was not proportionate, so that the Bauhochschule was able to record good profits out of it with the two items."[22] As it was, architect Erich Mendelsohn used more than a thousand Wagenfeld handles for his Columbushaus in Berlin in 1930, and the Bauhochschule was said to have received 3000 M in licence fees alone.[23]

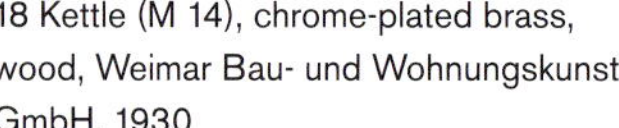
18 Kettle (M 14), chrome-plated brass, wood, Weimar Bau- und Wohnungskunst GmbH, 1930

The chronology of the objects is eloquent of the change described by Moholy-Nagy under the significant title of "From the Wine-Jug to the Lamp". The metal workshop at the Bauhaus had begun with customary tableware and accessories much as other schools produced; under Moholy-Nagy's hand, the emphases shifted. As he wrote, he succeeded after some time in "steering work at the workshop in that direction that later established the Bauhaus's leading position in designs for the lamp industry."[24]

It was not only in the lighting appliances that the school turned to everyday objects. Between 1922 and 1925 the metal workshop was the creative source of no less than five samovars, or, if the Wagenfeld mocha machine is included, since it belongs to the same species, six, at any rate, of a product type much in favour even among the reform movement of the pre-First World War years. In the fat/lean sauce boat, Wagenfeld coined a genuine innovation in table accessories. The kettle, much too little noticed, his door mountings and a cloakroom wall set have all extended the domain of conscious design from the set table to the kitchen and the house, that is, to the mundane things in domestic life.

Wagenfeld's achievement while at Weimar consisted in having derived from a restricted field of activity one of universal application. This transition of scale he achieved by concentrating the broad programme of the

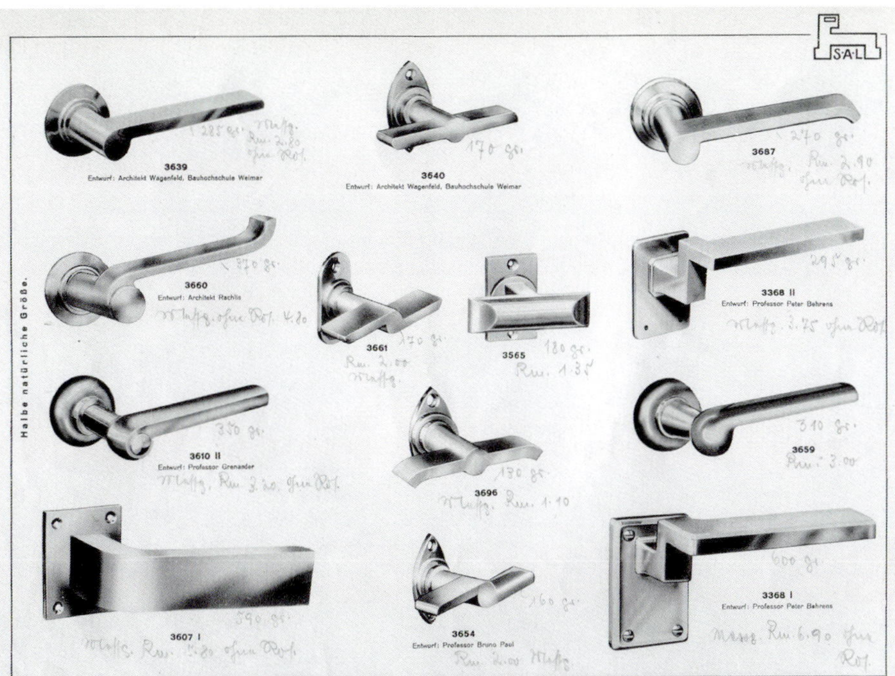

19 Door handles and window latch (above left and centre), illustrated in: *Bronzewarenfabrik S. A. Loevy,* catalogue no. 6, Berlin, no vol. no. (1930)

20 Display panel with door handle types (above left), S. A. Loevy/Berlin, 1928, illustrated in: *Die Form,* vol. 6, 1931

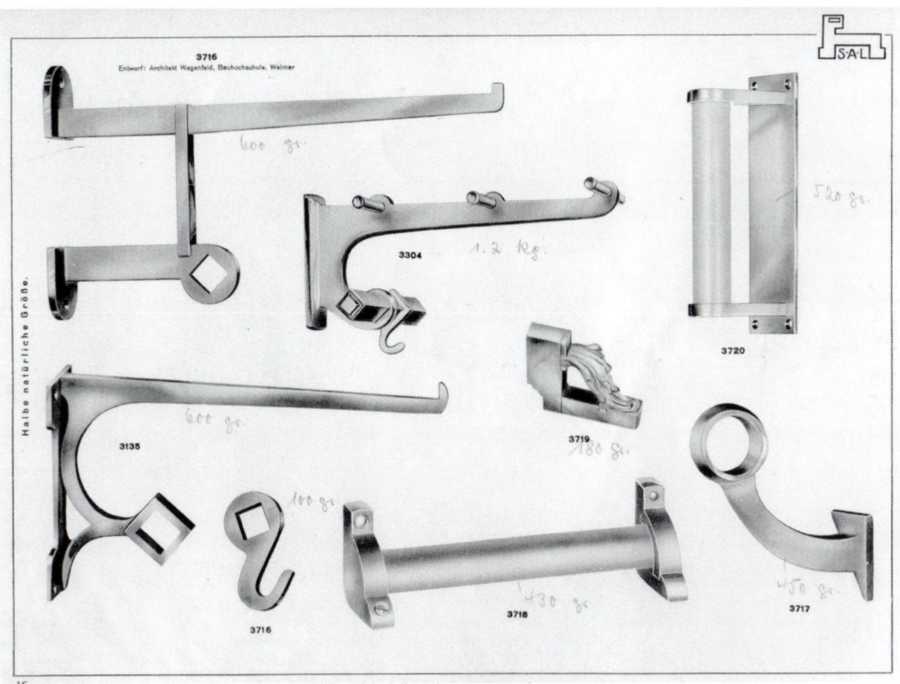

21 Wardrobe wall fixtures, illustrated in: *Bronzewarenfabrik S. A. Loevy,* catalogue no. 6, Berlin, no vol. no. (1930)

design of industrially manufactured utility objects on the model, with the manufacturing technique and the aesthetic and finally, also practical aspects in mind – the model in the experimental workshop of the designer who would anticipate in the reference model the subsequent phases of production and use. True, that broad programme had been postulated by Gropius as theory, so that to that extent, Wagenfeld could be said merely to have appropriated it; true, too, that it took him to the end of his time at Weimar before he could relinquish the strict formalism of his constructivist forms. But Wagenfeld it was who first developed Gropius' statements into a practical technique of model-based design fit for industry.[25] Recalling that the Bauhochschule placed *man* in the foreground of the ideals of designing and making, Wagenfeld's own development at Weimar might be characterised as a path from form to man. But in 1930, this idea had not yet fully crystallised. He would not strike upon his dictum of beautiful utility in everyday life until his subsequent activity as a designer in the glass industry.

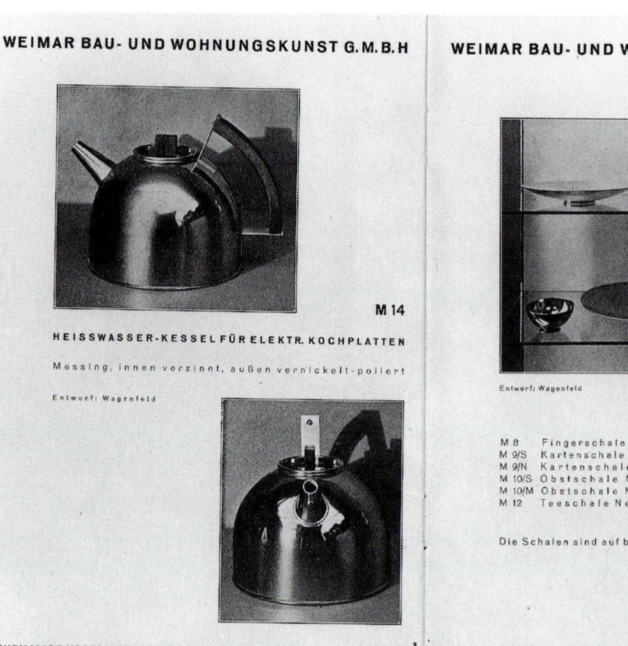

WEIMAR BAU- UND WOHNUNGSKUNST G. M. B. H

M 14

HEISSWASSER-KESSEL FÜR ELEKTR. KOCHPLATTEN

Messing, innen verzinnt, außen vernickelt-poliert

Entwurf: Wagenfeld

EHEMALIGE VERTRIEBSORGANISATION DER STAATL. BAUHOCHSCHULE

WEIMAR BAU- UND WOHNUNGSKUNST G. M. B. H

M 12
M 10
M 9
M 8
M 10
M 8

Entwurf: Wagenfeld

SCHALEN

M 8	Fingerschale Neusilber versilbert poliert	Ø 12 cm
M 9/S	Kartenschale Neusilber versilbert poliert	Ø 16 cm
M 9/N	Kartenschale Messing vernickelt poliert	Ø 16 cm
M 10/S	Obstschale Neusilber versilbert matt	Ø 32 cm
M 10/M	Obstschale Messing poliert oder matt	Ø 32 cm
M 12	Teeschale Neusilber versilbert poliert	Ø 16 cm

Die Schalen sind auf besonderen Wunsch verchromt lieferbar

EHEMALIGE VERTRIEBSORGANISATION DER STAATL. BAUHOCHSCHULE

22 Kettle and bowls, illustrated in: *Metall,* catalogue of Weimar Bau- und Wohnungskunst GmbH, 1930/31

NACH MODELLEN UND ENTWÜRFEN VON WILHELM WAGENFELD-OBER-WEIMAR (THÜR.) UND RICHARD WINKELMAYER-FRANKFURT A. M. IN ZUSAMMENARBEIT MIT DER WEIMAR BAU- U. WOHNUNGSKUNST G. M. B. H. HERGESTELLT VON DER FA. WALTER & WAGNER, METALLWARENFABRIK, SCHLEIZ. VERTRIEB DURCH DIE WEIMAR BAU- UND WOHNUNGSKUNST G. M. B. H. WEIMAR. ANFRAGEN ÜBER ENTWURF UND AUSFÜHRUNG VON SONDERAUFTRÄGEN AN DIE WEIMAR BAU- U. WOHNUNGSKUNST G. M. B. H.

METALL

WEIMAR

BAU- UND WOHNUNGSKUNST G. M. B. H

EHEMALIGE VERTRIEBSORGANISATION DER STAATL. BAUHOCHSCHULE

WEIMAR

23 Teapot-warmer and lamp, illustrated in: *Metall,* catalogue of Weimar Bau- und Wohnungskunst GmbH, 1930/31

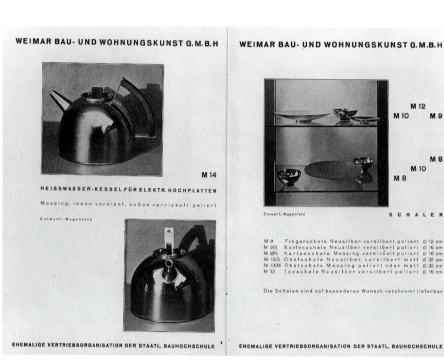

Notes

I am grateful to Reinhard Sänger of the Badisches Landesmuseum Karlsruhe, Ernst and Gine Weber (goldsmiths and silversmiths at Krefeld), Klaus Weber (Bauhaus-Archiv, Berlin) and Klaus-Jürgen Winkler (Bauhaus-Universität Weimar).

1 *Die Metallwerkstatt am Bauhaus,* ed. Klaus Weber, exh. cat. Bauhaus-Archiv Berlin, Berlin 1992 (referred to below as *Die Metallwerkstatt am Bauhaus); Das andere Bauhaus. Otto Bartning und die Staatliche Bauhochschule Weimar 1926–1930,* ed. Dörte Nicolaisen, exh. cat. Bauhaus-Archiv Berlin, Berlin 1996 (ref. below: *Das andere Bauhaus),* on the works in metal see especially Klaus Weber, "'Dienende Geräte'. Die Metallwerkstatt der Bauhochschule", pp. 105–121.

2 See Beate Manske's treatment of the subject in this book, pp. 24 ff.

3 It was as a consequence of the Art Schools Reform instigated towards the end of the First World War that the "Einheitskunstschule" for architecture, painting and sculpture first proposed by Bruno Paul was realised with the founding of the Bauhaus at Weimar in 1919. A good general idea of these developments can be gleaned from *Kunstschulreform 1900–1933. Bauhaus Weimar Dessau Berlin – [...],* ed. Hans M. Wingler, Berlin 1977; Katja Schneider, *Burg Giebichenstein. Die Kunstgewerbeschule unter Leitung von Paul Thiersch und Gerhard Marcks 1915 bis 1933,* 2 vols., Weinheim 1992, vol. 1, esp. pp. 17–23; Dörte Nicolaisen, "Otto Bartning und die Staatliche Bauhochschule in Weimar 1926–1930", in: *Das andere Bauhaus,* esp. pp. 16–23.

4 Walter Gropius, "Grundsätze der Bauhausproduktion", in: *Neue Arbeiten der Bauhauswerkstätten* (Bauhausbücher, vol. 7), Munich (undated; 1925), p. 7; see Dörte Nicolaisen 1996 (see note 3), pp. 22 f.

5 See Beate Manske, "Biografie Wilhelm Wagenfeld", in: *Wilhelm Wagenfeld: gestern, heute, morgen. Lebenskultur im Alltag,* published by the Wilhelm Wagenfeld Stiftung, Bremen; Bremen 1995, pp. 10–12.

6 *Staatliche Bauhochschule Weimar 1929,* Weimar 1929, p. 37; on the attribution of the casket to Wagenfeld, see Beate Manske, "Zwei Lampen sind nie gleich. Wilhelm Wagenfeld in der Metallwerkstatt des Staatlichen Bauhauses Weimar", in: *Die Metallwerkstatt am Bauhaus,* p. 89, note 5.

7 See Beate Manske 1995 (note 5 above), p. 12.

8 "It is a different and better affair where the originators of the purchased designs participate in taking charge of or working on the preparations at the plant. Proceeding in this way vouchsafes sound collaboration between technician, artist and salesman." Wilhelm Wagenfeld, "Künstlerische Formprobleme der Industrie" (1941), in: W. Wagenfeld, *Wesen und Gestalt der Dinge um uns,* Potsdam 1948, p. 85.

9 Wilhelm Wagenfeld, "Das Staatliche Bauhaus – die Jahre in Weimar", in: *form,* no. 37, 1967, pp. 17–19, quoted here from *Täglich in der Hand. Industrieformen von Wilhelm Wagenfeld aus sechs Jahrzehnten,* ed. Beate Manske and Gudrun Scholz, Worpsweder Verlag, Worpswede 1987 (referred to below as *Täglich in der Hand),* p. 27.

10 See Klaus Weber, "'Vom Weinkrug zur Leuchte'. Die Metallwerkstatt am Bauhaus", in: *Die Metallwerkstatt,* p. 39, note 83; and cat. no. 204 for the candelabrum.

11 See Dieter Opper, "Lehrjahre und graphische Arbeiten", in: *Täglich in der Hand,* p. 206.

12 Wilhelm Wagenfeld 1967 (see note 9), in: *Täglich in der Hand,* p. 28.

13 See Klaus Weber, "'Sachliche Bauart. Höchste Qualitätsarbeit.' Christian Dell als Lehrer, Silberschmied und Gestalter", in: *Die Metallwerkstatt am Bauhaus,* p. 57.

14 Both the crater-shaped beaten prentice piece MT15 and the cylindrical model MT 50 were listed at the Weimar Bauhaus as models for serial production nonetheless.

15 *Gold und Silber. Deutsche Goldschmiedearbeiten der Gegenwart,* compiled and introduced by Wilhelm Lotz, Berlin 1926, p. 13 (Bücher der Form, 3).

16 Wilhelm Wagenfeld, "Zu den Arbeiten der Metallwerkstatt", in: *Junge Menschen,* special issue, *Bauhaus Weimar",* vol. 5, 1924, no. 8, p. 187.

17 Wilhelm Wagenfeld, "Kleine Betrachtungen" (1938), in: Wilhelm Wagenfeld 1948 (see note 8), p. 31.

18 See Siegfried Gronert, "Wilhelm Wagenfeld. Weimarer Wehen", in: Gronert, *Türdrücker der Moderne. Eine Designgeschichte,* Cologne 1991, pp. 28–31.

19 See Klaus Weber 1996 (see note 1), pp. 111–113.

20 *Die Form,* vol. 6, 1931, no. 10, p. 395; see Siegfried Gronert 1991 (see note 18), pp. 30 f.

21 Information from *Bronzewarenfabrik S. A. Loevy,* catalogue no. 6, Berlin; no vol. no. (1930), no. 3639.

22 Wilhelm Wagenfeld, "Bauhochschule Weimar, Beginn meiner Industriearbeit" (1986), in: *Täglich in der Hand,* p. 28.

23 Note by Wagenfeld on 4. July 1985 (Wilhelm Wagenfeld Stiftung, Bremen); Wagenfeld states the amount in a letter to Nikolaus Pevsner in London, 15 December 1950; see Beate Manske 1995 (see note 5), p. 16, note 19.

24 László Moholy-Nagy, "Metallwerkstatt. Vom Weinkrug zur Leuchte", in: *Bauhaus 1919–1928,* ed. Herbert Bayer, Walter & Ise Gropius, exh. cat. The Museum of Modern Art, New York 1938 (quoted after the German ed., Stuttgart 1955, pp. 134–139, quote p. 134).

25 There was also the question as to how suitable this model technique is for more complex and technical implements. In the 1950s and 1960s that debate was pursued notably by Wilhelm Braun-Feldweg. See *Form und Industrie. Wilhelm Braun-Feldweg,* ed. Siegfried Gronert, Frankfurt am Main 1998.

A Design Makes History
Wilhelm Wagenfeld's Bauhaus Lamp

Beate Manske

"The table lamp – a type suited to machine production – achieved the greatest simplicity in its form and the greatest economy in its use of time and materials. A round base, a cylindrical tube and a spherical shade are its most important constituents."[1] With these brief words written in 1924 Wilhelm Wagenfeld characterised one of his earliest industrial designs, created at the *Staatliches Bauhaus* in Weimar, with which he wrote himself into the history books of everyday 20th-century culture.

The significance of lamps was recognised very early on, by designers and architects in particular: this was a product with a "past", of which there were many forerunners – not only the traditional petroleum lamps with porcelain or metal bases and glass shades but also the numerous electrical table lamps which emerged after the turn of the century and which in their sophisticated design were clearly part of the arts and crafts movement.[2] Yet at the same time, Wagenfeld's lamp pointed to the "future": despite the features still strongly reminiscent of the craft industry (soldered-on pull switches etc.), the break with the arts and crafts tradition was complete and an independent aesthetic standard was formulated which was expressly geared towards industrial production.

The eventful history of the two Bauhaus lamps with their many variations, new editions, copies and plagiarisms, and not least the copyright battle over the glass version,[3] has increased their popularity and led to them being internationally linked with the name Wilhelm Wagenfeld whilst the buyers of his designs – of which there are millions in circulation – are often only aware of the firm which manufactured them.

The special position of Bauhaus lamps in Wagenfeld's work deserves a chapter of its own – a chapter which intends at the same time to give an insight into the endeavours and the design work of the Weimar Bauhaus.

In October 1923, Wilhelm Wagenfeld applied to the *Staatliches Bauhaus* in Weimar. In his home town of Bremen, he had completed a sound apprenticeship as an industrial draughtsman at the silverware factory Koch & Bergfeld; a stipend enabled him to continue his education and become a silversmith and graphic designer at the drawing academy in Hanau (to which a precious metals school was annexed) which he left with a Master's title in 1922. Reports of the 1923 summer exhibition of the Bauhaus, which Gropius had opened with a lecture entitled "Art and Technology – a New Unity", reached Wagenfeld in Worpswede where he had settled as a freelance graphic artist.[4] The exhibition made it clear that the Bauhaus was principally concerned with creating an autonomous, stylistically independent industrial culture by means of a holistic formal design principle which embraced all areas of life – a desire expressed in particular in an experimental show house, the *Haus am Horn*, built and furnished by the school. Wagenfeld, who had learnt during his apprenticeship that workmanship and craftsmanship in the making of objects were continually being repressed in favour of cheaper machine production, was immediately enthusiastic about the idea of influencing machine production and improving the product in both usability and form.

Wilhelm Wagenfeld was immediately accepted into the Bauhaus metal workshop and included in its design work right from the start. At that time, the artist, typographer and photographer, László Moholy-Nagy, an extraordinarily keen experimenter, was head of form and the silversmith, Christian Dell, was head of the workshop, someone whom Wagenfeld already knew and respected from his time in Hanau.

From the monthly reports of the workshop[5] which have survived – reports written chiefly by Dell – it is possible to trace exactly what each of the apprentices, journeymen and students taking the Basic Course was working on at a given time; however it also makes clear which difficulties the school faced during this period. Neither teachers nor pupils were prepared for the transition to a "productive operation" in which prototypes for industrial manufacture were designed and were to be offered to the appropriate companies for purchase. Nobody was really familiar

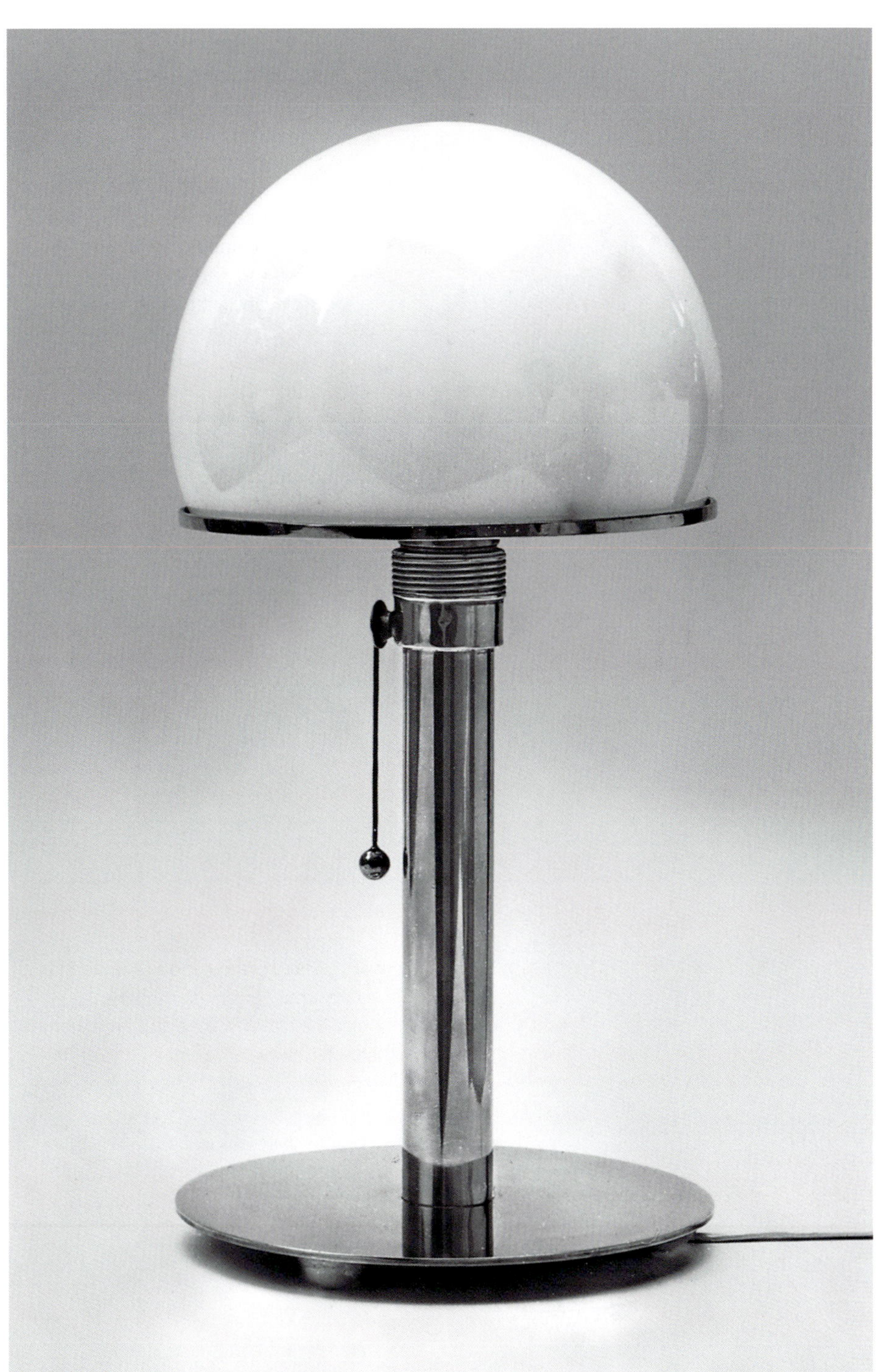

1 Bauhaus lamp, metal version,
Bauhaus Weimar, 1924

with the requirements for machine production and scant consideration had been given to which types of product were particularly suitable for production in large numbers. Consequently no new utensils were developed, born of the technological possibilities of the 20th century, rather objects with often centuries-old traditions were recreated using conventional techniques: tea and coffee sets, trays, candelabras, wine jugs, pieces of jewellery etc. For the apprentices, who were all required to have a proven record of work experience, it was not the objects themselves that were unfamiliar but the manner of teaching, the intensive search for the fundamental principles of a modern machine aesthetics, the free experimentation with a canon of forms reduced to the "essence". Thus in a rather primitively equipped workshop, objects were created with no pretensions to technical perfection made chiefly out of base, non-ferrous metals and largely unsuitable for serial production.

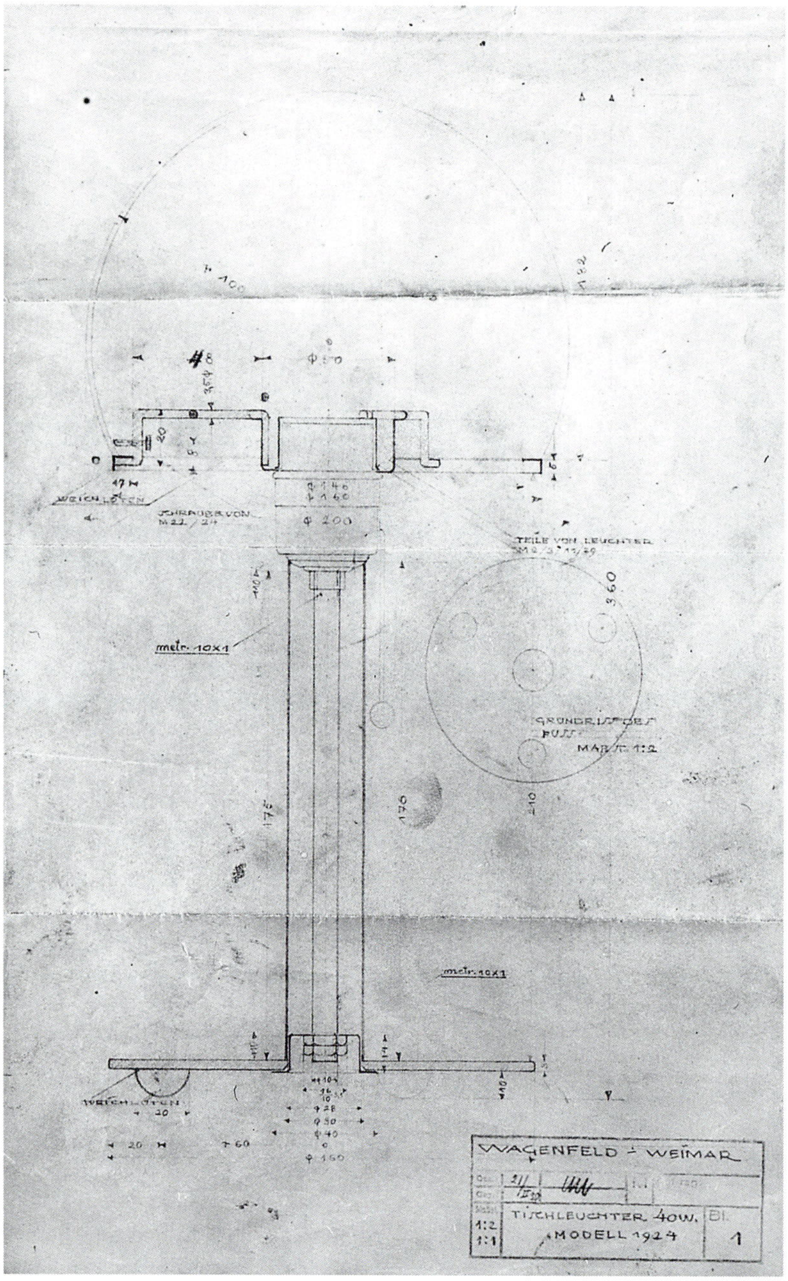

2 Later working drawing of the glass version of the Bauhaus lamp, dated and marked, "2/II 30, WW, Tischleuchter, 40 Watt, Modell 1924"

In this context Wagenfeld – directly after his final journeyman's examination on 3 April 1924 and his formal acceptance to the metal workshop – was given a project which was a particular hobbyhorse of the heads of the school: the development of lighting appliances. They hoped that this field would be the most likely to arouse the interest of industry, whose orders were urgently needed to finance the school. At the Spring Trade Fair in Leipzig in 1924 they had been unable to offer any prototypes – as Gropius remarked in his critique of the fair, "We are lagging a long way behind as far as lighting appliances are concerned […]." He went on to say that it would only be possible to make up for this delay "if the workshops adopt to a greater extent than they have to date the outlook required for reproducible products and their commercial constraints."[6]

As Wagenfeld remembers it, the Bauhaus lamp was created on the day after that final exam,[7] "[…] when he [Moholy-Nagy] then suggested I work on a table lamp made from metal. I had already visited his studio often and gazed at his paintings and glass and metal sculptures, whilst he talked a great deal about the visible and tactile properties of these materials which he allowed to work together in dissonance and harmony. […] When, kindly supervised by the head of the workshop, I was then able to put the finished 'Bauhaus lamp' on the work table in front of us, and delighted in seeing how the dimensions of the most significant parts as intended on paper were now set to advantage spatially and also how well the contrasts of the materials worked together – the lampshade of opaline glass, the nickel-plated polished shaft of the lamp and its dark oxidised base – I believed and was only too pleased to hear from my teacher that I was the creator of the lamp and that it was well suited for industrial use."[8]

Wagenfeld, who always stressed the contributions made by his teachers, nevertheless makes it clear in this description that it was not the material specifications that were responsible for the impact of this lamp, which has become so well-known, but the sympathetic rendering of Moholy-Nagy's world of ideas. The harmony of forms and proportions and the contrast of colours and materials are the design elements that make the lamp so distinctive: the dull black iron base rests on three metal spheres so that it appears to float above the table. The cylindrical silvery metal shaft is optically finished off by the rings of the screw fitting; conversely

3 Bauhaus lamp, first metal version with black iron base, Bauhaus Weimar, 1924. Shown here is the re-issue produced by Bremen-based Tecnolumen from 1994 onwards

4 Bauhaus lamp, glass version, Bauhaus Weimar, 1924

these grooves direct our gaze to the suspended metal ring which corresponds in shape and diameter to the base and which supports the spherical segment of the white opaline glass dome. The pull switch soldered on at the side with its silver chain and ball forms a sculptural element that breaks up the even geometrical proportions of the whole, thus drawing one's attention to them and simultaneously increasing their impact. Wagenfeld's teachers were very enthusiastic about the lamp and immediately obtained permission from Walter Gropius to duplicate the new type; by April 1924 the first fifteen copies of the lamp had been produced. With a view to the autumn trade fair in Leipzig, they attempted right from the start to develop a variety of types from the basic model. In May the wood workshop evidently produced a wooden version of the metal lamp for which the metal workshop supplied the hemispheres for the bases.[9] Wagenfeld himself used a nickel-plated brass plate as an alternative to the iron base, which, reflecting the shaft, gave the whole lamp a greater sense of lightness. An object of entirely different character came about, on the other hand, in a material variant in which base and shaft are of transparent glass. The suggestion for this version came in 1923 from Moholy-Nagy, who had already encouraged Bauhaus student Carl Jacob Jucker to experiment with glass lamps but without satisfactory and industrially usable results. We will return to Jucker's designs again in a later section as these have led to disputes over the copyright of the Bauhaus lamp albeit after a large interval of time; at this point we shall simply note that Jucker conducted the leads "openly" through the lamp shafts, i.e. without disguising them, whilst Wagenfeld used a narrow metal tube for conducting the cables for aesthetic reasons but also to give it the required stability.

Gropius set so much store by the Bauhaus lamp that in mid-June he had already registered it for its own stand at the Leipzig fair, in the "Grönländer Messhaus" which was showing electrical lighting.[10] He favoured the metal lamp which was produced in larger numbers and a copy of which (a present from the metal workshop for his birthday) he placed conspicuously in his Directorial office.

Wagenfeld himself manned the stand in the "Messhaus" and noted down the numerous queries and wishes of the dealers. The report he wrote afterwards highlights the dilemma of the Bauhaus in producing "industrial prototypes"; "We had a tremendously good stand situated on the first floor of the "Grönländer Messhaus" near the stairs. It was only narrow – barely 50 cm wide – and only 3 m long. The four variations of the electric table lamp covered it completely, there was no room for anything else. Some 30 lamps were placed in two rows between two illuminated lamps, one taller one and one separate one. We had expected that this arrangement of the manual products of our workshop would implicitly indicate machine work processes but we had completely disregarded the inevitable collisions with the prices we had fixed. They were the reason that the number of lamps ordered was lower than in the Grassi Museum. [...] In my opinion, the last fair here provided the best opportunities for spreading the word about our electric table lamps; quite the best propaganda for them was their strong contrast to the rest of the lighting appliances. My notes showed that we could immediately expect sales of between 1,500 and 2,000 items on the electrical market, if cheaper production methods could reduce the price to 8–12 M whilst the manual products were only of interest to the arts and crafts trade."[11]

Moholy-Nagy agreed with his pupil's assessment of the situation, urging that "The Bauhaus must try with all its might to build up a relationship with industry. It must try to produce its most useful and rationally produced goods by taking matters into its own hands where necessary and finding cheaper and reliable small manufacturers (workshop-factories). This is the issue with top priority and the work of the Bauhaus stands and falls by it. The Bauhaus has indeed achieved its given aim of producing models of useful products which truly serve modern living, we now need to concern ourselves with their commercial exploitation."[12] In Weimar as in Dessau it was still to be a number of years before they were able to truly offer the industry models ready for production.

Subsequent to the not particularly high sales results of the lamps at the fair, Wagenfeld recalls them being at least partly offered to members of the Bauhaus at cost price.[13] Since it was evident that the Bauhaus was receiving occasional inquiries about and orders for the lamps, additional metal and glass lamps were produced until at least November 1924. After this period the reports of the metal workshop break off. In October a larger version of the glass lamp is mentioned for the first time.[14] It is possible that improvements were also made at this time to previous models, including raising the shades slightly, which cracked easily due to the heat developed by the large light bulbs used during this period. It was not possible, however, to really standardise the lamps, on account of the small numbers produced: the domes were used as they came from the glassworks in Jena and different fittings were evidently used depending on what stocks were currently available in the workshop.

When the Bauhaus was driven out of Weimar in 1925 for political reasons and moved to Dessau, there was still enough material left for 50 glass lamps, and as opinion at the metal workshop had it, "there is always a market for the lamps." [15] Thus it is not surprising that the Bauhaus secured the property rights to the Bauhaus lamp in the apportionment negotiations with the Thuringian ministry. In Dessau the lamps were among the first products manufactured by the new Bauhaus GmbH, the sales organisation for the various workshops' designs, as is clear from the model codes ME1 and ME2. Between 1928 and 1930 the Berlin-based company Schwintzer & Gräff took over the serial production of the lamps from the metal workshop, including the large and small glass version. [16]

Like all pupils, Wagenfeld had no right to use his designs, which formally belonged to the state. The state, however, could in turn sometimes transfer them to the school; and in Weimar, as the intellectual originator, he had been given a share of the royalties. In Dessau the product was completely severed from its creator, who was no longer able to influence the form, size or finishing of the

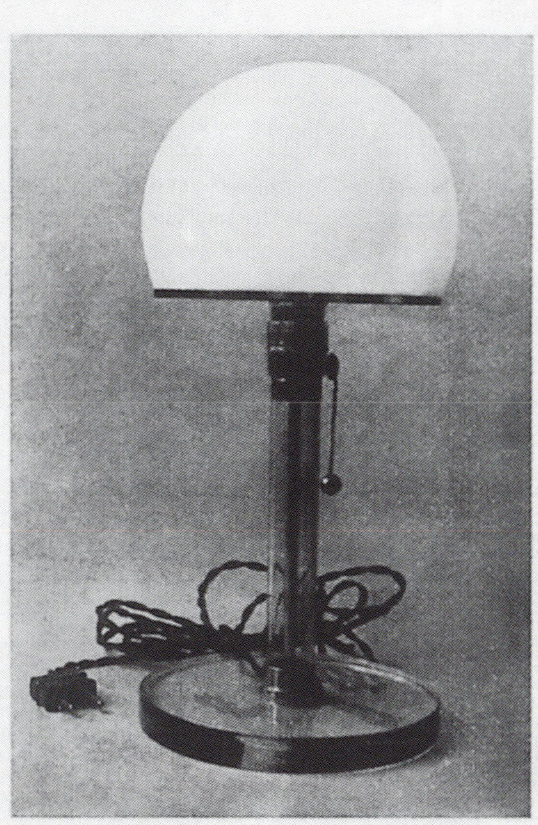

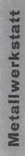

gesch.
Höhe ca. 35 cm

AUSFÜHRUNG

Kristallspiegel-Glasplatte, Felsenglasrohr, Glasschirm, Zugfassung

TISCHLAMPE AUS GLAS

VORTEILE

1 beste Lichtzerstreuung (genau erprobt)
2 sehr gefällige Form
3 besonders schönes Licht
4 praktisch für Schreibtisch, Nachttisch usw.
5 Glocke festgeschraubt bleibt in jeder Lage unbeweglich

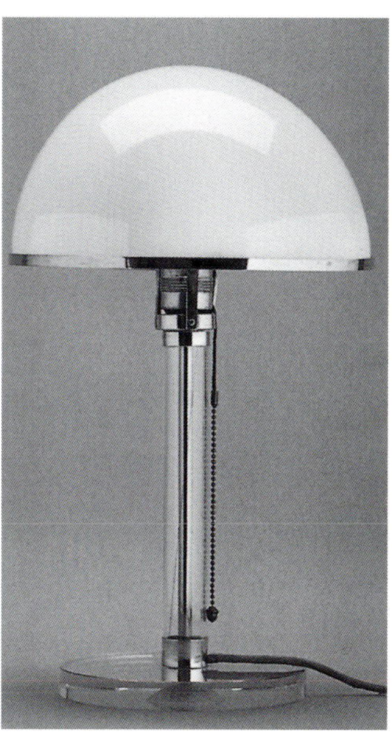

5 Bauhaus lamp, large glass version, Bauhaus Weimar, 1924

6 Herbert Bayer, insert (front) to *Katalog der Muster,* Bauhaus GmbH, Dessau 1925, glass version of Bauhaus lamp

product and was not named in connection with it.

Nevertheless Wagenfeld was quite at liberty to develop considerable parts of his design and to develop it further technically. On 16 April 1925, directly after the Bauhaus was closed down, Wagenfeld patented an invention to improve the glass version, a socket which was fitted between shaft and lamp fitting and made assembly cheaper and better. According to the entry at the Patent Office in Berlin the invention was concerned with "the well-known electric table lamp [...]. The lamp consists in the familiar manner of a base A, the glass tube shaft C as a cladding

7 Glass lamp with parchment shade, type 2, Bauhochschule Weimar, 1925/26

and the fitting B."[17] This patent registration caused some stir in Weimar and Dessau as Gropius wrote from Dessau to the former Administrator at Weimar, Dr Neckar, "You are most certainly mistaken if you think that we have ordered plates for a model lamp that was patented in the name of Wagenfeld in Berlin. On the contrary, Wagenfeld signed that regardless of whether he accompanied us to Dessau or not, he would hand over his formal right to use his designs to us in Dessau. As a result it is with perfect justification that we continue to manufacture and sell the lamps to date. He has patented his new lamp. To what extent this is based on the old version I am not in a position to judge. Furthermore he has not been in contact with us regarding this matter. But following discussions with him in person and in writing, I see no difficulties. I shall not act small-mindedly in this matter."[18] Wagenfeld thus developed other lamps on the basis of his Bauhaus lamp. In 1925 he decided to remain in Weimar. "Outward reasons were the trigger. Inwardly my remaining was a personal necessity."[19] Until December of the same year he continued to work together as "floor mate" with Christian Dell in the workshop at the school which had been taken over by the architect Otto Bartning and was reopened under the name of State Architectural School (*Staatliche Bauhochschule*) on 1 April 1926. Beginning on the same date Wagenfeld was given a new contract of employment as assistant to the metal workshop now headed by Richard Winkelmayer, from whom he took over the reins from 1 April 1928.[20] His first design at his new workplace was a table lamp with a parchment shade, glass shaft and glass base; he used this same combination of materials for further lamps with plastic shades. In April 1930, the Weimar architectural school was also closed by the National Socialists and the entire teaching staff dismissed. "After long negotiations, at least the copyright" was returned to Wagenfeld for his models and designs. On 10 April 1930, he writes, "It is now possible for me to make free use of these works".[21]

A new chapter in the chequered history of the Bauhaus lamp now began since the regained utilisation rights also included the rights to the Bauhaus designs in which the Dessau school no longer had any interest.

As early as May 1930, Wagenfeld presented the first specimen of his technically considerably improved metal lamp to the public. There were also some alterations to the dimensions.[22] In the autumn this was followed by the new version of the glass lamp, which was five centimetres taller than the metal version. In contrast to the earlier designs the most striking change is the extremely high glass dome which is rounded off almost to a five-eighths globe – a feature which was almost certainly due to the problem of the strong heat developed by more powerful light bulbs as mentioned above.

The new Wagenfeld lamps – this time "patented", as the advertising brochure proclaimed – were manufactured for the Dresden-based Architekturbedarf GmbH and marketed by them and another Dresden company, Neue Kunst Fides GmbH. They complete the series of table lamps developed at the architectural school. As Klaus Struve has convincingly explained (see his chapter "Diversity and Consolidation", p. 66–85), Wagenfeld deliberately did not want his designs to compete with the movable and adjustable desk and office lamps as developed by Christian Dell in Frankfurt or Marianne Brandt and Hin Bredendieck at the Dessau Bauhaus, but chose the domestic lighting sector which had been completely neglected by the industry up to that point. Not surprisingly, the remarkably graphic impact of the Bauhaus lamp – even when it is switched off – has always been emphasised by critics.

The profound knowledge in the field of electrical engineering that Wagenfeld had gained during his years at the architectural school allowed him to offer the metal lamp at an initial price of 22 Reichsmark, later 18, and to offer the glass lamp for 28 (in contrast the small Dessau glass lamp had been priced at 55 Reichsmark).[23] Delighting in the pride of possession, Wagenfeld named his "recovered" lamps W1 and W2. Gropius showed the new metal version at the Werkbund show in Paris in 1930[24] – or rather in the German section of the "20. Exposition de la Société des Artistes Décorateurs" at the Grand Palais, where rooms were also designed by Moholy-Nagy, Bayer and Breuer.

businessman Walter Schnepel of the Bremen-based Tecnolumen to bring out another edition of his first work from 1924. A fruitful dialogue began: the lamp was modernised insofar as it was absolutely necessary in order to comply with modern safety regulations and Wagenfeld made some changes to the proportions of the lamps which were important to him but are barely perceptible to the layman. In contrast to today's frequently reissued replicas of design classics, the "new" Bauhaus lamps produced from 1980 onwards occupy a special position. Although they are very true to the original design, they also bear the hallmark of an experienced designer and display an assured balance.

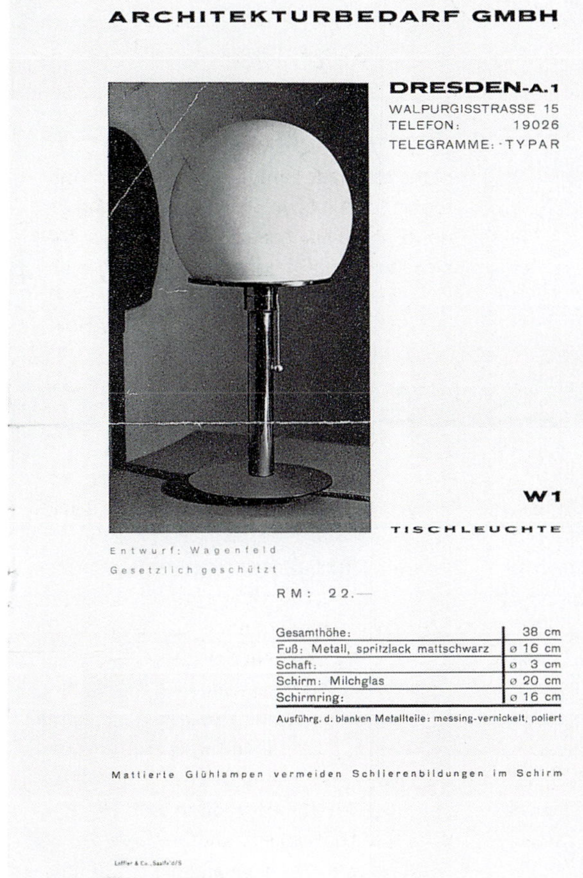

ARCHITEKTURBEDARF GMBH

DRESDEN-A.1
WALPURGISSTRASSE 15
TELEFON: 19026
TELEGRAMME: TYPAR

W1
TISCHLEUCHTE

Entwurf: Wagenfeld
Gesetzlich geschützt

RM: 22.—

Gesamthöhe:	38 cm
Fuß: Metall, spritzlack mattschwarz	ø 16 cm
Schaft:	ø 3 cm
Schirm: Milchglas	ø 20 cm
Schirmring:	ø 16 cm

Ausführg. d. blanken Metallteile: messing-vernickelt, poliert

Mattierte Glühlampen vermeiden Schlierenbildungen im Schirm

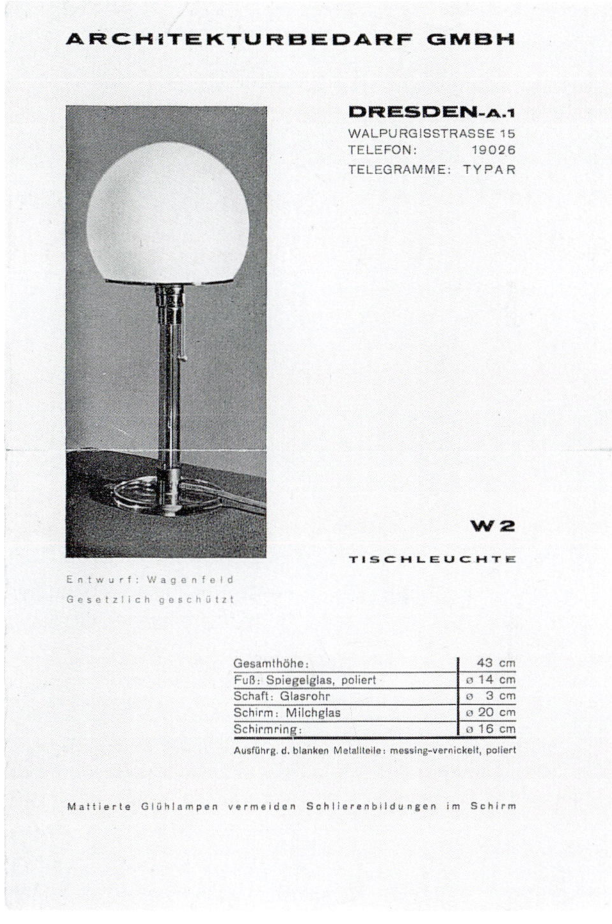

ARCHITEKTURBEDARF GMBH

DRESDEN-A.1
WALPURGISSTRASSE 15
TELEFON: 19026
TELEGRAMME: TYPAR

W2
TISCHLEUCHTE

Entwurf: Wagenfeld
Gesetzlich geschützt

Gesamthöhe:	43 cm
Fuß: Spiegelglas, poliert	ø 14 cm
Schaft: Glasrohr	ø 3 cm
Schirm: Milchglas	ø 20 cm
Schirmring:	ø 16 cm

Ausführg. d. blanken Metallteile: messing-vernickelt, poliert

Mattierte Glühlampen vermeiden Schlierenbildungen im Schirm

8, 9 Advertisement inserts (each front page) by the company Architekturbedarf GmbH Dresden for the altered new issue of the two Bauhaus lamps, 1930

In 1933 the manufacture of Bauhaus lamps was finally discontinued. Under the changed political circumstances a product so clearly linked with the Bauhaus did not have a chance – even without being expressly banned.

It was not until the 1960s that the fundamental achievements of the Bauhaus were acknowledged in Germany through publications and exhibitions and were gradually drawn to the attention of a wider public. Wagenfeld, who made a considerable contribution to the development of contemporary lamps from the early 1950s to the early 1970s, was suddenly confronted in 1979 with a surprising proposal from

The worldwide attention and accord occasioned by the lamp's reissue not only resulted in numerous copies and imitations but also triggered off disputes over the intellectual copyright. The verdict pronounced by Hamburg's intermediate court of appeal on 4 March 1999 has now clarified the matter legally; the key phrase being: "Wagenfeld is to be considered the sole creator of the 'glass lamp' in the legal sense [...]."[25] Since art publications continue to attribute the lamps to different creators notwithstanding, we would now like to briefly outline the complicated facts of the matter.[26]

Former Bauhaus students, Gyula Pap and Carl Jacob Jucker, who left the school in autumn 1923 and never met Wagenfeld, both claimed in retrospect – over fifty years later – to have been party to the genesis of the glass version. Since the only accepted and valid blueprint of the lamp was developed for the metal lamp in 1924 by Wagenfeld and not transferred to a glass version until later, the question of joint copyright is not relevant. The issue at stake is rather how to assess the alleged or real "preliminary work".

In the case of Gyula Pap, it was evidently no more than working on "similar" glass pieces. With a view to the planned

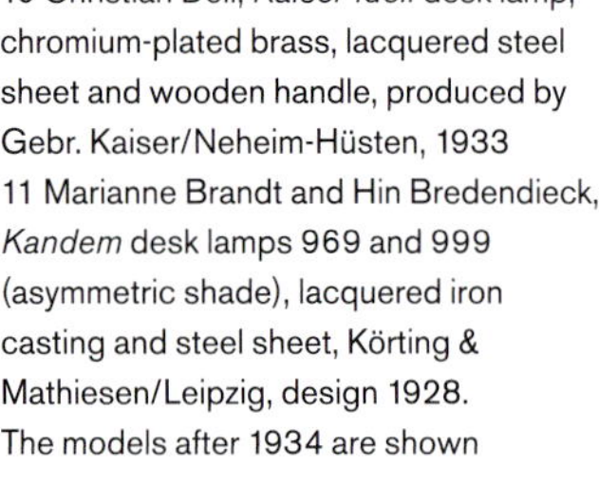

10 Christian Dell, *Kaiser-idell* desk lamp, chromium-plated brass, lacquered steel sheet and wooden handle, produced by Gebr. Kaiser/Neheim-Hüsten, 1933
11 Marianne Brandt and Hin Bredendieck, *Kandem* desk lamps 969 and 999 (asymmetric shade), lacquered iron casting and steel sheet, Körting & Mathiesen/Leipzig, design 1928. The models after 1934 are shown

summer exhibition the entire workshop was involved in fitting out the experimental show house in 1923. As is clear from the monthly reports, Pap was occupied with designs for standard lamps but his practical work consisted almost exclusively of improving a glass samovar, which however he did not finish because "too many things about it were not quite ready".[27] Pap maintains he gave Jucker the parts for this samovar, which he had ordered but which did not arrive until just before he was due to leave, "to make a table lamp with". Allegedly, these parts consisted of "four glass tubes intended as feet, a thick round glass plate intended as a base and an unusable frosted glass globe which was too small and the walls of which were too thin." [28] Jucker has denied this version of matters or rather called it "completely fictitious"; [29] and indeed insofar as it can be compared with the facts which have been handed down, it is certainly not very credible.

At the beginning of the year, Jucker was the only member of the metal workshop who was working on lighting appliances for the *Haus am Horn*. With the help of the head of the workshop, Christian Dell, he developed angle-poise or extendable metal lamps, which, despite a recognisable attempt to seek distinct "technoid" forms, were extremely awkwardly constructed and later laughed at as "dinosaurs". When Moholy-Nagy took over the workshop in early April 1923 the developmental work was put on a new footing: all the lamps were to be uniformly designed from metal and glass. The designs, which have been handed down to us as photographs, show how fundamentally the approach changed at Moholy-Nagy's instigation: the pupils no longer tackled "appliances" but sought to make the phenomenon of "electricity" their theme. Pap's standard lamp consists of a broad, flat base and a tall, very thin shaft which ends in a flat glass disc.[30] The light bulb has no covering of any sort but is simply mirrored – an aesthetically convincing design. The six table lamps made from glass on the other hand, which according to the monthly reports were being worked on by Jucker, are clearly geared towards an experiment to "dematerialise" the lamp: the round base plates and cylindrical glass shafts are virtually invisible or rather allow our attention to be drawn solely to the coloured electrical wires which are openly led through the glass tube up to the light bulb. The left lamp in fig. 12 shows the approach most clearly; here the light bulb is completely unprotected. The remaining studies serve the attempt to moderate the dazzle-effect by means of small screens, moveable metal plates or simply by mirroring. There is no sign of any technical preparation whatsoever for the possibility of covering the light bulb with a traditional glass dome nor is it in any sense in keeping with the concept. The only design which was actually executed and exhibited in the *Haus am Horn* is the right-hand lamp with the hinged metal shade (fig. 13) which comes closest to Pap's standard lamp; it is the only one to which a pull switch was soldered. A contemporary critic described it very clearly, "The table lamp cannot be used as the light bulb is completely exposed on top of a glass disc and dazzles the user. In order to emphasise the 'technology' the shaft of the table lamp is made of a glass tube, which conducts the electrical wires. The base consists of a circular glass plate. We ask ourselves why? And the technicians from Weimar will maintain that glass is the only material possible for a table lamp."[31]

Closer inspection of the six glass lamps reveals above all a fundamental difference to Wagenfeld's design. The lamps are studies used to act out an idea with no consideration for formal coherence. This played a secondary role since only those materials were used which were to hand at the time: thus the base plates and glass shafts are of varying diameters and heights and none of them achieve harmonious proportions.

designed his metal lamp and this material variant was pointed out to him.

Pap's attempt to lay claim to the idea of the appearance of the Bauhaus lamp is contradicted by the chronological and factual sequence of events. Jucker left the Bauhaus on 18 August 1923, three days after the exhibition was opened showing his lamp that we have described above. Pap therefore could not possibly have given him the idea, at the end of August, of making a glass lamp with an opaline glass dome. [32]

The claims put forward by Jucker from 1980 onwards have also been disproved: for example, maintaining that he only created

12, 13 Carl Jacob Jucker, studies of six glass table lamps, Bauhaus Weimar, 1923

The metal workshop evidently found no way of developing a usable range of lamps out of this undoubtedly interesting but unfinished approach after Jucker left. The parts were left untouched until Wagenfeld had

one single glass lamp and that he ordered the materials personally for this from the glassworks in Jena; but that the opaline glass dome belonging to the piece did not arrive until after the Bauhaus exhibition in

Weimar had begun. [33] He also maintained that the lamp was not exhibited there for long since it soon landed in the Director's office. As proof of this he cites a photograph of Gropius' desk, yet this photograph shows a lamp which is beyond a shadow of a doubt Wagenfeld's metal lamp.[34]

The continuing art historical dispute over Jucker and Wagenfeld's "joint authorship" of the glass lamp – a dispute conducted independently of questions of legal copyright – is difficult to comprehend in view of the above. It is based on information contained in a Bauhaus publication and the context of this publication requires explanation.

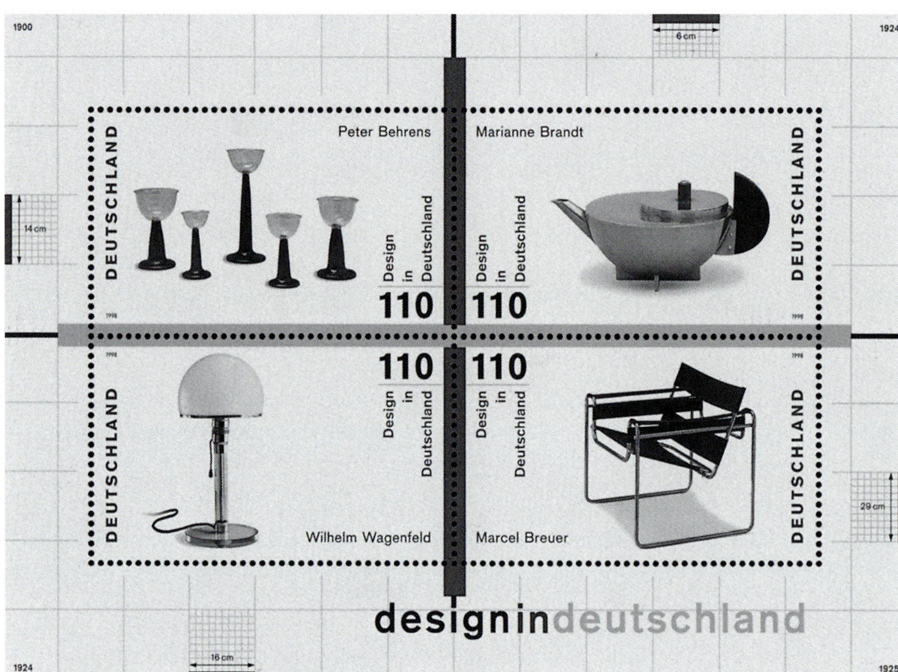

14 Ingo Wulff, *Design in Germany* block of stamps I, 1998

In the series of Bauhaus books edited by Walter Gropius and Laszlo Moholy-Nagy, Volume 7 of the series entitled *New Works of the Bauhaus Workshops* was drafted in 1924 and did not appear in print until 1925. In this volume a picture caption attributes the metal lamp to Wagenfeld alone but the glass lamp to Jucker and Wagenfeld. This was at the instigation of Wagenfeld himself. Shortly before the book went to press on 11 October 1924, Wagenfeld had applied to the "Meisterrat" or senate of the Bauhaus that all Bauhaus products be published or exhibited under the name of the school or workshop only, as he had strongly internalised the element of teamwork in the workshop and supported it wholeheartedly. The angry letter written by Erich Dieckmann protesting at such a "notion" and signed by a large number of members of the Bauhaus is reprinted virtually in full by Karl-Heinz Hüter.[35] In a second letter, written a few days later, Dieckmann informed the senate of the Bauhaus that the representatives of the workshops unanimously wanted the work of journeymen and apprentices to be published together with their names.[36] This wish was taken note of and the Bauhaus made a particular effort from then on not to neglect any of the "authors". We have to believe Wagenfeld, whose intention it had been to stress the aspect of teamwork at the workshop, when he said that he himself "had wanted Jucker's name to be included too" [...] "having in mind the lamp he had seen by him".[37] Since the teacher's contribution to the design idea was never mentioned on principle, the picture caption pays tribute on the one hand to Jucker's 1923 experiment in creating lamps entirely out of glass, and on the other to Wagenfeld's achievement in giving this idea a convincing form, namely as a material variant of his own design in 1924, irrespective of what Jucker may have designed. This is the only conclusion that is of significance for any art-historical attributing of the authorship of the designs.

In the eyes of all those involved, Jucker's mention in the publication did full justice to his rights. He received no royalties from the Bauhaus lamp and the apportionment agreement was not signed by Jucker but by Wagenfeld (see Walter Gropius' letter dated 31 August 1925 mentioned on p. 30).[38]

At a much later date, in 1970, Jucker used his earlier designs as a starting point for the development of two new lamps, which were produced by the Milan-based company, Imago dp. One metal table lamp with a mirrored light bulb and a swivel reflector is a replica of the *Haus am Horn* lamp but made of different materials. The other is a glass lamp with an opaline glass dome which is mounted on a metal ring.[39] Despite using the same basic elements as the Bauhaus lamp, a completely different product has been achieved: "Coarse proportions and a squat dome are a visual affront", wrote Magdalena Droste in her monograph on the Bauhaus lamp.[40] If Jucker, as he later maintained, was the co-author of the "real" Bauhaus glass lamp or at least believed he was, why did he not publish it at this point unchallenged and without competition? Why did he try to prove that he was the sole creator ten years later in the ways described above, maintaining that Wagenfeld simply added technical improvements?

Evidently it was the triumphal march and commercial success of the Wagenfeld lamps that triggered Jucker not only to claim the use of glass parts as his own "invention" but also to lay claim to the lamp's visual design. The court verdict above has produced the desired clarity in this matter; the only thing that remains is to point out that not one of the competing designs ever achieved anything close to the quality of Wagenfeld's lamp.

Notes

1 Wilhelm Wagenfeld, "Zu den Arbeiten der Metallwerkstatt. Service und Tischlampe", in: *Bauhaus Weimar,* Special supplement to *Junge Menschen,* Vol. 5, No. 8, 1924, reprinted Munich 1980.

2 These lamps often have imaginatively designed bases and bowl-shaped white glass shades. A selection, including designs by the Wiener Werkstätte and Josef Hoffmann can be found in: Magdalena Droste, *Die Bauhaus Lampe von Carl Jacob Jucker und Wilhelm Wagenfeld* (Design Klassiker, 8), Frankfurt am Main 1997, p. 40 f.

3 See Beate Manske, "Zwei Lampen sind nie gleich. Wilhelm Wagenfeld in der Metallwerkstatt des Staatlichen Bauhauses Weimar", in: *Die Metallwerkstatt am Bauhaus,* ed. Klaus Weber, exh. cat., Bauhaus Archiv Berlin, Berlin 1992, pp. 79–91.

4 *Wilhelm Wagenfeld. Handzeichnungen und Druckgraphik,* exh. cat., Barkenhoff Worpswede, printed in the series of papers by the Barkenhoff-Stiftung Worpswede, Worpsweder Verlag 1996.

5 Thüringisches Staatsarchiv, Staatliches Bauhaus 176.

6 Document dated 5 March 1924, Thüringisches Staatsarchiv, Staatliches Bauhaus 59.

7 Wilhelm Wagenfeld, "Die Geschichte meiner Bauhaus-Lampe", in: *Bauhaus-Lampe 1924,* brochure by the company Tecnolumen, Bremen 1980, unpaginated.

8 Wilhelm Wagenfeld, "Das Staatliche Bauhaus – die Jahre in Weimar", in: *form,* vol. 37, 1967, p. 19.

9 Illustrated in: Beate Manske 1992 (see note 3), fig. 110.

10 Report by Theodor Bogler dated 19 June 1924, Thüringisches Staatsarchiv, Staatliches Bauhaus 61.

11 Handwritten manuscript, Archiv Wilhelm Wagenfeld, Stuttgart. The lamps had already been presented at the Stuttgart Werkbund show "Die Form" (June/July 1924) and the Frankfurt Autumn Fair and offered for sale at 23 and 28 M respectively. For the Leipzig Autumn Fair, which was considered to be an important test, the price was reduced to 18 M. In comparison to the machine-produced lamps by the other suppliers this price was still much too high.

12 Report dated 4 September 1924, Thüringisches Staatsarchiv, Staatliches Bauhaus 59.

13 Wagenfeld too obtained a copy of "his" metal lamp to give to his parents as a present; it later came into his possession again.

14 In keeping with the numbering of the metal version with the model number MT8 and the glass version with the number MT9, the large version was given the number MT10. The model numbers were not assigned from the beginning but were introduced at the earliest in July 1924. This later selection meant that only those of the designs created from October 1922 onwards were chosen which were considered suitable for further reproduction.

15 Thüringisches Staatsarchiv, Staatliches Bauhaus 183.

16 See the draft which has survived for Sample Sheet No. 1708, *Bauhaus-Modelle,* by Schwintzer & Gräff, reproduced in: *Die Metallwerkstatt am Bauhaus* (see note 3), fig. 106 f.

17 Printed in: *Täglich in der Hand,* ed. Beate Manske and Gudrun Scholz, 4th edition, Bremen 1998, p. 278 f.

18 Thüringisches Staatsarchiv, Staatliche Hochschule für Handwerk und Baukunst 90; original in lower case letters.

19 Wilhelm Wagenfeld, "Kleine Betrachtungen" (1938), in: Wilhelm Wagenfeld, *Wesen und Gestalt der Dinge um uns,* Potsdam 1948, identical reprint Worpsweder Verlag 1990, p. 26.

20 Contracts of employment, Archiv Wilhelm Wagenfeld, Stuttgart.

21 Letter from Wilhelm Wagenfeld to Dr Erhard, Director of the Kunstgewerbe-Museum für Edelmetall-Industrie e. V., Schwäbisch-Gmünd; original in today's Museum für Natur und Stadtkultur.

22 See note 21. Wagenfeld had been planning an exhibition of the works of the architectural school with a focus on the metal workshop with the museum since the beginning of January when he was taken by surprise by political events and the school's closure. The exhibition was opened nevertheless on 11 May 1930 but consisted almost entirely of designs by Wagenfeld supplemented with a few works by pupils. In a letter from Wagenfeld to the museum dated 2 May 1930 he wrote, "I am sending you the promised cloakroom console 3716 made by the S. A. Loevy Co. of Berlin, and also the candelabra W1 by today's express post. The candelabra left the factory only half-finished. The glass shade used I had made here specially.".

23 The prices of 18 and 28 Reichsmark respectively were listed by the Dresden company Neue Kunst Fides GmbH in: Wilhelm Lotz, *Wie richte ich meine Wohnung ein? Modern, gut, mit welchen Kosten?,* Berlin 1930, No. 216.

24 See advertisement by the company Architekturbedarf GmbH Dresden, in: *Die Form,* Vol. 5, No. 11/12, 1930, unpaginated.

25 Published in: *Zeitschrift für gewerblichen Rechtsschutz und Urheberrecht* (GRUR), No. 8–9, 1999, p. 714 ff.; extracts reproduced in: *Original und Serienprodukt,* ed. Beate Manske, exh. cat., Wilhelm Wagenfeld Haus Bremen, Bremen 1999.

26 Detailed description in Christian Wolsdorff, "Die Bauhaus-Lampe. Versuch einer Rekonstruktion ihrer Entstehungsgeschichte", in: *Design – Formgebung für jedermann, Typen und Prototypen,* exh. cat., Kunstgewerbemuseum Zurich, Zurich 1983, pp. 48–55, and Wolsdorff, "Designer im Widerspruch", in: *m. d. Möbel interior design,* No. 4, 1984, pp. 27–30.

27 Christian Dell on 4 July 1923, monthly reports (see note 5).

28 Gyula Pap, "Zeit des Suchens und Experimentierens" (1978), in: *form + zweck,* Special Edition, Vol. 11, No. 3, 1979, p. 57 (Bauhaus Booklet No. 2).

29 Letter from Carl Jacob Jucker to the Bauhaus Archives dated 28 November 1983, Bauhaus-Archiv Berlin.

30 According to Hubertus Gassner there were at least four design variants, which either had a disc-shaped glass globe above three light bulbs or a slightly concave shallow bowl or a flat sheet of mirrored glass underneath a mirrored light bulb (Hubertus Gassner, "Zwischen den Stühlen sitzend sich im Kreise drehen", in: *Wechselwirkungen. Ungarische Avantgarde in der Weimarer Republik,* exh. cat., Neue Galerie, Kassel, and Museum Bochum; Marburg 1986, p. 313 f.).

31 "Schön, neu und zweckmäßig. Zur Bauhaus-Ausstellung in Weimar im August 1923", in: *Fachblatt für Holzarbeiter,* November/December 1923, p. 163.

32 According to the interim report by the metal workshop dated 18 August 1923 (Thüringisches Staatsarchiv, Staatliches Bauhaus 1976), Pap intended to remain at the Bauhaus until the beginning of September; however in the following days or weeks he made a sudden journey to his sick mother in Transylvania and did not return to the Bauhaus. See *Bauhaus 3,* catalogue no. 9, Galerie am Sachsenplatz Leipzig, Leipzig 1978, p. 15 f.

33 Letter from Carl Jacob Jucker to the Bauhaus Archives dated 18 November 1981, Bauhaus Archives Berlin.

34 Letter from Carl Jacob Jucker to the Bauhaus Archives dated 8 September 1990, Bauhaus Archives Berlin. In this last statement Jucker refers to a photograph dated 1923 which was in Gropius' study. However it has been proven that the photograph was not taken until 1924. It is reproduced in: *Neue Arbeiten der Bauhaus-*

Werkstätten, 1925, colour plates after p. 16.

35 Karl-Heinz Hüter, *Das Bauhaus in Weimar,* 2nd edition, Berlin 1976, Doc. 97, p. 275 f.

36 Thüringisches Staatsarchiv, Staatliches Bauhaus 132, und Karl-Heinz Hüter (see note 35).

37 Letter from Wilhelm Wagenfeld to Willi Rotzler dated 12 January 1982, Wilhelm Wagenfeld Stiftung, Bremen.

38 Thüringisches Staatsarchiv, Staatliches Bauhaus 199. The piece of paper listing "property rights" found deposited in the file on apportionment negotiations between Weimar and Dessau has often been cited in support of Jucker's case. Yet, not only for the glass lamp MT9, which is attributed here to Jucker alone, the paper either wrongly lists only one name for each of the other "joint authorship" works or misrepresents the facts, not to mention other errors and omissions. The undated piece of paper, not signed by any of the members of the Bauhaus, is to be seen simply as a preliminary list – probably drawn up by the administration – not as an evidential document. A reminder of Gropius' phrase cited in the main body of text above, is appropriate here, namely that Wagenfeld signed that [...], he would hand over his formal right to use his designs to us in Dessau." (see note 18). This letter clearly refers to the glass lamp.

39 The Spanish company Metalarte manufactured Jucker's lamp under the name of *Valentino.* See Thomas Heyden, *Die Bauhaus-Lampe,* publ. Museumspädagogischer Dienst Berlin for the Bauhaus-Archiv Berlin 1992, p. 62, fig. 51.

40 Magdalena Droste 1997 (see note 2), p. 32.

The Experiment
Schott & Gen. in Jena
Walter Scheiffele

"The role played by the artist in industrial production" was the title of a survey for designers and industrial companies published by *Die Form,* the trade journal of the Deutscher Werkbund in 1930.[1] A very up-to-the-minute topic. Since the mid-1920s many sectors of industry had been introducing rationalised manufacturing methods. The mass product became a sign of the times. At colleges of art and design, such as the Bauhaus, the Bauhochschule and Burg Giebichenstein, courses were training the future product designers of prototypes and standard forms. The artist's participation in developing industrial products was at issue: would artists be able to set new standards, or would technical parameters and public taste remain the sole determining factors? While engineers were exclusively responsible for determining the functionality and design of the products at a portion of the companies in the survey, others had already been working in closer collaboration with designers for some time. Wilhelm Wagenfeld, one of the artists interviewed, referred to the connection between his Bauhochschule workshop and some small industrial firms, and told of a sophisticated range of procedures for the development of prototypes culminating in a carefully-prepared model. The time appeared ripe for an experiment in big industry.

At the "Neues Wohnen" ("New Living") exhibition in January 1931, the Jena art society showed an advanced programme of modern household appliances based on designs from teachers of the Bauhochschule. It was here that Wilhelm Wagenfeld first met Dr. Erich Schott. The scientific head of the Jenaer Glassworks was amongst the audience when Wagenfeld held the opening speech, "Machines and Handicrafts". "This speech," a critic of the *Jenaische Zeitung* wrote, "perfectly matched the room, it matched the style and the substance of the objects on show. How rare it is to find this quality in a speaker! – His words and phrases have sprung from the very same persuasion to which the room and the beautiful objects in the room owe their creation." Both the exhibition and the speech made a similarly strong impression on the visitors. The critic also noted, "The guests stayed on for quite a while, caught up in excited conversation: one could feel the thread connecting the objects, people and words in one common way of thinking. Truly a successful hour in the healthy atmosphere of a clear spirit."[2] It was in this atmosphere, Wilhelm Wagenfeld was to recall, that he had a conversation with Erich Schott about the dissatisfying shape of the Jenaer household glassware. In response to Wagenfeld's criticism of the fact that only scientists and not artists were involved in designing the glass, Schott offered to venture an experiment with the designer.

The world-famous glassworks had always held a great fascination for the artistic avant-garde. The pioneering work of Otto Schott, whose research placed glassmaking on a scientific basis, the borosilicate glass with its fantastic properties and ultimately, his turning the laboratory itself into a generator of all that was new, became for them a guiding principle on their way to modernism. From Henry van de Velde to Walter Gropius, artists' studios were reinterpreted as labs in which new instruments were created using systematic developmental procedures. In the kitchen of the *Haus am Horn,* which Georg Muche appropriately dubbed the "housewife's laboratory", prototypes from the artistic laboratories of the Bauhaus school came together with the household glassware from Schott's laboratory for the first time. The result was numerous attempts on the part of the Bauhaus designers to have an influence on the glassware of Schott & Gen. It was the "Sintrax" coffee maker by Gerhard Marcks that inaugurated the redesigning of the Jenaer glassware.

When Wilhelm Wagenfeld was hired by Erich Schott in 1931, the Jenaer household glassware range had not been updated since 1923, the year in which it had been exhibited at the *Haus am Horn:* there were baking dishes of various sizes and shapes fashioned after American samples, supplemented by tea and punch glasses as well as a coffee maker and a teapot by Marcks.

1 Teapot, Schott & Gen./Jena, 1931

2, 3 Functional household glass in Europe: Tea set from Czechoslovakia by Ladislav Sutnar, 1931, and baking dish from England by Harold Stabler, 1932

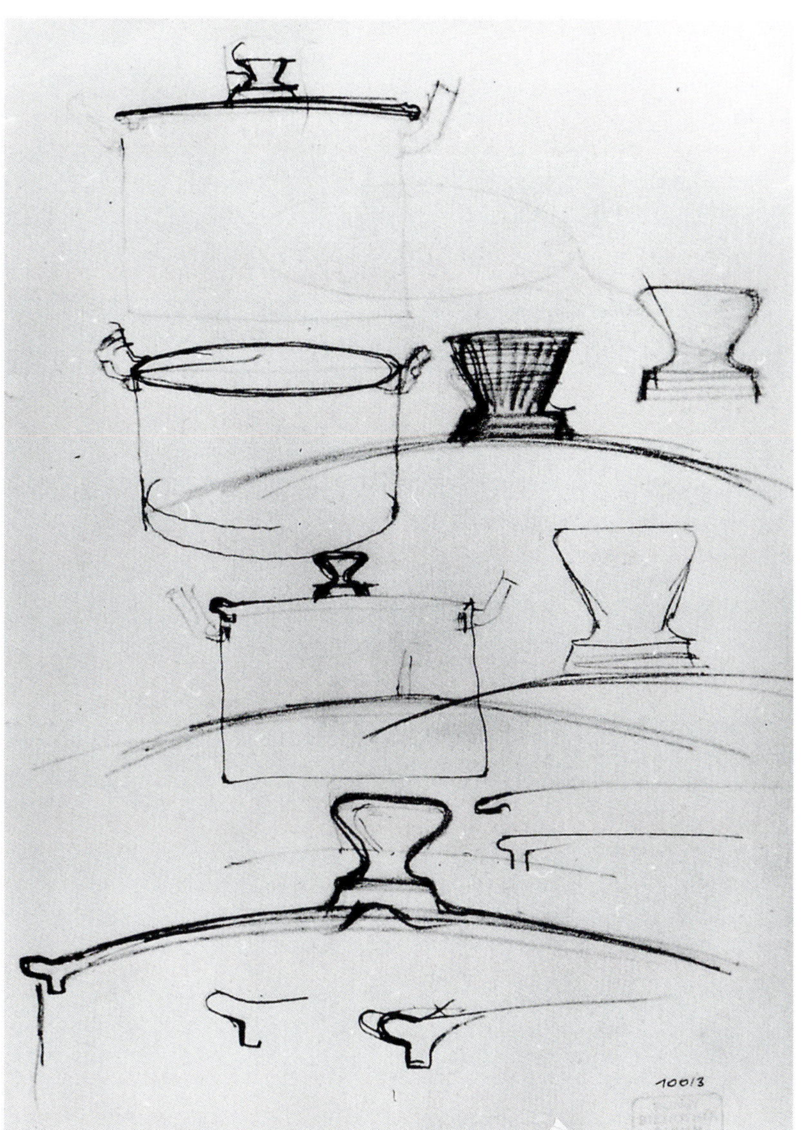

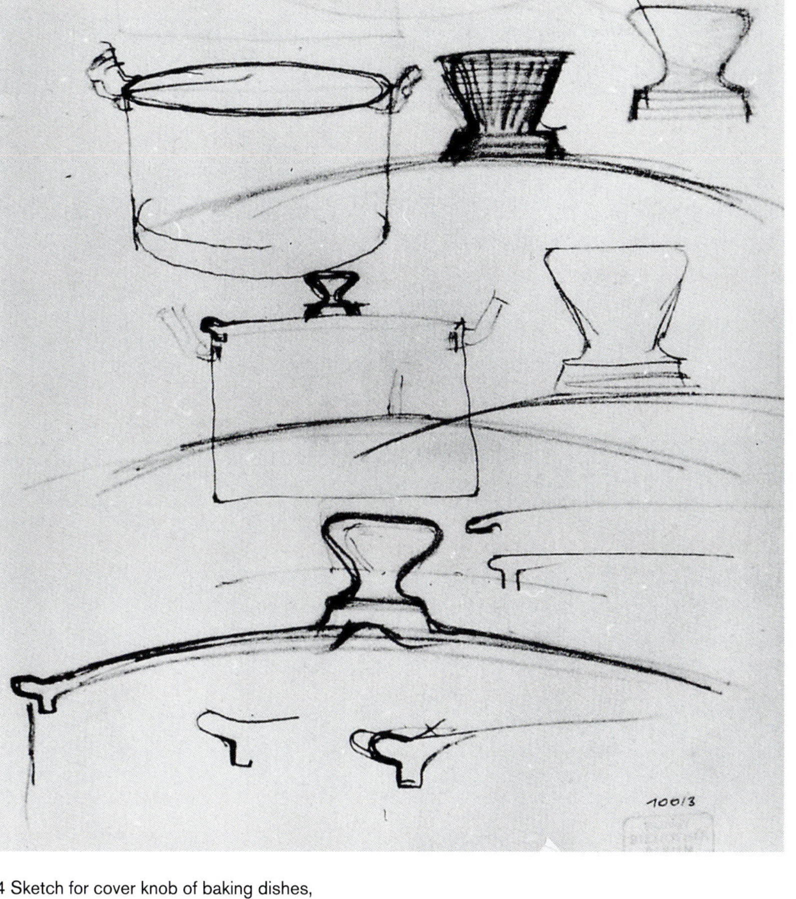

4 Sketch for cover knob of baking dishes, 1934/35

5 Baking dish and covered bowl on the gas cooker, photo: Albert Renger-Patzsch, 1935/38

6 Table set with Jenaer glassware, photo: Albert Renger-Patzsch, 1935/38

7 Atelier Moholy-Nagy, advert, 1932/35

In addition to the improvements already announced by Walter Gropius that were to be made to the baking dishes, which comprised the largest portion of turnover, further designs were yet to be developed before "oven-proof" glassware was to find its way into households everywhere. Although the heat resistance of the Jenaer baking dishes was astonishing enough in itself, a really spectacular feat was needed to ensure the popularity of this glassware. This was achieved by Wagenfeld with the design of his famous teapot. No other product has been able to exploit the transparency of this material so convincingly and effectively. Light and bright, almost floating and swaying, the body of the teapot, as a working drawing shows, is constructed of two intersecting discs. Possessing a similar light airiness with its conical shape and flat, widened top surface, the tea warmer lifts and enhances the volume of the "glass bubble". The shallow, wide-brimmed teacups, the saucers and cake plates similarly have no base ring. As a lucky coincidence, this vivacious tea set played a major role in a play by Oscar Wilde. When Hilde Hildebrandt served tea from Wagenfeld's teapot in *Lady Windermere's Fan,* it immediately became the talk of the day in Berlin and the metropolis was soon the bulk purchaser of this product.

8 Milk pots, Schott & Gen./Jena, 1931

9 Cocoa jug, Schott & Gen./Jena, 1933

The difficulties that the artist had surmounted in giving this form to glass are not in evidence in the tea set. The fact that Erich Schott found the introduction of a designer to the new material to be "toilsome", can be more easily understood in the transition from metal pots to glass baking dishes. The "metallic" shape caused problems and at the same time raised basic questions about industrial design. Still sketching the cylindrical shape, Wagenfeld became aware of how ill-suited the abrupt junctures between forms were to the properties of the new material. Suddenly the teachings of the Bauhaus school were also being put to the test. The Jenaer glassmakers taught the artist a lesson: "The student saw in the glassworks how little melted glass had in common with a cylinder, as long as it was still being swayed hither and thither at the end of the glass-blowing pipe and had not yet been forced into its intended shape in wooden or metal moulds. Nowhere could he discover a straight line, but rather curves as gentle and as taut as those he had only ever seen in creations of Nature."[3] Encouraged by these observations, Wagenfeld used an optical gauge to study the tension created in the glass bowls, and was able to develop designs which were largely free of tension in their organic development. This was a mark of the high quality of the new Jenaer glassware. The unification of art and technology was realised on the most advanced level.

Wagenfeld's designs are distinctive not only in their basic designs but also in every detail. The feature of forming the edge of a dish into a handle was borrowed from the early baking dishes. But now came a new kind of handle which brought with it the opportunity to introduce a closer, more emotional connection between hand and object. From the Jenaer baking dish to the pressed glassware of the *Vereinigte Lausitzer Glaswerke AG* (VLG) and the *Cromargan* bowls of WMF, this motif would be seen in many new variations. When the *Versuchsstelle für Hauswirtschaft* – the Testing Office for Home Economics – complained that the teacups were difficult to hold, Wagenfeld took the opportunity to develop a new kind of handle shape, which until then neither engineers nor artists had found. The somewhat protruding handle with an unusual upward curve protects the hand from the hot liquid and lends the cup a distinctive overall shape.

In the years from 1931 to 1935 a range of heat resistant household glassware designed by Wilhelm Wagenfeld was produced at the Jenaer Glassworks. In 1938 a final design was added: a baking dish with a flat cover that could also double as a plate. The twenty-three-piece product line was one of the first realisations of the Bauhaus programme. Not at all uniform and self-contained, it raised queries which Wagenfeld was only to answer at the VLG, and surprisingly it opened the door for the first initiatives in design organisation.

recruited for the advertising of Schott & Gen. A second experiment now took place in Jena: how could the experimental Bauhaus photography and typography be implemented in the advertising campaign of the manufacturer? Moholy-Nagy took part early in the process, even, as Wagenfeld recalls, in the discussions about the Jenaer Glassworks company logo: "With Moholy-Nagy's excellent and subtle changes to the graphic design, the new factory brand now bore only the name of the city famous in the history of glass-making."[4]

In Moholy-Nagy's Berlin studio, in which Bauhaus students such as Hajo Rose

11 Egg cooker, Schott & Gen./Jena, 1934

10 Sauce boat, Schott & Gen./Jena, 1931/32

By the time he was in Jena, Wagenfeld was already forming notions of the work of the designer in industry which surpassed the tasks of a model constructor as formulated by Gropius. Still following the latter's example, Wagenfeld was to present the newly-designed industrial products at exhibitions and champion them in magazine articles. But the "isolation" of the designer in the works, already noted during his time at the Bauhochschule, now struck him as a fundamental hindrance in his striving to unite art and technology, and this was a new perception. Despite the restricted sphere of his responsibilities, and from his weak position as freelancer, Wagenfeld set out to bring other designers into the Jenaer Glassworks.

His most surprising success in this endeavour was the hiring of László Moholy-Nagy. The teacher and Bauhaus master was

12 Cup filter, Schott & Gen./Jena, 1933

and the Neuner brothers worked, an abundance of advertising material was created for the Jena glassmakers. Moholy-Nagy's concept of the "typophoto", which took the increasing significance of optical media into account and ascribed photography a dominant role in visual communication, now demonstrated its suitability for designing advertising material. Excellent object photography formed the point of departure for the integration of typography and photography to a new form of medium which heralded the changeover from Gutenberg-style lead composition to phototypography. The best examples of such phototypes were done by Hajo Rose in Moholy-Nagy's atelier. For the range of preserving jars, Rose had the idea of inserting typographic film into the jars, against the round jar wall, as a simple solution for combining print material and photography into one unit.

A third designer of high standing also made his contribution to the public image of Schott & Gen.: Albert Renger-Patzsch. The leading industrial photographer of the Weimar Republic recorded the production processes in the glassworks, including the manufacturing phases of the teapot and the pressed baking dishes. Renger-Patzsch's photos, like those of Moholy-Nagy, show why German object photography was enjoying such esteem. It lent industrial serial products like these a memorable media presence. Wagenfeld also tried to bring a further photographer to Jena: Bauhaus master Walter Peterhans, by whom a photo of the Wagenfeld teapot survives. For the decoration of an exhibition room at Schott, Wagenfeld sought to enlist the participation of Ludwig Mies van der Rohe and his co-worker Lilly Reich. As artistic manager of the VLG he was later to work together with Lilly Reich again.

In their search for staff members to write texts for the arts columns of newspapers and magazines, in addition to the other advertising, Wagenfeld and Moholy-Nagy

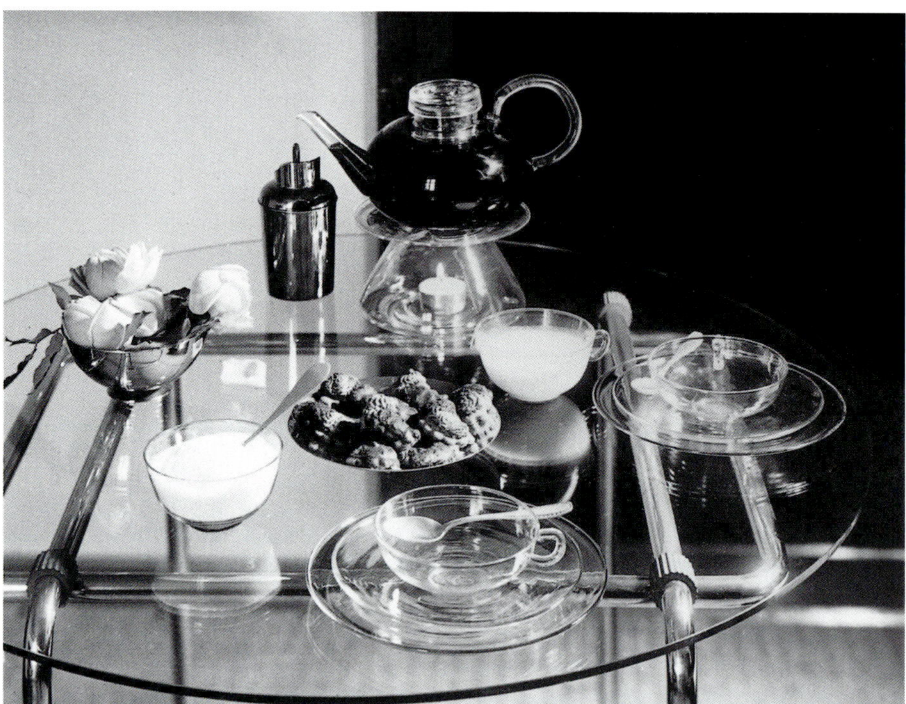

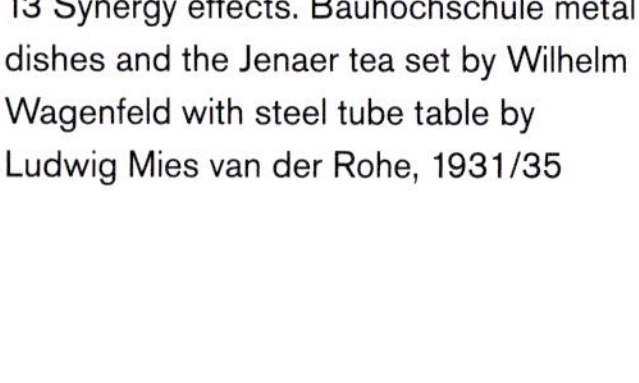

13 Synergy effects. Bauhochschule metal dishes and the Jenaer tea set by Wilhelm Wagenfeld with steel tube table by Ludwig Mies van der Rohe, 1931/35

also discovered Grete Schütte-Lihotzky, creator of the famous Frankfurt kitchen. She wrote an article in eloquent praise of the Jenaer baking dishes, which came very close to her idea of the kitchen as laboratory. In Irmgard Kraatz, a home economics teacher, Wagenfeld acquired another important participant for his cultural network. With her sense of modern economics trained by the rationalisation movement, Kraatz was a welcome critic of the new household glassware. In her household they were tested for their serviceability and ease of handling. For Moholy-Nagy, Irmgard Kraatz was the ideal scout for modernity in big city life. He placed her well-aimed and amusing observations with his adverts in the women's magazines and craft journals.

In the short time just before the Nazis came to power, many things culminated which had been initiated experimentally in the early 1920s. Now many avant-gardist ideas, coming together, proved their extraordinary aesthetic quality. Heinrich König, one of the first to market Jenaer glassware and Bauhaus products, wrote charmingly about the coming together of Jenaer glassware and tubular steel furniture: "The whole fascination of these glass dishes, the teapot by Wilhelm Wagenfeld, the cups, plates, jugs and sugar bowls, was immediately obvious to me. Nothing could better suit the new steel tube tables of Mies van der Rohe with their light crystal glass table tops."[5] Tableware and tables alike were the products of experiment which, similar to those of a scientific nature, undertook to break new ground, with little regard for tradition. Even for such well-meaning critics as Werkbund member Fritz Hellwag, in the case of Wagenfeld's glasses "the demarcation separating glass as a household item and glass as a purely utilitarian object (for example as required in the chemical industry) has almost been reached."[6]

The fact that laying new foundations at such a level could only succeed through the concerted efforts of like-minded people had already become clear to Wilhelm Wagenfeld at Schott & Gen., and by the end of his time in Jena he was not only the designer of the industrial product but also the organiser of a cultural network which formed the essential prerequisite for the unification of art and technology.

Notes

1 "Die Mitarbeit des Künstlers am industriellen Erzeugnis", in: *Die Form,* vol. 5, no. 8, 1930, pp. 197–221.
2 *Jenaische Zeitung,* 14 January 1931.
3 Wilhelm Wagenfeld, "Formschön, Anständig und Gut. Nachdenkliches über die Gestaltung unseres Hausrats," in: *Echo,* universal edition, 1944, pp. 21–30.
4 Hand-written note by Wilhelm Wagenfeld, archives of the Wilhelm Wagenfeld Stiftung, Bremen.
5 "Heinrich König an Dr. Erich Schott zu dessen 70. Geburtstag", in: *Werkzeitschrift Jenaer Glaswerk Schott & Gen., Mainz,* no. 2, 1961, p. 4.
6 Fritz E. Hellwag, *Wilhelm Wagenfeld. Formgebung der Industrieware,* published by Kunst-Dienst, Berlin 1940, p. 12.

The Model Precedent
The Lausitzer Glassworks at Weisswasser

Walter Scheiffele

In the year 1935 Wilhelm Wagenfeld was at a crossroads. With the range of Jena household glass, the Bauhaus designer had proven the significance of the artist for the industry in an impressive way. The Bauhaus programme had been made reality at least in part, and Wagenfeld had a considerable part in it. However, the future appeared uncertain. After four years of designing prototypes for the Jena works, the potential for developing innovatory household glassware there was largely exhausted. At any rate, it was unclear whether the work in collaboration with porcelain manufacturer Fürstenberg, begun in 1934, would be continued. This was the situation when a surprising new prospect opened up. In May of 1935 the largest German glass concern, the Lausitzer Glassworks (VLG), offered Wilhelm Wagenfeld the position of designer in their glass-making operations. But just how difficult this decision was for him is made clear by a letter from Wagenfeld dated 10 May 1935: "Yesterday, as soon as I had arrived in Oberweimar I had to continue on to Jena to talk to Schott about the latest offer from the VLG. They have agreed to meet my demands with a $^{1}/_{2}$-year notice period. Schott was very upset yesterday. We are to continue with the negotiations on Tuesday. Until then I can postpone making a decision while I give my answer to the VLG. The one-year contract period must also be observed from the beginning. Besides, I cannot start by 1 June but rather 1 August. Yesterday I realised for the first time just how much Jena values my work. It may be that the salary has been low, but you dealt with people and the working conditions there are very humane. The VLG is ruled according to capitalistic economic principles without consideration for the people working there. I can clearly see the difficulties I would encounter in my work in Berlin and at the Lausitzer, I know how they are always plotting and scheming against one another. But that can only be a useful lesson for me. The most important thing for me will always be the experiment of asserting myself under such conditions."[1]

Six months later – Wagenfeld had by this time begun his work in Weisswasser, the main site of the VLG – we read: "Since midday today I have been back working happily in my gold-diggers' town. Things are progressing slowly – that is dumb. But I must persevere. Eiff-Stuttgart [the artist-craftsman, Wilhelm von Eiff] has in the meantime become a member of the team, as per my plan. The people in sales are against me. I intend to carry out my plan in such a way that no one can ever claim I did not do everything necessary to win the battle against those mean-minded fellows. What has been newly created is clearer and more right than Fürstenberg. I am on the right track, I just need a bit more time and peace."[2]

Here, in the second half of 1935, Wagenfeld, yet uncertain and hesitant and already struggling against great adversity, followed his own path: the "path into the world of industry". A model precedent. No other person from the Bauhaus so consistently followed Gropius' programme for the unification of art and technology. And, as in Jena, Wagenfeld was to meet another strong-minded entrepreneur who would accompany the designer on his path in Weisswasser: supervisory board chairman of the VLG, Dr. Karl Mey.

The industrialist Mey was once thus described by AEG chairman Hermann Bücher: "I would like [...] here to say that you represent one of the few cases I have ever heard, of a man of importance dedicating himself not to following a company line but to the matter at hand."[3] Indeed, Karl Mey had made his mark in the way praised by Bücher on two global firms in two of the most important modern industrial sectors: Osram and Telefunken. As managing director of AEG, he was able to bring about the consistent development of high-technology products like the incandescent lamp and the valve, and in so doing became a "system builder", introducing co-ordinated decision-making to govern every aspect of industrial processes – including the designing of the products. In 1935 he rescued the VLG – a shared subsidiary of the AEG, Siemens and the Auergesellschaft – from a serious

1 *Warmbrunn* lemonade service,
VLG/Weisswasser, 1935

financial crisis. He then initiated a rehabilitation phase, during which the issue of a new look for the VLG product range came up. The industrialist brought up his idea at the Deutsche Glastechnische Gesellschaft, on whose expert committee for glass processing such designers as Wilhelm von Eiff, Bruno Mauder, Richard Süssmuth and Wilhelm Wagenfeld debated over the influence of artists on industry. At the VLG, "with its 2500 employees and an annual turnover of approximately 12 m. marks," Mey said, "there is not one single person [...] with authority and commitment to artistic quality to take charge of the design of the product in pattern and shape."[4] In the same circle of glass-makers, Wagenfeld would speak of his success at Schott & Gen. in Jena as the first "industrial designer" in the glass sector. For Karl Mey this very probably tipped the balance for taking Wagenfeld on at the VLG.

In the negotiations over the terms and conditions of the employment contract, the directors of the VLG offered Wilhelm Wagenfeld a "full-time position as artistic consultant in our firm, to work in close collaboration with the plant and sales management of our company." Wagenfeld, however, was not satisfied with this formula-

2 *Oberweimar* goblet service, VLG/Weisswasser, 1935

3 "Herzvasen," VLG/Weisswasser, 1935

tion and amended it: "I changed the word consultant to the word manager."[5] At long last the designer's demand for emancipation from the technicians and sales people was being voiced. But how was this artistic management to operate with the product range of a major concern, which in 1935 included an astonishing 60 000 different items of glassware and whose hollow glass works alone produced 50 000 tumblers and 35 000 goblets daily? Wagenfeld would have quickly realised that to keep pace with such dimensions he would have to reorganise the designing process. In the first few weeks after the signing of his contract, he travelled extensively, visiting the workshops and studios, professional classes and glass cellections of Bruno Mauder, Wilhelm von Eiff and Hermann Gretsch. He began to develop his tactic of assuring himself of the progressive standards in Stuttgart and Zwiesel while protecting the company from unwelcome competition by making them proposals of co-operation.

Thus Max Hagl, a glass cutter from von Eiff's class, and Erich Jachmann, the glass engraver who had studied under Bruno Mauder, came to Weisswasser. Prototype-designers Wilhelm Görtler and Friedrich Bundtzen were taken from the VLG works and brought to Wagenfeld's workshop. Together with sculptor and porcelain maker Heinrich Löffelhardt, Wagenfeld adopted new methods of designing glass. Accustomed to testing the designs and functional properties on a model, his experience with Fürstenberg, where plaster models traditionally preceded production, encouraged him in his intention to similarly integrate models into his glass designing. Wagenfeld recorded the sequences of this creative process with the example of the *Hermsdorf* jug. The design sketch now led to the plaster model and the technical drawing – also a novelty in the glass industry – and then to a glass prototype from a wooden mould, after which the metal moulds for serial production were made.

Thus, during 1935 and 1936, there developed at Weisswasser an artistic workshop which Wagenfeld, recalling the experimental workshops of the Bauhaus, sometimes also dubbed "artistic laboratory". Here, in plaster and grinding workshops the models for the new glassware were created. After Wagenfeld's decision to move permanently to Weisswasser, the workshop, which was located on the grounds of the firm's plant management, also became a venue for museum curators and journalists who were to introduce the new glassware to the public.

Wagenfeld soon realised that to entertain the idea of turning upside down the overwhelmingly large product range of the VLG at a blow would be pure folly. He cleverly relieved himself of the responsibility for the entire range, turning considered retreat into an audacious advance. "There is nothing to reform. We must drive a wedge of new quality into the existing overall range."[6] To that end and in the style of an experienced brand manager, he created a brand of his own, the "Rautenmarke" (i.e., "Diamond Brand"), with which hallmark the "Rautengläser" exclusive to his workshop would be traded. Thus insured,

4 Richard L. F. Schulz, *Troll* liqueur glass set, VLG/Weisswasser, 1935/39

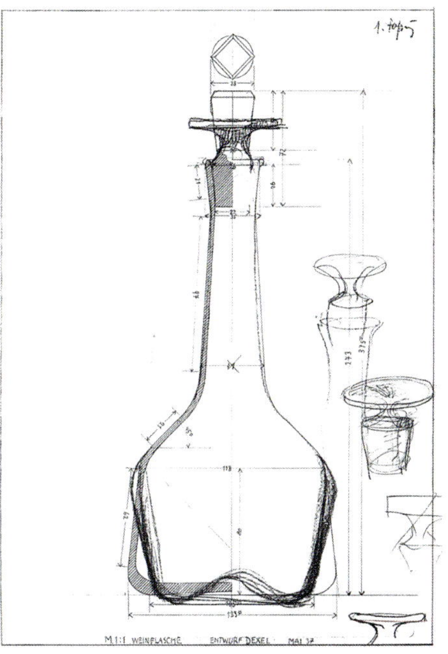

5 Walter Dexel, drawing of a wine bottle with corrections by Wilhelm Wagenfeld, 1937

Wagenfeld could now proceed with the development of new glasses.

His very first set of goblets, the *Oberweimar* series, immediately characterised the new line of the Lausitzer Glassworks. Glasses as delicate and thin as only the "muslin"-ware of a Josef Hoffmann had ever been before, attested to the standards of high-quality design and craftsmanship. The VLG, the largest stemmed-glass manufacturer in Europe, now had a set of glasses which met the most exacting taste. The glasses of the *Warmbrunn* lemonade set, another of VLG's mass production items, were similarly thin and elegant and formed a unit with the unique form of the decanter. Like these series the vases styled "Herzvasen" ("heart-shaped vases") were also created in the year 1935. As in the case of the *Warmbrunn* jug, the fascinating silhouette of these vases made for a convincing new design.

Even during his time at Schott & Gen. Wagenfeld had tried to reinforce the significance of art in industrial operations through the hiring of further designers. The first network had been established. As artistic manager of the VLG, Wagenfeld again sought collaboration with the most renowned designers of the day. While Bruno Mauder and Wilhelm von Eiff supported him in setting up his workshop, Richard L. F. Schulz contributed with many designs to the creation of the "Rautenglas" collection. From the co-founder of the Deutscher Werkbund, in addition to vases, bottles, wine cups, tea jars and the *Chiemsee* goblet set, came the *Bunker*, *Einsiedel*, *Lotse* and *Troll* liqueur glasses. Hermann Gretsch, porcelain designer and head of the Württembergisches Landesgewerbemuseum, designed the *Arzberg* goblet set. Walter Dexel, Constructivist and leading historian of vessel design, was denounced "degenerate artist" and suspended from school service in 1935. He designed the *Jena* goblet set. Wolfgang von Wersin, who was discharged from the administration of the Neue Sammlung München in 1934, was amongst the leading commercial artists in southern Germany. In 1938 he designed the *Regensburg* goblet set for the VLG. Even Charles Crodel, who first came to Weisswasser in 1935, was branded a "degenerate" artist and lost his professorship at the Burg Giebichenstein school. He and Wagenfeld would debate intensely on a suitable decoration for serial and also unique products. The guilloche-engraved cups from the series marked with the letters C-R-O-D-E-L were, as Erika Wagenfeld recalls, meant as a pendant to the collectors' porcelain cups. Decorated with translucent enamel painting and delicate line engraving, Crodel's designs became eye-catchers at trade fairs and in museums. By bringing Josef Hoffmann to Weisswasser Wagenfeld acquired one of the leading commercial artists of Austria. This pioneer of modern glass design, who had designed the most beautiful glassware for Lobmeyr, summed up around 1939: "We had to teach ourselves everything and there was almost no one who was in a position to help us. It was only with constant effort that we made any progress. All we had was sure instinct and little else. You are blessed with an excellent, solid foundation and you are predestined to create definitive products of flawless quality."[7] For the VLG, Hoffmann designed a comprehensive series of vases which were as delicate and thin as were his last designs for Lobmeyr.

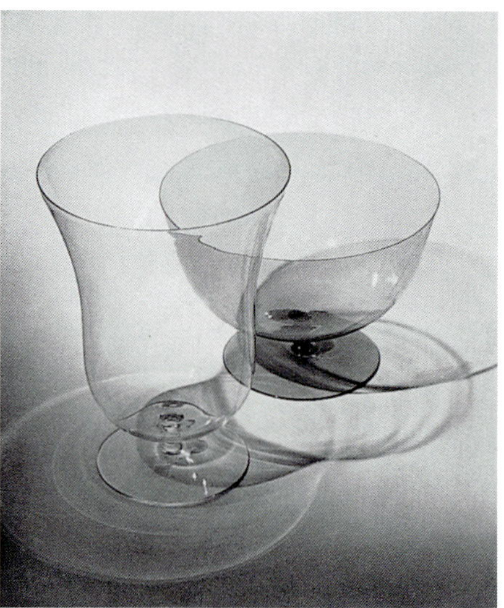

6 Charles Crodel, "C-R-O-D-E-L" beaker series (patterns), VLG/Weisswasser, 1935/39

7 Josef Hoffmann, vases, VLG/Weisswasser, 1935/39

The more distinctive the collection of "Rauten" glasses became, the more noticeably they contrasted with the VLG assortment. Wagenfeld himself criticised the works' blueprints harshly and wrote, "There are only clear options: on the one hand there is the rubbish, the intellectual property of the mean-minded, and on the other, creativity entirely conscious of your responsibility in every sense of the word, with the aim of producing only the best quality possible, under the given conditions, for the retail trade. Every intermediate solution is a waste of time and effort."[8] This strict differentiation between conventional commercial goods and the new glassware which, with its overriding attention to both beauty and utility, could be termed cultural goods, had a logical consequence in a clear demarcation running through advertising and distribution. Wagenfeld would speak later of a "third-way advertising campaign" that aimed at the cultural sphere; but the artistic manager of the VLG was destined to go this path alone. Based on the "Rauten" brand, Wagenfeld developed a brand mission which emphasised the high artistic, technical and craftsmanship quality of the "Rauten" glasses and at the same time underscored their impor-

8 VLG catalogue, *Faktotum* ashtray, 1939

ASCHENSCHALE „FAKTOTUM"

„Endlich einmal eine schöne Aschenschale, die man gern und mit gutem Gewissen verschenken kann", sagte ein Besucher der Entwurfswerkstatt, als er das neue Modell in die Hand nahm, das nach Angaben von Prof. Wagenfeld entwickelt wurde. Für Zigarre, Zigarette und Pfeife ist das „Faktotum" gleich praktisch. Es wird in den drei Farben Hell, Altgrün und Stahlblau geliefert.

Fotos: Dore Barleben, Berlin
B. G. Teubner, Leipzig-Dresden

Aschenschale „Faktotum"

Höhe 65 mm Durchmesser 164 mm Preis RM

VEREINIGTE LAUSITZER GLASWERKE A.-G., WEISSWASSER O/L · VERKAUFSLEITUNG: BERLIN SO 36, LAUSITZER STR. 10-11

tance for the general public: "Even the simplest glass can be beautiful."[9] Not only did Wagenfeld, himself a consummate graphic artist, create the best VLG advertisements, he also developed a promotional campaign for the VLG brand which would make it a dominant hallmark of quality in the glass industry. The third-way advertising campaign approached customers through publications, articles in magazines, catalogues and exhibitions. An unending stream of people interested in the arts flowed to Weisswasser and met in the nearby park of Prince Pückler, formed their impressions of "Rautenglas" production and passed these on to an interested public. Wilhelm Lotz, the representative from the Werkbund, wrote the VLG book *Die Reise zu den Glasbläsern.* Under the pseudonym of Thomas Brackheim, Theodor Heuss, later to be the Federal Republic's first president wrote articles for the *Frankfurter Zeitung* and, together with Wagenfeld and Mey, planned the publication of a journal for the glass industry. Museum directors such as Siegfried Asche and Walter Passarge chose "Rauten" glasses for their collections and exhibitions on contemporary consumer merchandise.

9 Lilly Reich, glass shelves for the "Rauten" glasses in the Grassimuseum, 1937

But the most important emporium for the growing "Rautenglas" assortment was offered by the spring and autumn trade fairs in Leipzig. In the "Zentralmessepalast", the VLG presented their glassware to the trade public. Wagenfeld describes his recollection of their approach: "There was a relatively large room so chock full of the conventional and also the new products of the VLG that the individual objects could hardly be recognised. I observed that the buyers here were primarily retailers to whom the glasses had only an indifferent monetary value."[10] Here Wagenfeld found a more favourable exhibition platform for his "Rauten" glasses, the Grassimuseum, in which high-quality craftsmanship was presented concurrently with the Fair. Now he was finally able to fulfil his long-standing ambition of collaborating with Lilly Reich, probably the most important exhibition designer of the day. The glass cabinets, shelves and tables of glass and chrome which Reich designed for the "Rautenglas" collection in the Grassimuseum, were a further contribution to that synergy effect of modern design which Heinrich König had noted in the combination of Jenaer glassware and the steel tube furniture of Mies van der Rohe. The next year Reich's glass cabinet displays of Wagenfeld's glassware were also to be seen in the "Zentralmessepalast": cultural objects were now meeting up with dealers in their own territory.

The world exposition in Paris gained international recognition for Wagenfeld's "Rauten" glasses. In just two years, the VLG had risen from being a nameless plant for mass production goods to one of the culturally leading glass manufacturers in Europe. A brilliant success for Wilhelm Wagenfeld, who simultaneously won the Grand Prix and the gold medal for his Jenaer glassware, and an equally impressive confirmation for Dr. Karl Mey and his modernisation measures. England's renowned art magazine *The Studio* wrote about the *Lobenstein* goblets, "open bowls balanced elegantly on square-cut solid stems, [it] is charming to look at and attractive to touch, the faceted stems less likely to snap than the thin rounded stems of glasses so tempting to twiddle between courses."[11]

In Paris the VLG glasses could be compared on an international level. Besides Lobmeyr (Austria), Orrefors (Sweden) and Leerdam (Holland), modern glass was now also being presented by Karhula-Iittala (Finland), Rückl (Czechoslovakia), Barovier

10 Alvar Aalto, *Savoy* vase,
Karhula-littala Glassworks, 1936

11 *Lobenstein* goblet service,
VLG/Weisswasser, 1937

12 Andries D. Copier, water carafe,
Leerdam Glassworks, 1937

13 Ludvika Smrčková, breakfast service,
Rückl, 1930–1936

(Italy) and Powell & Sons (England). The Leerdam glassworks came closest to the VLG as an industrial plant. Like Wagenfeld, their leading designer, Andries D. Copier, was interested in creating simple glass designs for a mass market. With the *Gildeglas* he succeeded in creating a first standard wineglass which would be widely used all over Holland. The carafe with water glasses of 1937 again embodied the successful combination of sophisticated design and simple utility glassware; but Leerdam also produced the *Unica,* unique artistic pieces which Copier conceived parallel to the industrial design.

Amongst the German glass designers, Bruno Mauder and Richard Süssmuth were at the same time predecessors and contemporaries of Wilhelm Wagenfeld. In the 1930s they too were searching for simple designs which were suitable for industrial production. Mauder, who had made a major contribution to glass design with an understanding for the material, now began to experiment with engraved ornamental bordering, which he supposed would be cheaper to manufacture than painted line decorations. However, at the same time he was looking for alternatives to mechanised glass production and his glasses formed

14 Bruno Mauder, set of glasses with carafe, Glasfachschule Zwiesel, 1930s

15 Richard Süssmuth, covered dishes, Penzig, 1930s

freehand at the oven set an early precedent for the masters of studio glass. Richard Süssmuth, who ran a workshop for art glass cutting, now designed simple, undecorated household glasses. In Paris Süssmuth was awarded a silver medal for his designs.

The Karhula-Iittala glassworks were highly successful in Paris, in particular with Alvar Aalto's *Savoy* vases. Created for the world exposition, they set new standards in modern design. Like Wagenfeld, Aalto was shifting in the 1930s from a constructivist to an organic design approach, moving away from the symmetry of the centrifugal mould and developing completely free designs. Aino Aalto, on the contrary, designed with *Bölgeblick* the first pressed glasses of beauty in the shapes, predecessors of the pressed "Rauten" glasses.

The Czechoslovakian glass-makers, too, enjoyed great success at the Paris world exposition: Ludvika Smrčková was also awarded the Grand Prix and the gold medal. Like Peter Witt and Ladislav Sutnar, she developed for the consumer co-operative Krásná jizba, which was a base for functional design in Czechoslovakia, beautiful utility glass for mass production. Her breakfast service, produced by Rückl, and the tea set designed by Sutnar and produced by Kavalier, were amongst the outstanding creations of the Czechoslovakian avant-garde movement.

When *The Studio* published an overview of the "New Table Glass in Europe and America" in the spring of 1938, Wilhelm Wagenfeld's *Lobenstein* goblet service was placed first, followed by a service by Andries D. Copier. A "fight for supremacy",[12] as the magazine postulated? Certainly during those years one would have been forgiven for thinking so. More than any other European workshops or distributors of cottage industry glass, more than any glass factory, Leerdam and the VLG had realised the most consistent industrial standards combined with high-calibre artistic design. Production across the range and in all its aspects was increasingly affected and placed under artistic direction. Thus the "Rauten" brand in 1938 comprised some 179 products, including 14 services and sets – and all designed by Wagenfeld! After the Paris world exposition the *Oberweimar* series of glasses was joined by the *Lobenstein* service. The bowl, of equally thin glass, but with a wider opening, stood on a square-cut faceted stem, giving the service its distinctive design. Parallel to his elegant goblets, Wagenfeld also created short-stemmed and stable glasses such as the *Hochstadt, Bremen* and *Tiefurt* series. The next step, in the *Reichenhall* and *Hallstadt* glasses of 1938/39, was to subsume the stem altogether in a squat, upward-tapering foot. Then there were the vases – besides the popular "Herzvasen", the large *Paris* vase, for example, whose voluminous body was complemented to perfection by the neck opened out gracefully from it. Of the numerous vases, the large floor vases *München, Berlin* and *Wien* stand out. Vases like the *Münster* were now produced with press glass technology. The methodology and creative power with which Wagenfeld and his workshop created this wide assortment was awe-inspiring. Material properties were well researched and adeptly exploited – the thin-walled glass out of its tension against the steady breath of the glass-blower, the thick-walled out of the tough viscosity of the glass mass, or the finely engraved net structure and the sparkle of assertive cutting and polishing. A colour spectrum of bronze-green, steel blue, pale yellow and aquamarine made the "Rauten" glasses lucid and light. The shape of the "Rauten" glasses was characterised by a sure instinct for arresting three-dimensional form, by carefully-worked details and a clear concept of functionality. Wagenfeld was freeing a traditional area of much of its clutter; but in the field of pressed glass he was breaking new ground. This industrial glass, burdened with the stigma of being cheap and of poor quality, now became the designer's central challenge. Wagenfeld's inventive talents, from designing to providing legal protection for registered designs and production patents, in short, his comprehensive striving for high quality, characterised the pressed glasses of the "Rautenglas" assortment. The most beautiful and at the same low-priced glasses produced by the VLG could now be discovered in a medium and market niche that until then would not have received a second glance. Whether ashtrays and wine-coolers for restaurants, saucers for plant pots, egg cups, apple graters, lemon squeezers or jam jars for household use, Wagenfeld would search meticulously for a solution with a high level of utility for every one of these. The ashtrays were so deep that the ashes could not fly out; the edge for resting the cigarette was ribbed to prevent condensation moisture from forming. The egg cups had attached saucers for the egg spoon and the eggshell. The saucer for plant pots was equipped with ridges on which the pot rested. The lemon squeezer was a two-piece creation; only the dish was brought to table.

Wagenfeld's greatest success with pressed glass was with the *Cube* food storage dishes: a miniature building block system. The "squared circle" contours of the freehand sketch (Pl. 13, 14, p. 113), given a tauter interpretation toward the square in the actual glass, made for a refreshing, sculptural quality in this cube-based container set for larder and refrigerator. It became a market success without rival and, along with the Bauhaus lamp and the Jena tea set, became a further design classic.

16 Vases, VLG/Weisswasser, 1935

In Weisswasser a new dimension of Wagenfeld's cultural concept became evident. He now took up a central problem over and above the designing of products: the distortion of human labour in industry. How could beautiful glass be created in an antiquated industrial sector? How could high-quality glass be produced where the art of glass-making was degraded as a

17 *Paris* vase, VLG/Weisswasser, 1936

18 *Münster* vase, pressed glass, VLG/Weisswasser, 1938

semiskilled occupation? It was not a coincidence that, in 1936, a job analysis from social worker Anneliese von Borsig was to be found on Wagenfeld's desk. Anneliese von Borsig was the granddaughter of a legendary locomotive tycoon. In the glassworks of the VLG, von Borsig discovered conditions which she summarises succinctly: "Favourable working conditions over and above the basic essentials are lacking almost everywhere."[13] She noted the lack of the most elementary standards. Disorderly work stations, poor work organisation, outdated technology and insufficient provisions for effective breaks all explained, and their pride in having been part of the production of an extraordinary product. With his thoughtful consideration and his uncompromising criteria of quality, "the professor", as they called him, had won their respect.

A high point in Wagenfeld's efforts to improve industrial working conditions came when he succeeded in introducing Ernst Neufert, one of the important modern architects, to the VLG. Neufert, who had managed Gropius' site office and taught at the Bauhochschule, built a glassworks and a central warehouse in Weisswasser. This modern industrial plant marked the influx of

19 *Granada* lemon and orange squeezer, pressed glass, VLG/Weisswasser, 1937

according to her report, the low quality of the products. Wilhelm Wagenfeld also looked to the way work was organised in his efforts to raise the its quality. He became involved in the training of the glass-makers, and on his suggestion, at each working area "a master was stationed who made sure that every man was given work best suited to his capabilities."[14] In the canteens of the VLG the workers were informed about the success of the "Rauten" glasses. Wagenfeld's entire efforts were geared to reinstating the "working pride" of the glass-makers. They never forgot their struggles for better wages

modern industrial engineering into the glass industry. This was a starting point for Wagenfeld's later visions of a different working world: "If only a spirit of adventure were the motivating power, the desire for what is new and the need to venture into unknown territory. Then all the glassworks would be lit up and the temperature would be moderate despite the ovens, and the factory halls would be lit and the air in them clean, nowhere would glassware be lugged about in cases or rolled on carts, and there would be no wasting of material and time through errands and transporting over

20 Wine cooler, pressed glass,
VLG/Weisswasser, 1938

21 *Greifswald* dishes, pressed glass,
VLG/Weisswasser, 1938/39

23 Table set with *Kubus* dishes and *Daphne* tea service (Rosenthal), late 1930s

22 *Kubus* dishes, VLG/Weisswasser, 1938

unnecessary distances, the office staff would be reduced to a minimum and the science of industrial engineering would no longer be an unknown field of knowledge."[15] In the brief phase of departure fever after the war, and in the circle of the town planners working with Hans Scharoun, culture finally became an imaginable concept as an entity, the synthesis of labour and living. Together with Siegfried Asche, Wagenfeld tried to interest Hans Scharoun in some new urban development plans in Weisswasser – a project of industrial culture as had not been realised or even considered since Wilhelm Osthaus' time in Hagen.

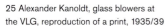

24 Ernst Neufert, new glassworks of the VLG, 1936

25 Alexander Kanoldt, glass blowers at the VLG, reproduction of a print, 1935/39

If Wagenfeld had always rejected the restricting view of design as an isolated discipline, it was because, since his Bauhaus days, he had always considered the connection to the arts to be so essential. It was no coincidence that the remote town of Weisswasser became a refuge for many artists in the 1930s. These were artists who were branded as degenerate by the NS cultural policy and accused of tending to "cultural Bolshevism". Alexander Kanoldt, who had protected Wagenfeld from similar allegations at the art academy in Berlin, now found himself in difficulties. Upon Wagenfeld's initiative, along with Ludwig Gies and Konrad von Kardorff, he found work and a new subject in the factories of the VLG. Their prints and drawings were given to staff as anniversary presents – instead of portraits of the "Führer" – and their works were collected by the VLG management. Sculptor Walther Wolff did a likeness of Karl Mey; on Mey's 65th birthday Wagenfeld presented him with a portfolio of the artists' works. Reinhold Ewald, Wagenfeld's teacher at the drawing academy in Hanau, also sketched at the VLG glassworks and worked on compositions dealing with the diversity of glass-making processes. In a speech at the opening of an exhibition of Ewald's works, Wagenfeld found himself walking a fine line between culture and politics: "He who feels called upon to sit in judgement over art, to point to Another Way, to separate what might be the chaff from the wheat, should take a very close look indeed at his own capabilities in carrying out such a task. He who judges others must himself have a big heart and a generous spirit, and must be familiar with the laws of the land. Anyone who sits in judgement over works of art must be like such a judge and be aware of the sublime meaning of all art and its high intended purpose."[16]

A similar tightrope was walked by the circle of Wagenfeld's friends and fellow workers, for example when VLG staff met up with high-ranking National Socialists at the Hotel Prenzel. As Konrad Sage relates, "Time was when there would be a table regularly reserved in Weisswasser, with you, Neufert, Jockisch, the Gestapo officer Blume, and SS officer Egloffstein. These were incredibly cosy evenings, during which I needed to muster all my strength to hold my tongue. Because – having been forbidden to work – I only existed thanks to Neufert's highly admirable discretion as construction supervisor."[17] In similar vein, Wagenfeld noted: "Later Egloffstein and Aschoff came. – If I could manage only one thing – to keep silent more!"[18]

In the Weisswasser of that time, when perpetrators, hangers-on and the persecuted associated with one another in close proximity, Adolf Reichwein, a member of the German Resistance, also played a part. Wagenfeld's appointments diary from this time shows many meetings and telephone calls with him. From the departing train at Weisswasser Reichwein called, "Active through passive resistance, Wagenfeld!" Soon afterwards he was hanged in Plötzensee.[19]

A calm oasis in this circus of insanity was provided by the "Insel", as the house of the Wagenfeld family was called – The Island. Within these protective walls the circle of friends and colleagues read, listened to music and talked. Very inventive warning devices at the windows prevented unwanted ears from listening in. The letters from VLG co-workers at the front reflect an image of the "Island" as the distant symbol of another world full of peace and culture.

The "Rautenglas" programme fell apart with the outbreak of the war. From the year 1939 we find six new sketches among the working drawings, from 1939/40 there are seven and from 1940 only three. How ironic that in this very year the "Rauten" glasses were awarded the Grand Prix at the Milan Triennale. Heinrich Löffelhardt, Wagenfeld's closest colleague, was conscripted in 1939, and the others over the course of the first few years of the war. During the war Wilhelm Wagenfeld fought an exhausting battle to retain the core of qualified glass-makers in the VLG and – in collaboration with Richard Süssmuth – to ensure the quality of glass production in the glass industry of Lower Silesia. Although a particular object of scrutiny under the watchful eye of the "National Socialist Labour Party" (NSDAP), Wagenfeld was shielded by the VLG management. When he was conscripted in the autumn of 1942 the commercial manager at VLG, Wilhelm Bremer, nominated him to the firm's Board, which enabled Wagenfeld to return to his workshop in March of 1943. Mid-1944 saw increased confrontations with the NSDAP. His refusal to join the party resulted in his being sent to the front, where he was taken prisoner of war.

The post-war years, despite the general hardships, offered the opportunity to thoroughly think about culture and its forms of organisation. Building upon his experience as artistic manager of a major company, Wagenfeld rehearsed constructions which looked beyond the bounds of a private firm and took every aspect of culture into consideration. How could culture, the state and business be combined in a relationship which would not only cover people's basic needs but also pave the way for a new product culture? Even during the last stages of the war, such a project that inherently transcended the four walls of the glass concern was mooted. In the emergency programme envisaged by Wagenfeld and Süssmuth, a wartime line of pressed glass was to be designed that would be produced by all the glassworks in Lower Silesia. The concept of the planned economy for rebuilding industry in the Eastern Zone also lead to the idea in 1947 of making "Rautenglas" into an obligatory programme for all East German glass producers. Bauhaus graduate Franz Ehrlich, who was also involved in the plans for reconstruction, actively favoured the programme. As late as 1949 such plans were still being discussed. By then, however, Wagenfeld was fast dissociating himself from planning that he was already convinced was inflexible, and tried to redirect it instead into an organic increase of the quality output.

In the place of visionary plans came the exhausting rebuilding of the VLG, which had been bombed during the war. As the Eastern Zone made the transition into a planned economy, the VLG, renamed Oberlausitzer Glaswerke or OLG, became the core of the collective combine for the entire GDR. In 1947 the Oberlausitzer Glassworks again took up the production of "Rautenglas", with an increased use of optical

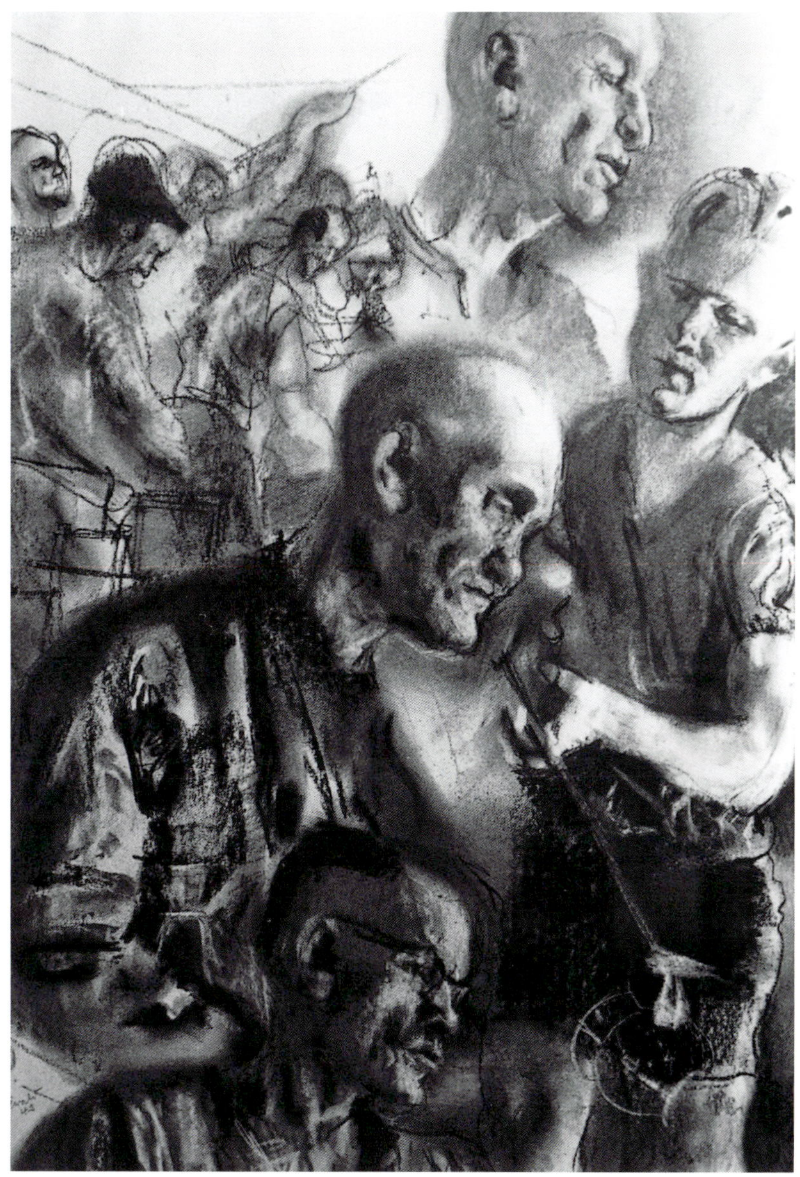

26 Reinhold Ewald, glass-makers at the VLG, print, 1935/39

patterns and cutting, necessarily, to compensate the inferior quality of the melted glass. The *Amorbach* cut, for example, was created during this time. Wagenfeld's orientation westward and the formation of two separate German states meant that contractual agreements with him on the production of "Rauten" glasses, licenses and so on lost all meaning. Nevertheless, "Rautenglas" ware continued to be produced in Weisswasser until the 1960s, and the quality glass sector was maintained by Wagenfeld's colleague Friedrich Bundtzen until well into the 1970s.

Wilhelm Wagenfeld was always aware that his activity at the VLG would go down in the history of industrial design as a precedent. Whenever product and market strategies were being forged, in firms such as WMF, Peill & Putzler or Lindner, he would fall back on his wealth of experience at Weisswasser, reminding people about the exemplary support he had received from the Chairman of the Supervisory Board as a designer. Ideas from the advertising plan for 1938 can be found again in *Vorschläge für die WMF-Werbung,* which describe a third-way advertising strategy for high-quality merchandise. Inspired by the *Hallstadt* glasses, the *Greif* service was produced by Peill & Putzler; the WMF *Doria* series was created as a revival of the *Oberweimar* goblet set. This is the deeper meaning of an "organic" design: the objects mature and develop in their utility properties and designs over a long period of time. As standards and prototypes they make their mark in the cultural landscape of society. This was what Walter Gropius had had in mind when he wrote to his former student: "I assure you that you and your works are the quintessential model of all that the Bauhaus strove for. I appreciate your work and the path you have unwaveringly followed in your co-operation with industry in order to influence its production. Your work follows our first experiments at the Bauhaus to the letter."[20] When Wilhelm Wagenfeld wrote to Gropius that, "after the war, however, I never again had as much freedom to make decisions as during my time in Weisswasser",[21] it was a sign that the relationship between economy and culture had taken a turn for the worse.

Lewis Mumford had already expressed his opinion in 1930 on the logic of such tendencies, in the same issue of *Die Form* which first set off discussion in Germany about the role of the artist in industry. The cultural question, as the great American cultural critic stated, is irrevocably connected to economic and social factors: "Sooner or later every community must accept the truth, that automated production must be socially-oriented. Because it creates either useful durable goods and free time or else a lot of worthless goods that do not achieve either time or prosperity, other than for the money-makers."[22]

Notes

1 Letter from Wilhelm Wagenfeld to Joachim Kraatz, 10 May 1935, private archives of the author.
2 Letter from Wilhelm Wagenfeld to Irmgard Kraatz, 9 December 1935, private archives of the author.
3 Speech of Board Chairman Hermann Bücher on Karl Mey's 65th birthday, 11 March 1944, private archives of Karl Mey Jr.
4 *Glastechnische Berichte,* vol. 13, no. 1, 1935, p. 39.
5 Letter from the VLG management to Wilhelm Wagenfeld, 8 May 1935, and reply from Wagenfeld, 11 May 1935; both from the Wilhelm Wagenfeld Stiftung, Bremen.
6 Wilhelm Wagenfeld's conversation with Otto Sudrow and Walter Scheiffele, 6 April 1983.
7 Letter from Josef Hoffmann to Wilhelm Wagenfeld, undated (1939), Wilhelm Wagenfeld Stiftung, Bremen.
8 Wilhelm Wagenfeld, "Drei Jahre Aufbau und Entwicklung einer Entwurfswerkstatt in der Glas-industrie", in: *Glastechnische Berichte,* vol. 17, no. 8, 1939, p. 247.
9 Advertisement for "Rauten" glasses, in: *Die Schaulade,* vol. 14, no. 9, 1938.
10 Quote from Olaf Thormann, "Die Leipziger Grassimessen", in: *Wilhelm Wagenfeld: gestern, heute, morgen. Lebenskultur im Alltag,* published by the Wilhelm Wagenfeld Stiftung, Bremen 1995, p. 119.
11 Quote from "New Table Glass in Europe and America", in: *The Studio,* Vol. CXV, no. 541, 1938, p. 196.
12 *The Studio* 1938 (see note 11), p. 200.
13 Excerpt from a social report by Anneliese von Borsig on the A Works, from the year 1936, p. 2, Wilhelm Wagenfeld Stiftung, Bremen.
14 Wilhelm Wagenfeld, "Notizen: Künstlerischer Leiter der Vereinigten Lausitzer Glaswerke AG", typescript, 1977, p. 2 f.
15 Letter from Wilhelm Wagenfeld to the Office for Plant Reorganisation, Dresden, 29 July 1946, Wilhelm Wagenfeld Stiftung, Bremen.
16 Wilhelm Wagenfeld's speech at the opening of an exhibition of Reinhold Ewald's work in the city museum in Bautzen, February 1944, Wilhelm Wagenfeld Stiftung, Bremen.
17 Letter from Konrad Sage to Wilhelm Wagenfeld, 22 April 1985.
18 Wilhelm Wagenfeld in a personal calendar from 1939, Wilhelm Wagenfeld Stiftung, Bremen.
19 Note from Wilhelm Wagenfeld on 20 June 1979, Wilhelm Wagenfeld Stiftung, Bremen.
20 Letter from Walter Gropius to Wilhelm Wagenfeld, 14 May 1965, Bauhaus-Archiv Berlin.
21 Letter from Wilhelm Wagenfeld to Walter Gropius, 4 July 1960, Bauhaus-Archiv Berlin.
22 Lewis Mumford, "'Modern' als Handelsware", in: *Die Form,* vol. 5, no. 8, 1930, p. 223.

Diversity and Consolidation
Wilhelm Wagenfeld's Achievements in the Design of Lamps and Lucent Units

Klaus Struve

Wagenfeld: a Protean Designer of Lamps and Lucent Units[1]

What diversity of skills and how many facets of his personality did Wagenfeld have to develop in order to have created such a comprehensive range of designs for lamps, lucent units and even illuminants?[2]

Both in obeying the necessities of his work as a designer and in order to integrate the conditions peculiar to the industrial production of consumer goods for general use (for example at Schott & Gen./Jena, Lausitzer Glassworks/Weisswasser, Peill & Putzler/Düren or Lindner/Bamberg), Wagenfeld had to develop abilities in a number of different areas; and, over the course of half a century (1920s to 1970s), to constantly tailor and update these skills to meet ever new and concrete standards. In that versatility, five fundamental skills and personality traits emerge. –

- The willpower to design 'the objects around us' to meet civil,[3] private and social needs. Wagenfeld left no room for doubt that this was an 'ethically motivated' drive that led people "to a perpetual revision of past accomplishment".[4]
- The sensual perception of objects and the interpretation of these perceptions – their intellectual processing, with full consciousness of the emotional response, with the aim of grasping the 'destined use', for example of a piece of furniture or an appliance, "and its own given bounds".[5]
- The ability to explore the potential technical and constructive solutions in designing and producting of useful appliances, in this case lamps. This also includes the selection and assessment of the materials to be used under consideration of their properties.
- The ability to register and integrate the economic laws of the industrial production of 'utility goods' "that meet everyday needs on a large scale; and the design of these appliances has found its clearest form of expression when it completely fulfils the requirements of both, general use and the production processes."[6]
- The ability to listen, to communicate with everyone contributing to the successful outcome of the work, to the quality of the product of joint efforts, with "enthusiasm and good will", as Wagenfeld wrote. "Quality is therefore not the achievement of the designer, but rather the achievement of the factory, it is the fine outcome of the positive collaboration of everyone involved. The salesman is just as important for this as the plant manager, the technician, scientist, master craftsman and worker."[7]

"The simpler the industrial product is to be" – and many of Wagenfeld's lamps are truly of a simple nature –, "the more difficult it is to meet the conditions for it. Simplicity being that uncomplicated state which can only exist at the beginning and at the end, that comes from the unselfconsciousness that we know from children, and from the clarity that has overcome all willing and constraining."[8] Wagenfeld was satisfied with an industrial product which, by his "actions, only after its long transformation from the idea to the finished product," stands before one "like a stranger".[9]

Wagenfeld's personality encompassed all these and further capabilities which, in the arena between 'dynamic and static principles,'[10] were continually put to the test as tools adequate for mastering every new challenge in his work. In such literally and generally productive living and working circumstances, the only certitude for Wagenfeld and his co-workers lay in the fact that they 'proceeded from reality', and knew their 'point of departure to be firmly rooted in the everyday lives' of individuals in society.[11] There were, as Wagenfeld insisted, no general rules for mastering new challenges. If there were occasions when "a certain shape is the overriding idea, the next time it may well be the idea of a function. The purpose of a table lamp is to provide the most favourable local lighting possible in a dark room. The technical task of the lamp is thus defined and could probably be achieved quickly enough with a properly constructed reflector. And yet in most cases, such a lamp would only serve a meagre part of its purpose. For our eyes want not only a technically perfect source of light, but also a pleasing illumination effect, which is closely and inseparably connected with its form. How can we benefit from a calm and even light if the effect is marred by the poor design of its source? Or, conversely, what is the good of a design if it stands in the way of any efficient lighting? Here, perfect balance between functionality and design is absolutely crucial; because during the daytime, the table lamp should not stand about like some hideous stove in summer."[12]

The diversity and profundity of Wagenfeld's skills and personality traits qualified him as a pre-eminent vocational trainer, as an educationalist for the design and industrial production of commodities. He worked as an expert in vocational training, possibly without ever being aware of it, because he had an eye for the independence and 'autonomous' potential of the people around him and knew how to build upon it.[13] That also made him the severest critic of all who believed that the calamities of social and economic development could be remedied by "re-educating" the people. To Wagenfeld this urge was the 'foolish malady of Germans', which had also afflicted the 'people in the Werkbund, even back then'. "They are still trying to re-educate people today", he wrote in a letter to Mr G., "instead of working on the premise of influences which are essential for altering the course of events in industry, business and bureaucracy. But that would mean changing the spirit of industry, the spirit of the economy and the spirit of bureaucracy, it would mean taking action, making confrontations and intervening with a sense of political and social responsibility."[14]

What, out of the wide field of activities circumscribed as the design and industrial production of lamps and lucent units, was the niche that Wagenfeld not only discerned, but would then develop and redevelop for himself continually over many decades?

Wagenfeld's perception, be it of the work of the people and experts in his social and professional milieu, of natural phenomena, of the objects for everyday use, the cultural and artistic achievements within his broad horizons[15] or, most of all, of the results of industrial production, remained subtle and critical throughout the long span of his creative work. He was also very interested in the product lines of competitor companies in the lighting industry. Wagenfeld was always prepared for the fact that the others also followed market developments carefully and contributed to them, and that they took ruthlessly from the vocabulary of his designs,[16] but also produced useful, practical and beautiful products of their own.

Wagenfeld was no doubt familiar with every important product of the lighting industry from the 1920s to the 1970s. This includes, in particular, the highly specialised first solutions from the 1920s to lighting drawing and office work as well as production areas in workshops and factories. These were the essential tasks of the still-young lighting industry. Their master craftsmen had already been found, and the designers included Marianne Brandt, Hans Przyrembel, Adolf Meyer and Christian Dell. In this connection, the *MIDGARD* swivel lamps from the Industriewerk Auma in Thuringia and the product line of Körting & Mathiesen in Leipzig/Leutzsch deserve mention for their general significance.[17] Wagenfeld himself worked in the light of a *MIDGARD* swivel lamp.

1 Wilhelm Wagenfeld working in his workshop under the light of a *MIDGARD* swivel lamp, Stuttgart, around 1956

After he began working in industry again in Stuttgart (1950), in collaboration with Günther Peill and his wife, Wagenfeld was even more attentive to every development in the glassworks and the industry producing lucent units, lamps and glass for lighting purposes. He remembered from the 1930s, during his time as artistic manager for the Lausitz Glassworks and not least through his work for Schott & Gen./Jena, that "like household glassware, glass for the lighting industry presents its own challenges."[18] Particularly with regard to lamps and lighting for living spaces, flats and homes, before the Second World War the general requirements of the population were only partially being met,[19] in any case not with the help of any lighting glass that, in Wagenfeld's opinion, was worthy of the name. In 1941 he wrote about the artistic problems associated with designing in industrial production and was quite convinced that lamps, in terms of their design and their manufacture, did not belong to the category of 'electrical appliances [in] the home', and that, in contrast to the 'real' electrical appliances, the 'diverse [household] lamps' had not yet found their proper design.[20]

2 Curt Fischer, *MIDGARD* double table swivel lamp, Industriewerk Auma, Thuringia, before 1925

After the Second World War there was no longer any doubt, for Wagenfeld and others with a similar sense of responsibility, about which duties were now the most important for industrial production. "Never were we more urgently aware of it than when we were faced with the sight of the tattered belongings of homeless people after nights of bombing, and never more clearly than afterwards, when household goods were being made with poor materials and insufficient means in workshops and factories. Here all the barrenness of an unscrupulous greed lay exposed, here revealed the shortcomings of accustomed methods, in an unutterably sober light. Yes – one did not wish to deceive others, one was accustomed to deceiving oneself without even knowing it, and it was no different in terms of one's responsibility towards the goods. And let us not fool ourselves: in the factories where the junk is produced, and in the workshops, hardly anyone – down to the last work station – knows what meaningful work can be! Scarcely anyone thinks about the fact that working hours are also hours in their lives and that industrial goods of inferior quality are human life laid waste."[21]

Thus Wagenfeld sought and found his niche in the sector of designing lamps and lucent units for the 'residential house' of Germany's post-war citizenry, for the homes, the small flats with their small rooms, for living and sleeping, for bathing and for the children to play in.[22]

The ceilings were now no longer 340 centimetres high (over 11 ft.) as in the "Jugendstil" period, nor were they 275 (9 ft.) as in the 1930s. The ceilings in houses built after the war were high enough for a person 190 centimetres tall to reach up and touch it with his fingers, without standing on his tiptoes (the equivalent of 245 centimetres; barely over 8 ft.). This new standard already implied the necessary decisions about the dimensions and volume of ceiling lamps for the general lighting of living space. Lamps suspended from the ceiling on a rod were now only hung over tables or not at all. Wagenfeld catered for the usual range of accommodation between a small flat for a maximum of four people and more luxurious flats and houses for more elevated standards (1960s and 1970s) by developing a wide range of product lines. Wall lamps, not only for kitchens and bathrooms, but also for hallways and living rooms now formed the new element in the assortments of the lamp factories.

The question of which materials or material Wagenfeld would choose for his designs in the field of lighting for living space is a rhetorical one. Naturally he chose glass, the material which gave his entire work its coherence – and not only in the domain of light and lighting.[23] The glass industry had already become the mainstay of the manufacture of lamps and lighting fixtures in the 1920s,[24] but Wagenfeld consistently raised the use of this material for such furnishings to new standards. An apt turn of phrase for Wagenfeld's multifarious work with glass was found by Hans Schwippert from the Werkbund: "With you, Wagenfeld, it all began with baking glassware, followed by drinking vessels and then came chiefly flower vases. And now you are making vessels of light. That must be more than just a coincidentally well-ordered career sequence!"[25]

The industrial production methods specific to making glass, along with the specialised techniques for forming glass objects, were as familiar to Wagenfeld as to other experts in the field. However, his grasp of the essence of his materials, namely, glass and ceramics, and their numerous favourable properties, and his ability to put it into words, were as succinct as Brecht's in relation to learning or Neruda's to the scent of wood.

Wagenfeld's concern is "influencing and convincing, proving by doing"[27]

Design and production of lamps and lucent units based on the principles of the Bauhaus in Weimar

During his ten-year period of artistic creativity in Weimar (1923–1933), Wagenfeld was concerned with the designing and construction of prototypes and even the production of the series of lamps and lucent units he designed. The series as featured in the (probably) last catalogue of the 'Weimar

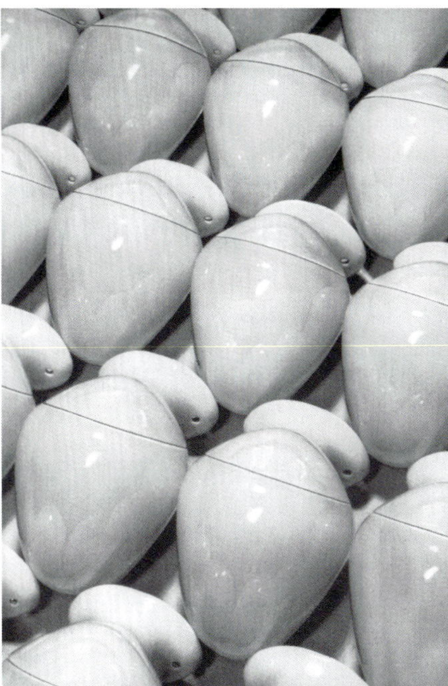

3 The wall lamps, No. 6020, 6021 (two sizes), form an unmistakable unit of porcelain and glass. Designed in 1954 for Lindner/Bamberg, screw-on glass surrounds (opal glass casing) manufactured by Peill & Putzler/Düren. In 1955 the lamps cost 11 and 15 DM apiece respectively

An Ode to Glass and Ceramics

"It is not only the state of solidified liquid,
the transparency
with which the [drinking] glasses so uniquely enrich the world of our senses;
almost more compelling is their fragility
and the careful gentleness
with which we must handle them.

As in the times of Ancient Rome, people today
are still searching for the unbreakable,
but all these efforts have distorted us from the real essence of glass
and the name is borne by what has been found without justification
but for the sake of a delusion.

Just how solid glass, despite its brittle nature,
has become thanks to scientific research,
along with porcelain and other ceramic materials,
is proven by its wide use in technical domains.

Ceramic materials, transformed by fire,
as we know them, thanks to research and sorting
in the laboratories of the institutes and factories,
have become increasingly tractable and inherently refined.

Their applications are more manifold by the day
and our ideas and concepts
are constantly finding new forms of existence for them,
expanding their intended purpose,
enhancing their properties
and placing them in the fore in unexpected areas everywhere."

Wilhelm Wagenfeld[26]

4 Hanging ceiling lamp, Model 54 (diameter 480 mm), Weimar Bau- und Wohnungskunst GmbH, matt and mirror-coated frosted glass. The glass fittings were created in collaboration with Wagenfeld at the Jenaer Glassworks Schott & Gen./Jena, 1931

Bau- and Wohnungskunst GmbH', the former marketing organisation of the Staatliche Bauhochschule in Weimar, comprised five table lamps (Models 41, 38, 29, 25, 2); a desk lamp, equipped with a Zeiss vertical mirror-glass reflector originally produced in series as a technical element for display window lighting (Model 42); an adjustable bedside table or wall lamp (Model 39); a wall lamp for strip lighting (Model 26); some eleven hanging ceiling lamps (Models 13, 57, 63, 61, 61S, 54, 60, 30, 31, 22, 24) and nine ceiling lamps (Models 59, 4, 27, 64, 66, 56, 53, 58, 55).[28] All in all, the series included twenty-eight different models. Moreover, it is worth remembering that Models 13 and 27 were available with a spherical glass surround (the lucent unit) in four different sizes (200, 250, 300 and 350-millimetre diameter). Additionally, Models 57, 63, 61S, 54, 60, 59, 64 and 53 were equipped either with a plane mirror or mirrored glass elements to intensify the illuminating effect of the lucent units or, for example, to produce the desired illumination but with bulbs of lower wattage.

The product range that Wagenfeld developed in collaboration with the metalworking firm of Walther & Wagner in Schleiz was not only very comprehensive but also very sophisticated in terms of the technology, construction and materials. With these products, they attempted to rectify the widespread opinion that the 'technical lamp' was suited for in working areas, in "offices, schools and similar buildings" whereas the 'craft-designed' item belonged in living rooms. In the only article in which Wagenfeld exclusively and fundamentally dealt with issues on the lighting of living space,[29] he analysed the difficulties associated with starting up the still-young lighting industry. "Like a new piece of machinery without a related predecessor to fall back upon, and which usually appears heavy and unnatural in its very first form, when we began to construct technically advanced lamps in keeping with the special preconditions associated with electric lighting, they were unwieldy and strange. Today, however, the leading industrial companies in this field have long since overcome such growing pains. They have produced lamps which can be deemed the synthesis of design and functionality."[30]

Of course Wagenfeld was also thinking of the *Weimar* series and of its potential for high turnover. Most of all, the range of at least eight different lamps, equipped with plane mirrors or mirrored glass elements, emphasised the high technical level of the production, as these lucent units were generally made up of three glass or mirrored elements. Moreover, the distribution, installation and even the maintenance of the lamps required the help of qualified staff, as the entire lucent unit had to be removed from the mountings in order to change a light bulb.

It was of utmost importance to Wagenfeld to establish a combination of "decentralised spot lighting and centralised room lighting in line with the wishes of interior decorators". "Light and shadow, bright and dark" must be deployed "as conscious elements in the design of an interior."[31] The problem of realising such objectives – regardless of whether the lighting is intended for working or living space – is today again a subject of discussion, many sites in the labour and production sector having too long and too often had blinding light flooding all their offices and places of work indiscriminately.

Based on the literature available and on statements made by Wagenfeld, it must be

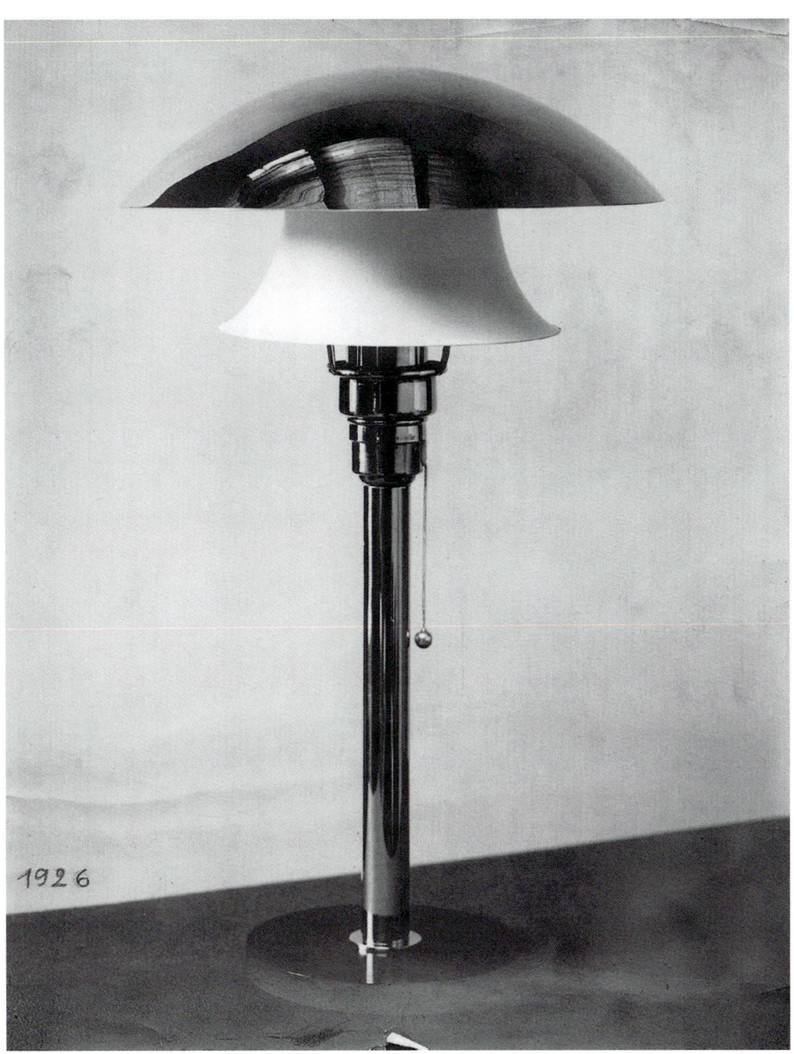

5 Table lamp, Model 38, Bauhochschule Weimar, 1926. Manufactured by Walther und Wagner/Schleiz. Distributed from 1928 by Weimar Bau- und Wohnungskunst GmbH

assumed that the body glass, other glass elements and possibly also the mirrored elements were manufactured by Schott & Gen..[32] Wagenfeld phrased it clearly: "The lamp glasses were produced in collaboration with the lighting technology department of the [Schott & Gen.] glassworks. Our task here was to create lamp glasses suitable for the home."[33]

Wagenfeld left no room for doubt that he employed the ideas and methods cultivated at the Bauhochschule in Weimar when he designed the *Weimar* lamp series.[34] Geometric bodies – the sphere and spherical segment, cylinders of various sizes, the cone and truncated cone – their combination and intersection dominate the drawings for this lamp series. The materials used for the lampshades, to distribute the light in the room and on the surfaces of the furniture in the room, to direct the light and then again, to screen off bulb glare, included, in addition to matt or frosted glass, the plane mirrors mentioned above, mirrored glass elements, lampshade card and, in particular for the table lamps, metal reflectors.

Among the various protagonists of the 'New Objectivity',[35] contradictions within the designing processes for lamps and lucent units were, generally speaking, relatively few; in any case they will not be dealt with in detail here. More significant in the context of the present discussion is that the lamp designs or lamp production in the orbit of the Bauhaus at Weimar and Dessau and likewise within Ferdinand Kramer's creative activity for the 'New Frankfurt', stood in irreconcilable contradiction to the traditional form of lamps, in particular the chandelier for living areas. As astutely as Wagenfeld analysed and condemned these traditions, he was equally certain that 'this situation' could only be handled through a concerted and consistent effort, "because during the many years in which the industry has been manufacturing products largely without a sense of responsibility, when large circles of dealers, with similar lack of responsibility, have never tired of distributing such goods to the people, we have reached a cultural low point which is not going to be rectified from one day to the next".[36] Although over the course of Wagenfeld's entire period of creativity (1920s to 1970s) there were few others who opposed mainstream fashions as he did, "large circles of buyers [search] in vain for industrial and hand-crafted products [...] that rise above the standard of the commercial norm."[37] Wagenfeld did not shrink from occasional sarcasm to allow his public an unveiled glance at the commodity society. "For every buyer has had to learn that he is the servant of commerce, the vassal of an authority that in this case is called the economy and makes its own laws, which no one can break with impunity. Commerce knows the public's taste, and the buyer must be the public. Within these boundaries he is allowed freedom of choice, freedom of expression and the freedom to live his life."[38]

To conclude the discussion on the *Weimar* lamp series, it must be emphasised, with Wagenfeld, that "the standard-model objectives of the Bauhaus of that time [...] were nothing new to the industry." "Nevertheless: the fact that these objectives could be extended to the objects in the home was denied emphatically. There was talk of the uniformity of life in the home being the ultimate threat to the freedom of living. And people also spoke passionately about the complete destruction of all individual existence."[39] Naturally, Wagenfeld had the best argument at hand to substantiate the exact opposite. No piece of furniture and no appliance could be uniform, "if it has been created with every attention to its destined use and its own given bounds."[40]

In contradiction lies the truth: Wagenfeld's designs for lamps and lucent units for Peill & Putzler Glassworks in Düren

More than one year of intensive co-operation lay behind the co-workers of Wagenfeld's workshop in Stuttgart, the glassworks in Düren under the management of the Peills and at the office of designer Jupp Ernst in Wuppertal, when at the end of April 1953, just in time for the trade fair, the new catalogue designed by Jupp Ernst was published;[41] and lamp production in the glassworks and the distribution of the lamps to the wholesale and retail trade could begin.[42] The new lamp range, presented with the help of the company newsletter, was organised into a three-tiered structure:

The first tier was formed by wall lamps – the smaller *Piccola* and *Media*, the larger *Majora* design and the shell-shaped wall lamp in two sizes. The shell lamps were intended respectively for living and auxiliary rooms in small flats or, when hung higher, for the standard general lighting of hallways and stairwells. The *Media* and *Majora* designs were available in different versions, such as opalescent cased glass with polished or satin finish; clear glass with satin finish and enamel painting; clear glass with matt finish inside, matt stripes with cut lines, etc. With

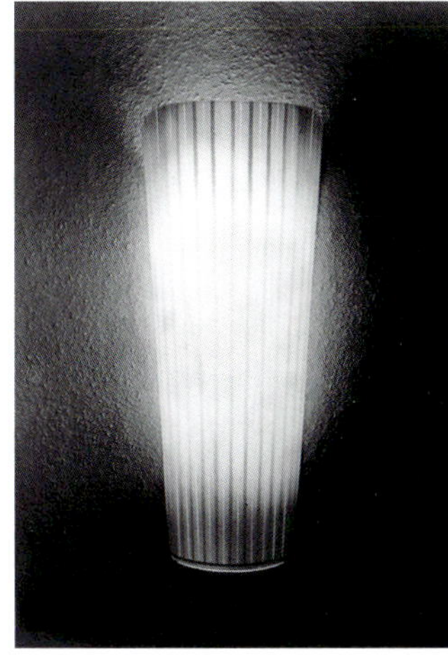

7 *Majora* wall lamp, Model No. 2685/0103, clear glass with matt finish inside, matt stripes with cut lines, Peill & Putzler/Düren, 1952

6 *Media* wall lamp, Model No. 2683, opalescent cased glass with satin finish, Peill & Putzler/Düren, 1952

its slim, 440-millimetre length, the *Majora* lamp was designed for public and luxurious rooms in hotels and restaurants, with the quality of lighting and of the light itself in mind. It could also be equipped with the (then) high-performance, U-shaped 16-watt neon tube.

Hardly was one developmental phase achieved, but Wagenfeld's thoughts would be on the next. In a letter to Günther Peill in February 1953 he reflects "how hard we must work and how well we are placed to progress a step further again next year than we have now in the first catalogue on our toddler's legs."[43] Perhaps his thoughts were already on the design of the asymmetrical *Daphne* wall lamp, which would later be added to the series.

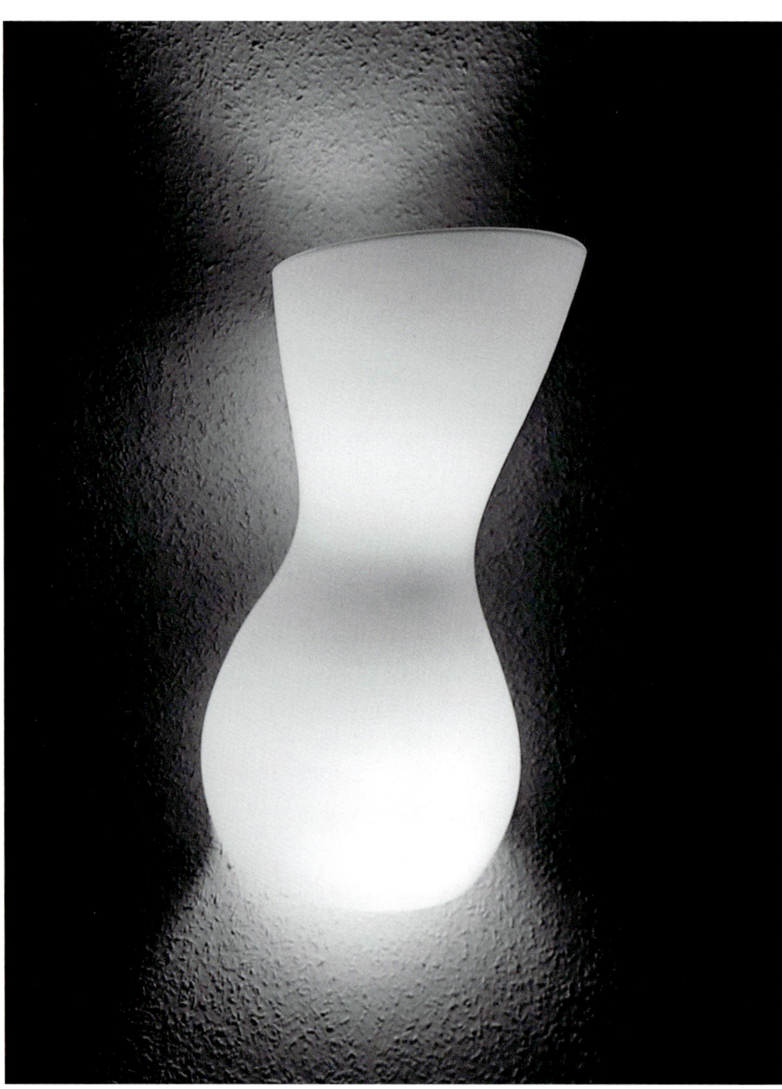

8 *Daphne* wall lamp, Model No. 3340, opalescent cased glass with satin finish, Peill & Putzler/Düren, 1954

The second part of the programme was formed by the hanging ceiling lamp with a one-piece (closed) opalescent cased glass body as the lucent unit, with polished or satin finish, derived from the geometric figure of the sphere but at the same time in an unmistakable, well-calculated contradiction to it. With these designs Wagenfeld had departed radically from the core design principles of the Bauhaus and his own approach at Weimar, and discovered taut, exciting forms which not only well suited the lamp glass of hanging lamps but, as designs, could also be protected by law. Thus Wagenfeld and his colleagues had also created a significant economic success for themselves.[44] Amongst the hanging ceiling lamps were the *Düren*, *Lunetta* and *Lucia* designs, the "teardrop lamp" and the "Segmentspiegelleuchte" with its "mirror [coated] segment" body. Later the cylindrical *Bonn* design, the *Bremen* (an open teardrop form for convenient changing of light bulbs) and the *Oslo* ('upside-down' open teardrop form) were added. The "segment mirror lamp" deserves special mention. In terms of the lighting technique[45] it forms a connecting element between the *Weimar* series and the part of the lighting range for the firm of Lindner known as the all-glass ceiling lamps. With the design for the segment mirror lamp (1952), Wagenfeld mentally anticipated the design concept of his Lindner all-glass ceiling lamp (1955); in both, that tension intimated in the slight "downward tug" to the arc of what would otherwise be a clear-cut spherical segment.[46]

The third part was formed by the hanging lamps which were intended by their designers to dominate, and in the end did dominate the German citizen's centre of living – the illumination area over the tables. But it must not go unnoticed that Günther Peill made sure that they would also be put to use in living rooms by adding the satin finish of the lamp glasses from the second group.[47] This third tier in the structure was initially small, and included the *Mandarin* design (a one-piece clear glass surround, with matt finish inside, matt stripes and engraved lines), the *Pomona* (the same), the *Cora* (two-part; opalescent cased inner shade, outside clear glass with matt engraved decorations) and the *Aura* (inner glass opalescent cased, matt outside finish with deep etching). In his design for the *Aura,* Wagenfeld's surface work extended to the outer glass, too. This surface appeared to be technically well-suited to the model (i.e. in its distribution of light through the outer glass shade). On the decorative element in the design process, however, there were surely differences of opinion between Wagenfeld and Peill, and they were brought to expression in their correspondence. In a letter dated 4 November 1952 Wagenfeld wrote to Peill about their

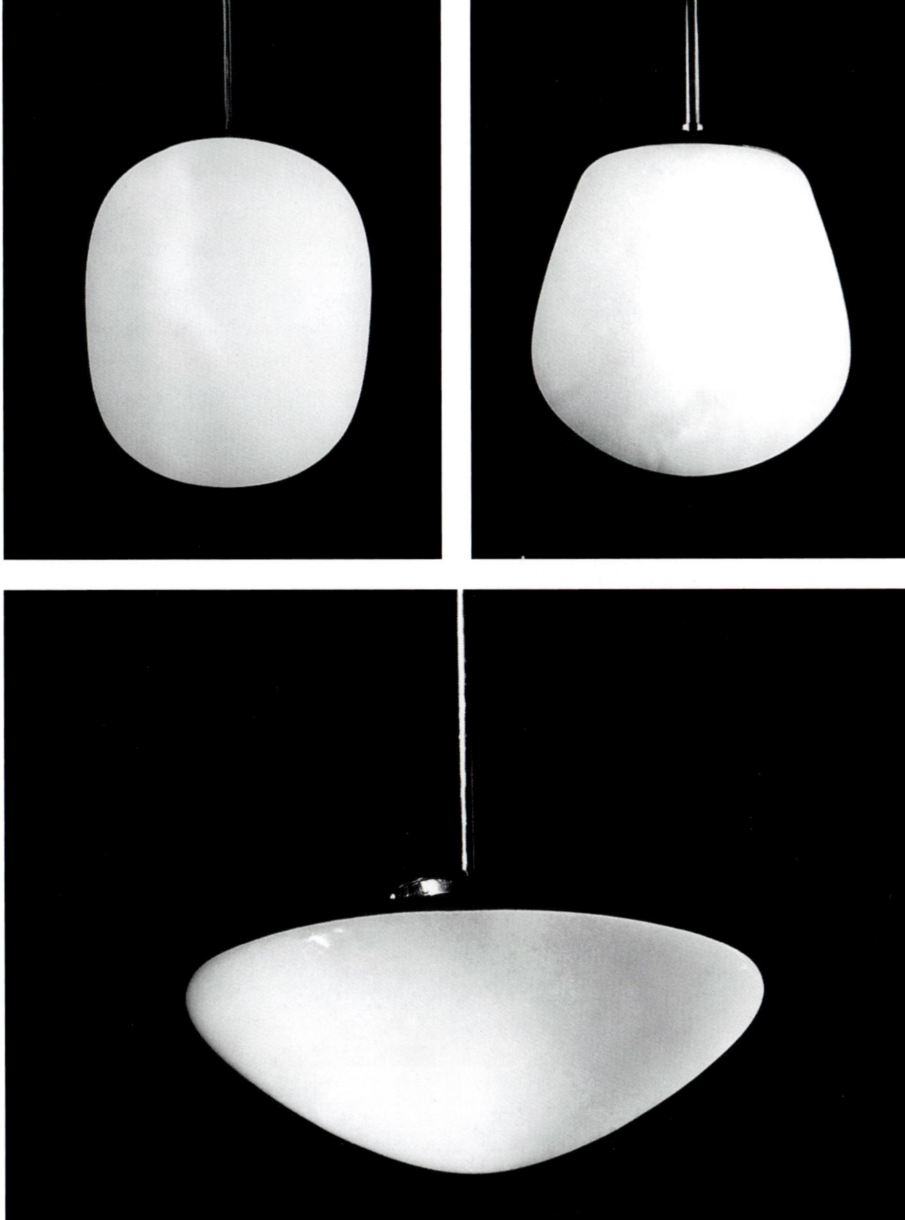

9 *Düren* hanging lamp, Order No. 2674–2676 (three sizes, largest diameter 300 mm, height 360 mm), opalescent cased glass with polished or satin finish, Peill & Putzler/Düren, 1952

10 *Lucia* hanging lamp, Model No. 2680 (one size, diameter 192 mm, height 190 mm), opalescent cased glass, polished or satin finish, Peill & Putzler/Düren, 1952. Fittings removed to the inside of the surround, this attached with the aid of the cowl on the suspension rod

11 "Segment mirror lamp", Model No. 2688 (one size, glass lampshade diameter 400 mm, height 182 mm), clear glass with matt finish inside, mirror coated, works design elaborated by Wilhelm Wagenfeld; Peill & Putzler/ Düren, 1952

12 *Aura* hanging lamp, Model No. 2679/M 699, clear glass with matt striated decoration, opalescent cased inner glass, Peill & Putzler/Düren, 1952

13 *Cora* hanging lamp, Model No. 2666/0104, clear glass with matt patterning, opalescent cased inner glass, Peill & Putzler/Düren, 1952

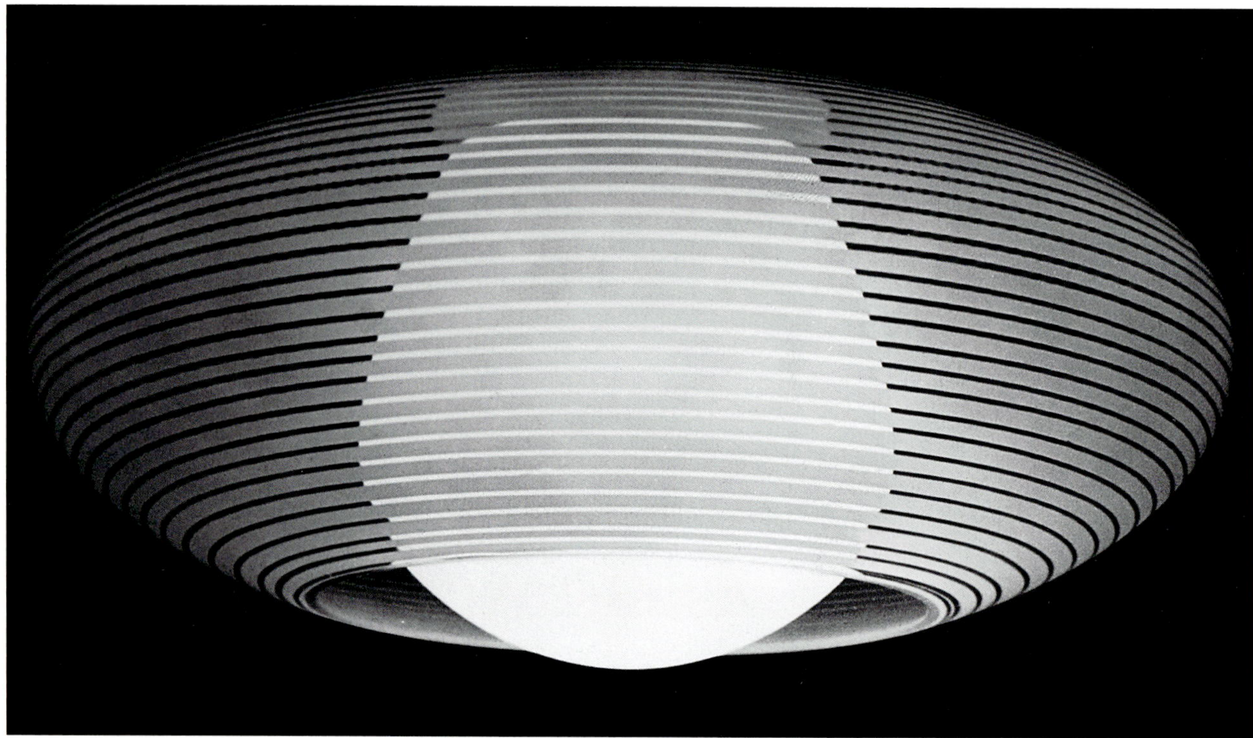

14 *Juno* hanging lamp, clear glass with white (Model No. 3306/M 865) or yellow (Model No. 3306/ M 866) stripes, opalescent cased inner glass, Peill & Putzler/Düren, 1954

"mutual worries about the lighting glass. I wonder whether we hadn't better put the pronounced decorative element more into ornate and yet, technically, for the lighting, right shapes for the glass."[48] This letter may be an indication that Wagenfeld had some problems with the matt glass finishes, in particular in the *Cora* design. After the initial successes initiated by the spring, 1953, range, several models were added to the third design group, for example the *Diana* and *Juno* lamps.

Every series of lamp glasses designed by Wagenfeld may legitimately prompt the question: which role models was he following? One insight has been gained thanks to a conversation between Walter Scheiffele and glass designer Heinrich Fuchs.[49] Fuchs, who transferred to the Phönix glassworks at Penzig in 1937, brought to our attention that "very little progress had been made in the area of lamp glass."[50] "The hanging lamps" produced under the direction of Fuchs were "entirely of glass. The inner cylinder was opalescent and the outer one crystal clear glass. 'Don't forget: at this time the tassel was still usual. Here too, blown forms – spheres, rounded cylinders and teardrops – were used throughout. The outer cylinders [or better, glasses] were also decorated in different variations with bands and lines. The lamps sold well, but the company could not have survived on these alone."[51]

Fuchs points out that he did not know Wagenfeld personally. It is, however, probable that Wagenfeld, as artistic manager of the Lausitzer Glassworks at Weisswasser, was informed about the product range of the works at Penzig, a centre located like Weisswasser, in the Lusatia (Lausitz) region of Silesia. While space does not permit an exposé on links in the companies' history, it is significant in the present context that the partners of the Peills in Düren, the Putzlers, also came from Penzig.

15 a, b Heinrich Fuchs's hanging lamps from the Phönix glassworks at Penzig, Silesia, 1937–1940, could have been models on which Wagenfeld based his work

The whole is more than the sum of its parts: Wagenfeld's activity as a designer for Lindner in Bamberg

The co-operation between Wagenfeld's workshop in Stuttgart and Lindner GmbH was multifarious and long-lasting. It was born of the work Lindner carried out for the Düren glassworks, as Lindner, specialising in glass-working, was the vital supplier of lighting glass for all manufacturers of lamps and lamp fixtures. Even the significant lighting industry in Neheim-Hüsten (in the Sauerland) bought most of their material from the Düren glassworks.

One of the most important specialist manufacturers of installation material for electricity and power plants – in particular as long as the hard, durable insulating material porcelain remained on centre stage of production and assembly work – is (or was)[52] Lindner GmbH in Bamberg. Wagenfeld and his co-workers were involved in the process of expansion and the diversification of the production of lamps (almost) entirely of glass and porcelain (see Pl. 3).

From 1955 on, everything Wagenfeld had developed until then in the way of lamps, lamp glass and lucent units was submitted in turn to a process of consolidation into its own contemporary form in at least four major waves of new designs for Lindner. Initially, he steered the developmental process still further away from the 'geometry of the Bauhaus'.

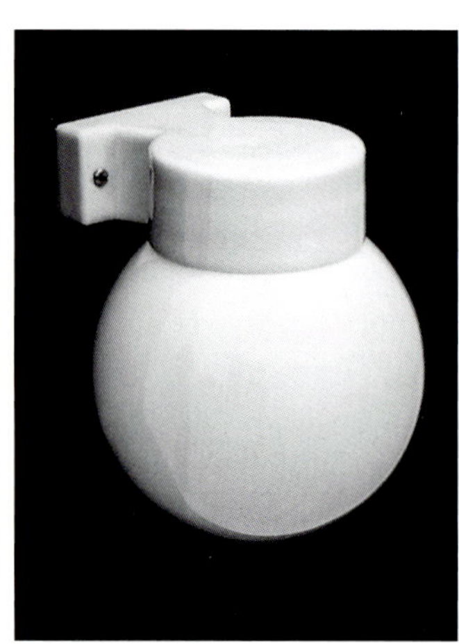

16 Wall lamp, porcelain and glass. Works design, Bünte & Remmler, 1930s. Precursor of Lindner Bamberg's porcelain lamps

The first examples of the renowned mirror lamps for bathrooms had a dynamic and off-centre quality. That which is consciously designed for people should not be allowed to be lost, not completely integrated in their lifestyles. We must not be satisfied with 'pure functionality' alone, wrote Wagenfeld.[53] He became aware of this design principle very early on, and always adhered to it. "Now [1938] functionality is no longer a problem for me in my work, but merely a prerequisite. If anyone recognises and emphasises the functionality in my work first off, I know that I have not solved the problem properly."[54]

Wagenfeld worked constantly to perfect the 'flowing-radius corners'[55] of his lamp body designs and from 1960 on, would regularly present to the public the mirror lamps for Lindner and much else besides fundamentally redesigned. He could certainly not be accused of any opportunistic devotion to successive fashion trends, however. Wagenfeld had long since had his own decisive influence on how 'the objects around us' could be at once useful and beautiful, "because it must be possible for any use to be beautiful; otherwise objects fail their purpose."[56] This close relationship between use and the capacity for beauty was also embodied by the colourful design of many lamps in the Lindner series. From 1957, porcelain elements for kitchen and bathroom lamps could be had not only in white or black, but also in ivory, light-green, pale blue, rosé and Lindner grey. Lindner grey became the preferred colour for exterior lamps.

A cornerstone of the designing of the "New Wagenfeld Lamps" (NWL series) in the 1960s was the wall lamp with the number 959. The NWL series brought out the straight line, the rectangle and the square. The corner curvatures could hardly have been sharper, and admirers of Wagenfeld's lamps from the first series would only be able to tell by looking at the sectional plan drawing of the 959, if at all, that Wagenfeld had designed it. The sectional drawing is identical to the overall shape – the vertical section – of the all-glass ceiling lamp from the first series. It had always doubled as a wall lamp as it protruded just 170 millimetres from the ceiling or wall, even in the largest size (350 millimetres diameter). In its design history, or rather, its inherited shape, this all-glass ceiling/wall lamp itself was none other than the segment mirror lamp from the series of hanging ceiling lamps for the Düren glassworks, now become one with the ceiling or wall. The all-glass ceiling lamp was the aesthetic and economic mainstay throughout more than twenty years of continuing lamp design and production for Lindner. In every catalogue from 1955 into the 1970s, the subsystem with the basic number 961 was specially featured with its many properties: it was dust-proof; resistant against moisture, salty air and acidic vapours; and, owing to the perpendicular position of the light bulb (contrary to most products of the competition), it cast no shadows on the glass surrounds.[57] Not least, with this lamp and its well-balanced design, which took up little space and was made of material that would stand the test of time, Wagenfeld freed the porcelain-and-glass lamp from the image of attic, pantry and cellar fixture. It was – and still is – used not only in houses and flats; both of the large all-glass ceiling lamps were used in hospitals, schools and youth hostels, etc. millions of times over in the 1950s to the 1980s, and are probably still in use today, insofar as they have not fallen prey to the throw-away mentality.

In 1970 Wagenfeld created his last range of lamps, the *Systral* series, for Lindner. It consisted of eight different dish-shaped porcelain elements which could be used with the *Elroyal* light bulbs, also designed by Wagenfeld, and at the same time functioned as their light reflectors. The idea for illuminating a room or part of a room consisted of connecting many similar elements, for example, to make bands, circles or other areas of light. Particularly the units with the numbers 6454, 6455 and 6456 are extremely suitable for creating bands of both the fittings and their light to match the architectural and room concept and give expression through forms, material and colour to the overall creative concept. In the 1970s strong, bright colours were used for interior decorating: red and green upholstery fabrics, panelled walls and brightly striped wallpaper. The *Systral* lamps asserted themselves in such surroundings, in particular through their design. With the two colours Seladon and Méditerrané or the white porcelain of the *Systral* units, the lamps fitted in well with every interior colour scheme. It was also possible to create colour highlights on light-coloured backgrounds, on ceiling and walls, into the furthest corners of the room.

The four designs essentially created from the circle or trapezium (6450, 6451, 6452 and 6459) were excellently suited for forming more or less large, circular, triangular and trapezium-shaped areas of illumination. These lighting fixtures virtually cried out to be used as elements in the design of large, public, luxurious or formal environments, in particular the walls. It is no surprise, therefore, that closer examination of

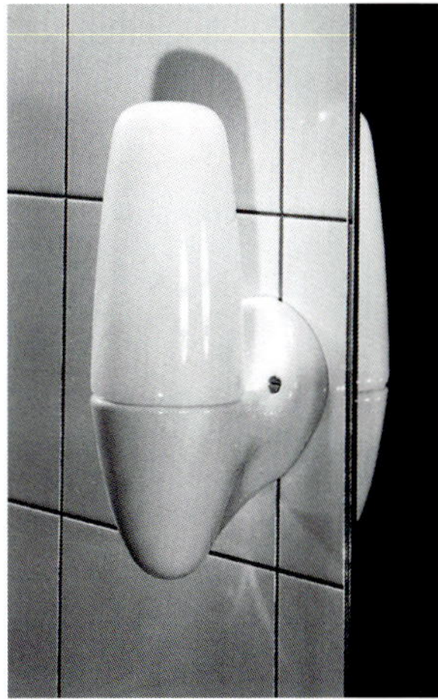
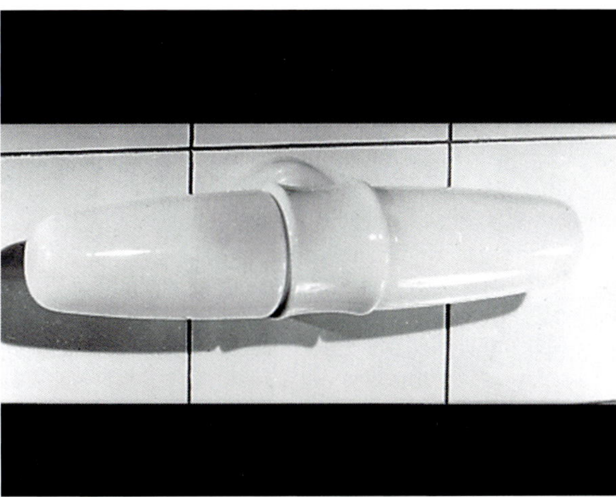
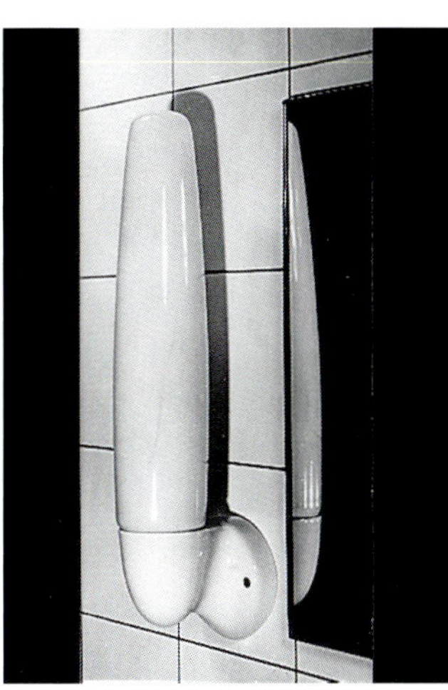

17 a–c Mirror lamps, Nos. 6065, 6066, 6060, glass and porcelain, Lindner/Bamberg, 1955

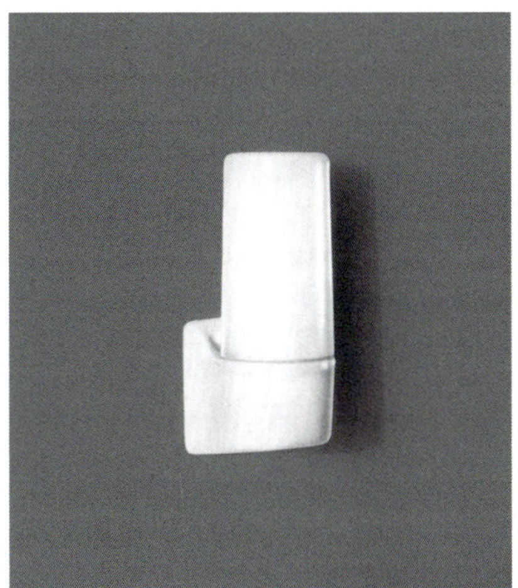
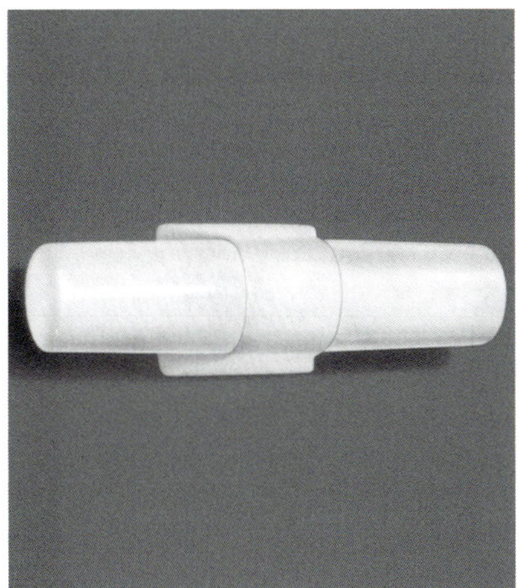
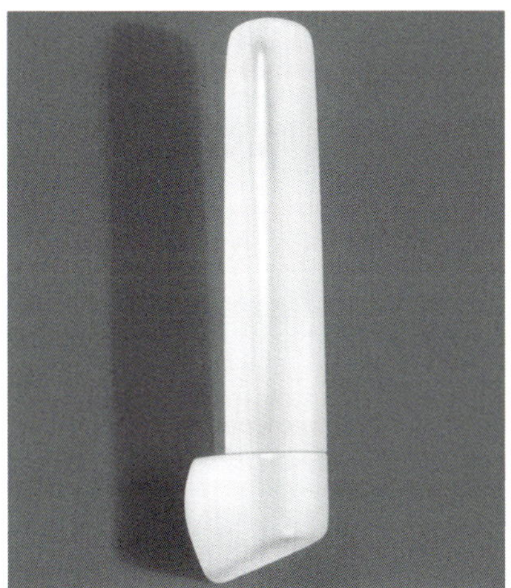

18 a–c Mirror lamps, Nos. 6063, 6064, 6061, glass and porcelain, NWL series ("New Wagenfeld Lamps"), Lindner/Bamberg, 1960–1963

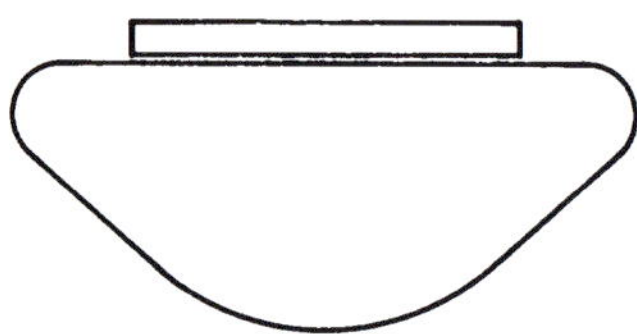

19 NWL wall lamp 959 for interior and exterior use, glass and porcelain, Lindner/Bamberg, 1962

20 All-glass ceiling or wall lamp, No. 961, glass light fixture in six different sizes and equipped with three different lighting technologies, Lindner/Bamberg, 1955

the *Systral* range tends to involve discussion on the real potential of 'Kunst am Bau' – [the state provisions for] 'Art in Architectural Projects'.

The *Elroyal* light bulb used by Wagenfeld for the lamps of his *Systral* range, was, like all the other *ELDECO* light bulbs he designed, at the same time a lighting fixture which did not blind people in the room, as the surface is cased with opal glass. A lamp consistently made of two parts – a porcelain reflector and the light bulb – this was a miniature revolution in terms of production technology, economy and design. Scarcely any other lamp was as easy to clean as the *Systral*. In the economical maintenance, the ease of changing the light bulbs, and the durability of the material, no lamp can better it. No matter how many good characteristics the *Systral* range and other lamp series by Wagenfeld are credited with, functionality is but one criterion in the creations of Wilhelm Wagenfeld.

21 a, b Partial view of a concertina leaflet advertising Lindner's *Systral* lamp system. The brand is equipped with the opalescent cased *Elroyal* light bulb. Lindner/Bamberg, 1970

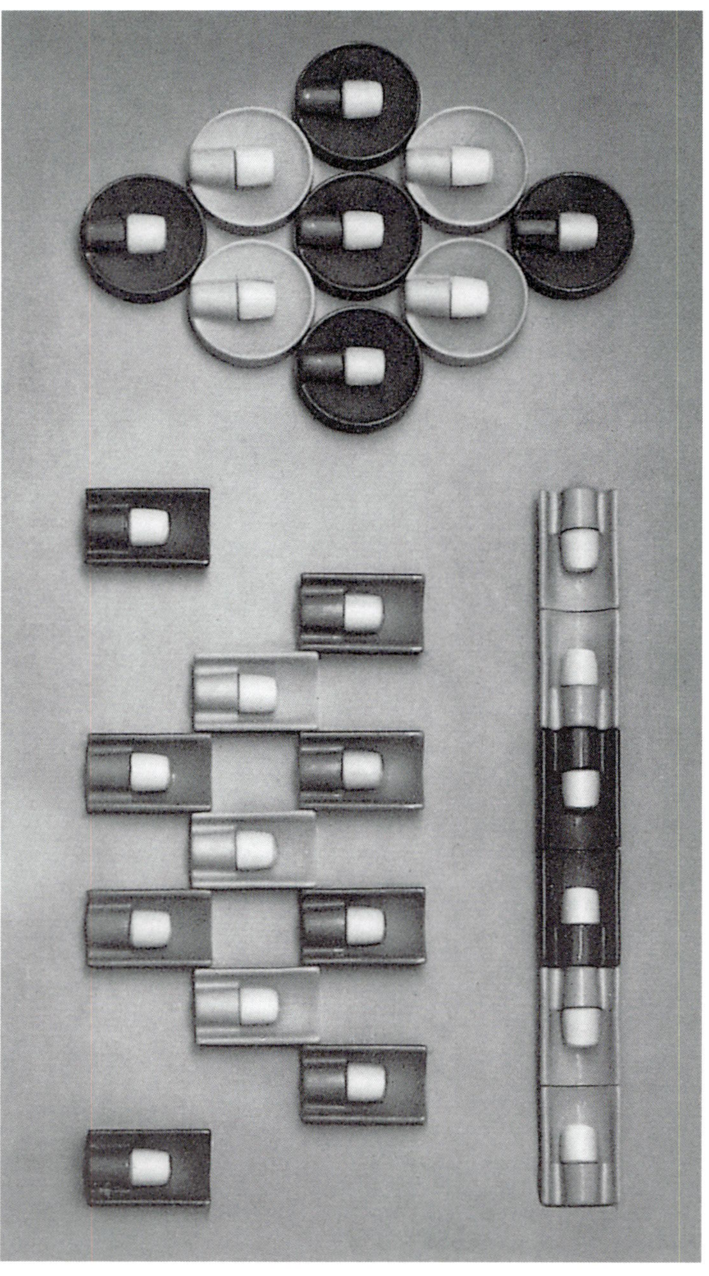

Notes

1 In the first section I look at Wagenfeld's general œuvre in the domain of 'light and lighting'. A 'systematic and logical' perspective and procedure is brought to bear. In the second section, with its three sub-sections 'Bauhaus, Peill & Putzler and Lindner', I place the emphasis of my survey on the various lamp series and several individual lamps ('personalities') from them.

2 In the 1960s Wagenfeld created a series of light bulbs (illuminants) for Lindner/Bamberg, which simultaneously fulfilled the function of the outer, lucent unit (compare section two on Wagenfeld's designs for Lindner, *ELDECO* light bulbs for the *Systral* range, p. 82)

3 For example, the letters from Wilhelm Wagenfeld to Walter Gropius of 4 August 1964 (in: *Täglich in der Hand. Industrieformen von Wilhelm Wagenfeld aus sechs Jahrzehnten,* ed. Beate Manske and Gudrun Scholz, Worpsweder Verlag 1987, 4th ed. Bremen 1998, p. 64–67) and to Mr. G., 21 August 1966 (in: *Wilhelm Wagenfeld. 50 Jahre Mitarbeit in Fabriken,* exh. cat. Kunstgewerbemuseum, Cologne 1973, pp. 9 f.) can give us an idea about why, and how resolutely, Wagenfeld consistently refused to participate in the slightest way in the building or decorating of 'beautiful barracks'.

4 Wilhelm Wagenfeld, "Raum und Lichtträger", in: *Die Schaulade,* vol. 8, no. 15, 1932 (hereafter referred to as "Raum und Lichtträger"), p. 645.

5 Wagenfeld, "Raum und Lichtträger", p. 646.

6 Wilhelm Wagenfeld, "Künstlerische Formprobleme der Industrie", in: Wagenfeld, *Wesen und Gestalt der Dinge um uns,* Potsdam 1948, unaltered reprint, Worpsweder Verlag 1990 (hereafter referred to as *Wesen und Gestalt),* p. 77.

7 Wilhelm Wagenfeld, ".. über: Die industrielle Formgebung", in: *Innen-Dekoration/Architektur und Wohnform,* vol. 63 ("Fachliche Mitteilungen") no. 1, 1954/55, p. 20.

8 Wagenfeld, *Innen-Dekoration* (see note 7)

9 Wagenfeld, *Innen-Dekoration* (see note 7)

10 Compare Wilhelm Wagenfeld, "Kleine Betrachtungen", in: *Wesen und Gestalt,* p. 30.

11 Compare Wilhelm Wagenfeld, "Brief aus der Werkstatt", in: *Wesen und Gestalt,* p. 58.

12 Wilhelm Wagenfeld, "Raum und Lichtträger", p. 646.

13 Compare the contributions of his co-workers Pfaender and Sammet, in: *Täglich in der Hand* (see note 3), pp. 250–256.

14 Wilhelm Wagenfeld, "Lieber Herr G.!", in: *50 Jahre Mitarbeit in Fabriken,* 1973 (see note 3), p. 9.

15 In a letter from the Wagenfelds to the von Pechmanns, Munich, of 20 June 1958 there is mention both of the work on the *Combal* lamps and of the impression made by two exhibitions: a glass exhibition at the 'Neue Sammlung' and a Rococo exhibition in the Münchner Residenz. By reading the correspondence sustained through the years between the Wagenfelds and the Peills, we can retrace exactly the exhibitions the couple visited (Wilhelm Wagenfeld Stiftung, Bremen).

16 Compare the letter from Wilhelm Wagenfeld to Günther Peill of 3 February 1953 (see note 15).

17 Compare Klaus Struve, "Leuchten und Licht im Arbeits- und Lebenszusammenhang. Anfänge einer Kultur der Beleuchtung mit elektrischem Licht", in: *Idee: Christian Dell. Einfache, zweckmäßige Arbeitsleuchten aus Neheim,* ed. Peter M. Kleine and Klaus Struve, Arnsberg 1995, pp. 26–37, especially pp. 28–30, and the bibliography and sources pp. 76–81.

18 Wilhelm Wagenfeld, "Glasfachsimpeleien" (1937), in: *Wesen und Gestalt,* p. 63.

19 In an assessment of the economic status of the year 1926, Jacques Goldberg points out the fact that even in the environs of "greater Berlin only one-fifth of households use electric lighting", in: *Licht und Lampe,* vol. 1, 1927, p. 12.

20 Compare Wilhelm Wagenfeld, "Künstlerische Formprobleme der Industrie", in: *Wesen und Gestalt,* p. 78.

21 Wilhelm Wagenfeld, "Von alltäglichen Dingen" (1947), in: *Wesen und Gestalt,* p. 43.

22 Compare Joachim Petsch and Wiltrud Petsch-Bahr, *Eigenheim und gute Stube. Zur Geschichte des bürgerlichen Wohnens. Städtebau – Architektur – Einrichtungsstile,* Cologne 1989 (neither of the main chapters of the book, "Die Nachkriegszeit" and "Vom Ende der 50er Jahre bis zur Gegenwart", mention the works of Wagenfeld).

23 Compare Walter Scheiffele, *Wilhelm Wagenfeld und die moderne Glasindustrie,* Stuttgart 1994.

24 Compare Klaus Struve 1995 (see note 17), pp. 30 ff.

25 Hans Schwippert in the company newsletter on the occasion of the launching of Wagenfeld's lamp series of Putzler glass, in: *leuchten aus putzler glas. Entworfen von Wagenfeld,* Düren, undated (1953), unpaginated (p. 6). It is to designer Jupp Ernst, then Director of the Werkkunstschule in Wuppertal, that the glassworks in Düren owe this excellent presentation of the lamp series, achieved with the help of superb photography, economy in the technical illustrations, exact measurements, flawless texts and precise descriptions of every lamp, including the name, type of glass used, its surface design, cut, colour, etc.

26 Wilhelm Wagenfeld, "Die Gegenwart in Architektur und Hausrat" (1946), in: *Wesen und Gestalt,* pp. 119 f. (title and text layout by Klaus Struve).

27 Compare Wilhelm Wagenfeld, ".. über: Die industrielle Formgebung" (see note 7), p. 18.

28 Compare Weimar Bau- und Wohnungskunst GmbH, Weimar, *Katalog über Leuchten und Metallgeräte,* Weimar, undated (around 1933).

29 Compare Wilhelm Wagenfeld, "Die Beleuchtung von Wohnbauten in unserer Zeit", in: *Spiegellicht Blätter* (special issue, Zeiss Ikon Werke A.-G., Goerz Werk, Berlin-Zehlendorf, for the Deutsche Bauausstellung show in Berlin, 1931), no. 8, May 1931, pp. 112–116.

30 Wagenfeld, *Spiegellicht Blätter,* pp. 114 f.

31 Wagenfeld, *Spiegellicht Blätter* p. 116.

32 Compare Wilhelm Wagenfeld, "Jenaer Glas", in: *Die Form,* vol. 6, no. 10, 1931, pp. 461–464. The journal is accompanied by seven leaflets advertising twelve hanging and ceiling lamps with the name *Astax-Spiegel* and the chimney logo of Schott & Gen.. (The name *Astax* is not to be confused with the Atrax Zweckleuchten GmbH in Berlin W 9, Bellevuestraße 6a, at what was formerly Potsdamer Platz.) The glass surrounds under the name *Astax* are almost identical to the *Weimar* range which Wagenfeld and Walther & Wagner produced.

33 Wagenfeld, "Jenaer Glas", p. 464. In a letter from Wilhelm Wagenfeld to Dr. Wildhagen (Ludwigshafener Glassworks) of 31 August 1951 he writes: "[In addition to my work at the VLG] I also worked for Zeiss-Ikon, designing lamps." In view of Wagenfeld's consistently exact use of the terms, I cannot view this as proof that he designed lighting glass for Zeiss-Ikon, because further up in the same letter, he writes that he "designed and developed, in addition to lighting glass, most of the well-known Jenaer dishes for the Jenaer Glassworks" (Wilhelm Wagenfeld Stiftung, Bremen).

34 Compare Wilhelm Wagenfeld, "Raum und Lichtträger", p. 645, and Klaus Weber, "Dienende Geräte. Die Metallwerkstatt der Bauhochschule", in: Dörte Nicolaisen, *Das andere Bauhaus. Otto Bartning und die Staatliche Bauhochschule Weimar*

1926–1930, published for the Bauhaus Archives in Berlin, exh. cat. Bauhaus-Archiv Berlin and Kunstsammlungen zu Weimar, Berlin 1996, pp. 105–121.

35 It is well known that Wagenfeld did not think much of the term of 'New Objectivity'. "The Bauhaus of 1923 was less objective than romantic. And this romantic joie de vivre was explicit in every expression of the Bauhaus of that time: in the building projects, in the workshops and on the stage", in: Wagenfeld, "Raum und Lichtträger", p. 645.

36 Wilhelm Wagenfeld, "Über die Aufgaben der Glasindustrie" (1936), in: *Wesen und Gestalt,* p. 71.

37 Wagenfeld, "Über die Aufgaben der Glasindustrie"

38 Wilhelm Wagenfeld, "Von alltäglichen Dingen" (1936), in: *Wesen und Gestalt,* p. 37.

39 Wilhelm Wagenfeld, "Raum und Lichtträger", pp. 645 f.

40 Wagenfeld, "Raum und Lichtträger"

41 *leuchten aus putzler glas* (see note 25). The company newsletter is more than just a catalogue of the lamp range designed by Wagenfeld.

42 Compare the correspondence between Wilhelm Wagenfeld and the Peills, their manager Dr. Hans Ahrenkiel and designer Jupp Ernst, especially from August 1952 to April 1953, Wilhelm Wagenfeld Stiftung, Bremen.

43 Letter from Wilhelm Wagenfeld to Günther Peill of 3 February 1953, pp. 1–3, here p. 1, Wilhelm Wagenfeld Stiftung, Bremen.

44 The scope of this essay does not allow for a detailed account of the increased profit balance at Peill & Putzler based on the designs by Wagenfeld. Retracing the development from a 'salary-based relationship to a licence-based one' between the Düren Glassworks and Wagenfeld's workshop alone would necessitate its own section (compare the correspondence between Wagenfeld and the glassworks in October 1956, Wilhelm Wagenfeld Stiftung, Bremen).

45 The inside surface of the top of the lucent unit is mirror-coated. This markedly increases the effect of the illumination, e.g. onto a table or work area.

46 Wagenfeld himself regarded the designing process in the Düren Glassworks as a matter of course and universally valid to the extent that he claimed no credit for them. He viewed the lamp as the ultimate development of a working drawing.

47 Compare page 3 of the letter dated 30 January 1953 from Günther Peill to Jupp Ernst containing all the details for the first comprehensive catalogue of April 1953, Wilhelm Wagenfeld Stiftung, Bremen.

48 Letter from Wilhelm Wagenfeld to Günther Peill of 4 November 1953, Wilhelm Wagenfeld Stiftung, Bremen.

49 Compare Walter Scheiffele 1994 (see note 23), pp. 141–144, conversation with Heinrich Fuchs on 10 August 1990 in Ingolstadt, pp. 192–197.

50 Scheiffele, 1994, p. 195.

51 Scheiffele, 1994, p. 196.

52 The factories of the Lindner company have also been closed down, sold and re-sold in the past few years. There were two main production lines: installation material and the Lindner lamp department, which included the production of light bulbs and porcelain-and-glass lamps for household, business and industrial use.

53 Compare Wilhelm Wagenfeld, "Glasfachsimpeleien" (1937), in: *Wesen und Gestalt,* p. 64.

54 Wilhelm Wagenfeld, "Kleine Betrachtungen" (1938), in: *Wesen und Gestalt,* p. 27.

55 Compare Bruno Winter, *Wilhelm Wagenfelds Leuchtenentwürfe,* diploma thesis in the faculty of Industrial Design of the Hochschule für bildende Künste, Hamburg 1992, p. 51.

56 Wilhelm Wagenfeld, "Glasfachsimpeleien", in: *Wesen und Gestalt,* p. 64.

57 *Lindner-Leuchten. Katalog aus dem Jahre 1966,* Bamberg 1966, p. 16.

followed in 1930. At the same time Berlin launched its mocha service called *Hallesche Form* designed by Marguerite Friedlaender, which by 1932 had been followed by a coffee and tea service and a dinner service called *Burg Giebichenstein*.[3]

Wilhelm Wagenfeld's Designs for the Porcelain Industry

Peter Schmitt

1 Artur Hennig, *Fortschritt* coffee and tea service, Friedrich Kaestner, Oberhohndorf, Saxony, 1930

Wilhelm Wagenfeld's designs for porcelain make up a relatively small percentage of the many designs that arose out of his "artistic collaboration with factories".[1] Over the course of some twenty-five years, only three services and a small number of vases and bowls were actually executed, other projects never managing to get beyond the design stage due to prevailing circumstances. Yet Wagenfeld was particularly attracted to porcelain, fascinated not only by the beauty of the material but also by the richness of the cultural heritage manifest in it. Both of these elements were united in an exemplary fashion in his eyes in the work of the Berlin Porcelain Manufactory, which had always shown itself to be sympathetic to contemporary artistic trends and had already made a name for itself since the turn of the century partly on account of this. From 1929 onwards, under Günther von Pechmann, it attempted once more to establish itself as a company paving the way for contemporary forms. This move at least earned it more attention than the Friedrich Kaestner porcelain factory in Oberhohndorf, which had previously ventured to commission Artur Hennig, an artist who taught at the ceramics school in Bunzlau, to design tableware with unadorned, functional forms. The first and also most consistent execution of this new range was the 1928 collection *Reform* – a set of tableware which had been "designed for the purpose with a rare determination".[2] The collection however found little favour with the public. *Fortschritt*

Wagenfeld's porcelain designs in the 1930s and 1940s

When Wilhelm Wagenfeld turned to porcelain in the mid-1930s, the advance of smooth, unadorned tableware was impossible to ignore. It was not so much that eclictic quotes in form or excessive novelty had completely disappeared but that slowly and surely almost every sizeable porcelain factory had augmented their range of products with simple, modern forms – a move also propagated by official sources after 1933. Fürstenberg, for example, had endorsed this trend as early as 1931 with Walter Nitzsche's *Diana 630*.[4] All of these tablewares were clearly inspired to a greater or lesser degree by the cylindrical vessels of Hennig and Friedlaender or Hermann Gretsch's oval *Arzberg 1382*.

Form "639" for the Fürstenberg porcelain factory

Wilhelm Wagenfeld's first china service explored a different avenue. The coffeepot is based on a baluster shape following an example set by the eighteenth century – evidently a deliberate allusion to the tradition of the formerly royal manufactory – however the body of the vessel is more elongated and shaped into a cylinder in the upper third. The pourer does not take the form of a small spout as in the historical models, but is long, slender and curved and begins where the curvature of the vessel is roundest. This contour is echoed by a rounded ear-shaped handle on the other side. The inset lid is only gently rounded and has a mushroom-shaped finial. On the teapot, the handle is fuller in shape in keeping with the character of the vessel. The tureen is designed along similar lines, but merges into the slightly flared rim at the point where the outline of the coffeepot curves inwards. Here too the lid is inset and has a mushroom-shaped finial; the handles are flat, slightly curved bands. The pieces styled "Serving Dish for Potatoes" and "Sauce Boat" in the sales brochure are of a similar design, but not so full-bellied. For the sake of a uniform overall appearance throughout the collection the sauceboat is round, a departure from the conventional shape.

Aside from historical specimens, the form of the coffeepot is possibly modelled

2 Marguerite Friedlaender, *Hallesche Form* tea service, decorated by Trude Petri, Staatliche Porzellanmanufaktur Berlin, 1931

3 *639* coffee service, Fürstenberg porcelain factory, 1934

4 Hermann Gretsch, *1382* coffee pot and creamer, Arzberg porcelain factory, 1931

on the pots designed by Otto Lindig, whom Wagenfeld knew from his time at the Bauhaus. Lindig had developed a series of pots for the Bauhaus exhibition in August 1923 that were based on baluster-shaped vessels, whilst the pourer in one case taking the form of a short spout (*L 16*), and in others a slightly curved long spout (*L 15*). Lindig's pots are more full-bellied, the neck is narrower and expands conically towards the rim.[5] The handle consists of a circular segment; the flat lid is set deeply into the rim of the mouth and has a cup-shaped finial. Overall the design of Lindig's pot is more austere, the contours are tighter, yet one must bear in mind that it is a single piece where the designer did not have to take into consideration the ensemble of a service.

5 *639* dinner service, Fürstenberg porcelain factory, 1934

The *639* collection came onto the market in August 1934. The journal, *Die Schaulade,* presented and commented in detail on the new collection, which augmented Fürstenberg's range of remodelled pieces from the eighteenth and nineteenth centuries: "But now young designers are at work who do complete justice to the inner need for honesty and clarity in these glorious times in which we now live – designers, who produce things that can rightly be described as being born in the spirit of national edification. One expression of this new aspiration is the *639* collection. [...] "Simplicity, unpretentiousness combined with a dignified manner" – this extensive range of tableware fully answers the "Führer's" call for all German products to be created in this spirit. The directors of the factory and the collaborating designer W. Wagenfeld, from Oberweimar, were both very clear from the outset that something had to be created here which would stand the test of time."[6]

The sales brochure presenting the new tableware expresses a similar sentiment. Nevertheless it dispenses with currying political favour, which probably coincided more with Wagenfeld's own attitude than the comments in *Die Schaulade.* The brochure, too, stresses, "The artist collaborating on this service was Professor Wilhelm Wagenfeld of Weimar", and goes on to say: "We did not consider whether what we were drawing and modelling was new or whether it had already been done. Things called 'new' now are soon called 'old', and things that are 'modern' today are outmoded and unfashionable in tomorrow's taste. Yet where fashion is not a criterion the acquired items continue to be of lasting value as long as they serve their purpose. We do not want to produce anything 'new' nor anything 'modern' but we want to create a service which does its job with a clear and simple design and thus proves its worth to the benefit and joy of the customer."[7]

Although the article in *Die Schaulade* cited above attributes the "extensive range of tableware" to Wilhelm Wagenfeld this is only partly correct. Wagenfeld himself vehemently protested at the collection as a whole being linked with his name. The factory had added a number of pieces to the service without authorisation in order to complete the range. Wagenfeld commented on the incident in a letter to Heinrich König in 1955: "The *639* service [...] has really been completely altered in its overall character. But not by making alterations to the pieces which I designed and that we then modelled together, but – equally [bad] or with more far-reaching consequences – by adding as 'des.[igned by] W.' a shorter teapot, sugar bowls with or without feet, a shorter milk jug, soup cups with lids, children's beakers, a bread basket, butter dishes, partitioned dishes, compote dishes, egg cups, bone dishes, cruet stands, sardine dishes, asparagus platters, a cake platter, a strainer rest with plate, a tray for sugar implements, sauce spoons, an oval sauce boat, sauce tureen, salad bowls with flags, fish entrée dishes and plates with soft rims – in fact, nothing but 'additions' of which I myself was only aware on looking at the catalogue. This has practically ruined the service [...]."[8] The Fürstenberg porcelain factory was evidently not prepared to put a stop to this fraudulent labelling. The pieces to which Wagenfeld took such objection continued to be listed in the consumer guide *Deutsche Warenkunde* under the designer "Prof. Wilhelm Wagenfeld, Oberweimar (Thuringia), Ilmstrasse 4a".[9] This is surprising because in the case of the coffee ware *644* the entry is listed correctly: "Works design with collaboration of Hubert Griemert, Halle an der Saale, Burg Giebichenstein, 1938".[10] Perhaps they did not want to dispense with the name of Wagenfeld since it was well-known at least to interested circles, more so still than that of the art school in Halle, despite the fact that it had an excellent reputation in the porcelain field due to its connection with the Berlin Manufactory.

If we wish to do justice to Wagenfeld's first service of fine china then we must limit ourselves to the comparatively few pieces clearly by his hand. These admittedly are the dominant pieces in the service: coffeepot and teapot, sugar basin and preserves dish, milk jug, cups and breakfast plates on the one hand, tureens, sauce boat, serving platters, dinner and soup plates on the other. They show Wagenfeld's endeavours not only to work the individual pieces through down to the last detail, but also to make them recognisably part of a whole.

Fritz Kreikemeier can be regarded as the initiator of the *639* design. He took over as head of the Fürstenberg porcelain factory in early 1934 after Arthur Mehner, who had managed the company for fifteen years, died on 1 January 1934.[11] Kreikemeier had previously been a senior executive at the Arzberg porcelain factory and business manager at Villeroy & Boch since 1932 and in both companies had pursued a new model policy for which he engaged Hermann Gretsch as the designer.[12] This did not necessarily cause a conflict of interests between Arzberg and Villeroy & Boch as one company produced porcelain and the other stoneware, i.e. each served different segments of the market. In Fürstenberg's case Gretsch could not very well act as designer himself as Fürstenberg was a competitor, even if it manufactured products in a somewhat higher price category.[13] For this reason, he probably recommended Kreikemeier to approach Wilhelm Wagenfeld, whom he knew from working together in the Werkbund.[14] Wagenfeld himself only mentions being recommended by Hermann Gretsch.[15] When and how the first contact with Fürstenberg came about is not mentioned. It must have been quite early on, otherwise the first models could not have been presented in August 1934 – models which Wagenfeld had to design parallel to his work for the glassworks in Jena and alongside his teaching commitments at the art school in Berlin, in a field with which he was unfamiliar.

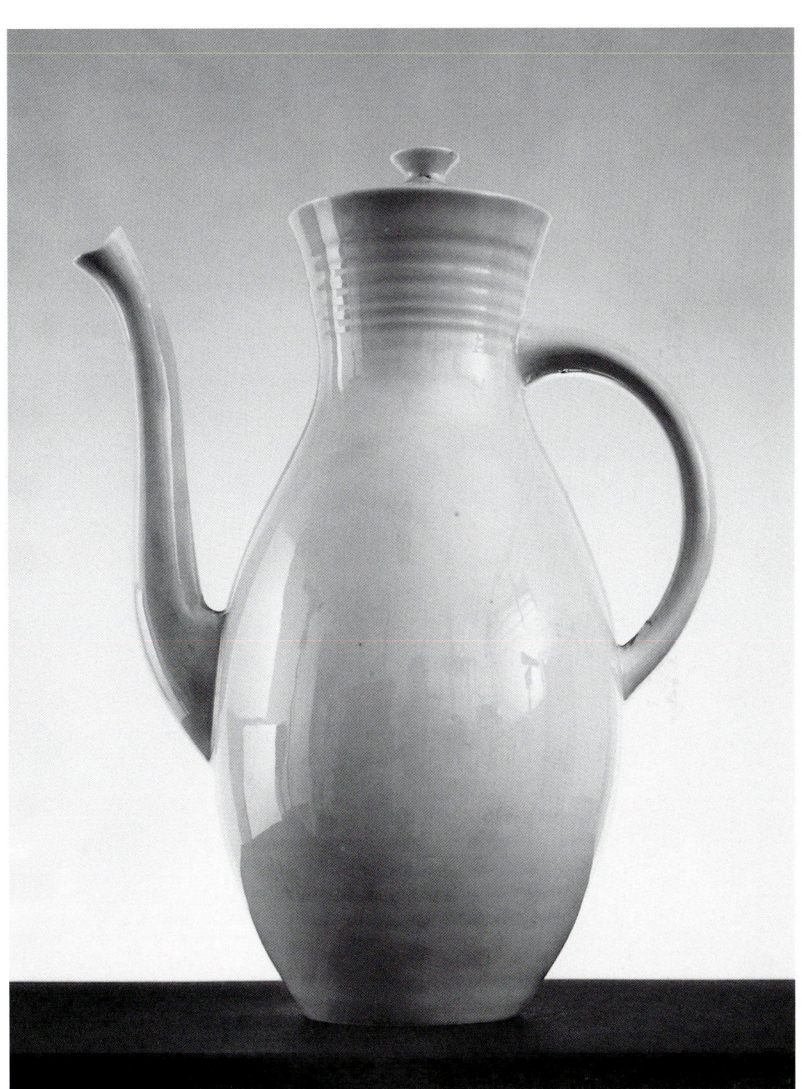

6 Otto Lindig, coffee pot *L 15*, Aelteste Volkstedter Porzellanfabrik, 1923/24

"Daphne" for the porcelain factory Philip Rosenthal, Selb

Whether his disappointment over Fürstenberg's unauthorized additions to the *639* service caused Wagenfeld to seek another partner in the porcelain industry or whether Rosenthal approached him of his own accord is still unclear. In any case, 1938 saw the launch of *Daphne* on the market – a move that represents an important step in Wagenfeld's work with porcelain. It is clearly a further development of *639*. The tea and coffee pots are based on a baluster form, the upper part of which is almost cylindrical. The high domed lid ends at the base with a flange. The contours of the body of the pot are broken merely by a fine edge beneath the lid. Spout and handle emerge gently from the body of the pot. An indentation highlights the mushroom-shaped finial as an independent design element, clearly concluding the upwardly striving contours of the pot.

The handles of the tureens are formed as flat bands as with the *639* design and grow organically out of the curvature of the body of the vessel but stand out as a design element in their own right by virtue of their square outline slightly rounded off at the corners.

The soft organic forms, still unusual at the time of *639,* had meanwhile established themselves. They can even be found in the tableware designed by one of Wagenfeld's employees Heinrich Löffelhardt as canteen ware for the Amt "Schönheit der Arbeit", part of the National Socialist "Deutscher Arbeitsfront" – tableware undeniably descended from *639*.[16]

Daphne embodies the late 1930s preference for refined simplicity that can be observed across the board in the porcelain design field.[17] An acquaintance of Wagenfeld's had spoken of "cultivated Puritanism" which Wagenfeld quoted with approval.[18] This trend towards more elegant, flowing forms extends right down to the cheaper services intended for a wider market, created by anonymous designers, as a glance at the *Deutsche Warenkunde* confirms. It gives the impression that as early as the mid-1930s a tendency was beginning to assert itself to bid farewell to rustic heaviness and to seek forms which, all severity aside, could give porcelain back something of its original elegance. Wilhelm Wagenfeld was one of the first to give expression to this changing need (the roots of which we shall not speculate on here).

7 *Daphne* Coffee service, Rosenthal porcelain factory, Selb, 1938

Unexecuted designs for C. M. Hutschenreuther, Hohenberg an der Eger

Wagenfeld's contacts with the Hohenberg-based porcelain factory C. M. Hutschenreuther fall in the final years of the war. The director of the company, Werner Heckmann, was interested in a complete set of table and coffee ware. Wagenfeld evidently had already prepared some designs previously, which he presented in Hohenberg in the December of 1943.[19] The china was originally to have been manufactured in the Bohemia porcelain factory,[20] which had been taken over by the SS, but Wagenfeld succeeded in releasing himself from the contract with Bohemia in November 1943 – a contract that had been entered upon under a certain amount of pressure – so that he was able to make free use of his designs.[21] A collection of tableware of noble elegance had been planned as embodied by the Berlin Porcelain Manufactory. It is reminiscent of Trude Petri's *Urbino*, particularly the sugar basin, but on the whole is rather longer in the body – a design element also stressed by the form of the handles.[22] Although the preliminary work had obviously made good progress, negotiations dragged on due to the events of the war and the increasing shortage of raw materials and could not be brought to a conclusion.

Parallel to his ideas for a set of table and coffee ware, Wagenfeld had also been working on heat-resistant cookware since February 1944 – a field in which C. M. Hutschenreuther hoped to develop a new market. The market leaders in this sector had previously been the porcelain factories Gebr. Bauscher and Walküre, nevertheless a change in eating habits had made the idea of expansion not unreasonable. The advantages of porcelain cookware were obvious – like their forerunners made of Jena glass: "Due to their pleasant appearance suitable for the dinner table, cooked or roast dishes no longer need to be transferred to serving dishes, in addition no heat is lost."[23] Much to Wagenfeld's distaste, C. M. Hutschenreuther issued a collection in 1950[24] based on initial sketches by Wagenfeld and several models made under his supervision – a service from which he firmly distanced himself. In a letter without a personal salutation, he argued: "I would be most grateful if in future you would desist from publishing this collection together with my name. As you will recall, several of the above-mentioned pieces were produced on the basis of my sketches only and were put on sale before I myself had seen the finished designs."[25] Hutschenreuther evidently did not take any notice of Wagenfeld's suggestion to redesign the tableware in line with his ideas. The collaboration, of which Wagenfeld had initially had such high hopes, was not continued.

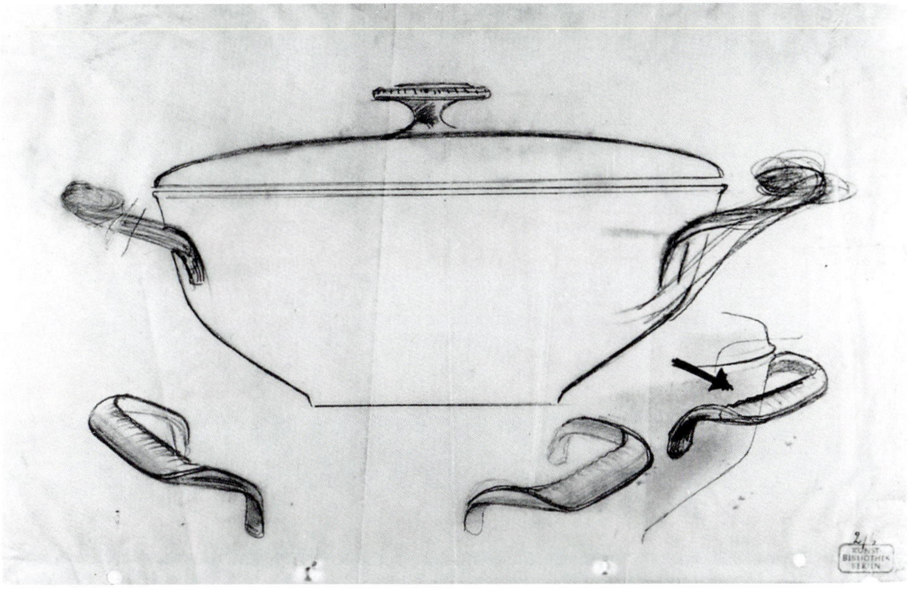

8 Sketch for soup tureen belonging to the *Daphne* collection, 1938

9 Hermann Gretsch, *1840* coffee service decorated with stars, Arzberg porcelain factory, 1938

10 Heinrich Löffelhardt, canteen ware for the Amt "Schönheit der Arbeit", 1938/39. The service was manufactured in various factories, including Rosenthal's works in Bahnhof Selb.

The porcelain designs of the 1950s

In retrospect, Wagenfeld was dissatisfied with the porcelain work he had done to date on account of a teacup designed by Marguerite Friedlaender which he admired

11 Plaster model of a coffee service for the Bohemia porcelain factory, later for C. M. Hutschenreuther, Hohenberg, after 1940

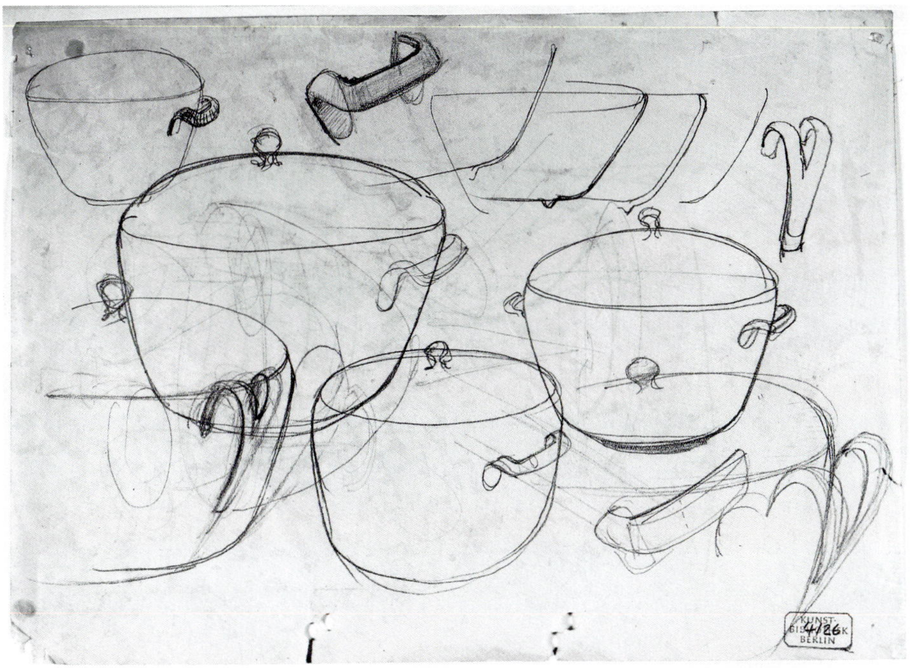

12 Sketch for soup tureens for C. M. Hutschenreuther, Hohenberg, circa 1944

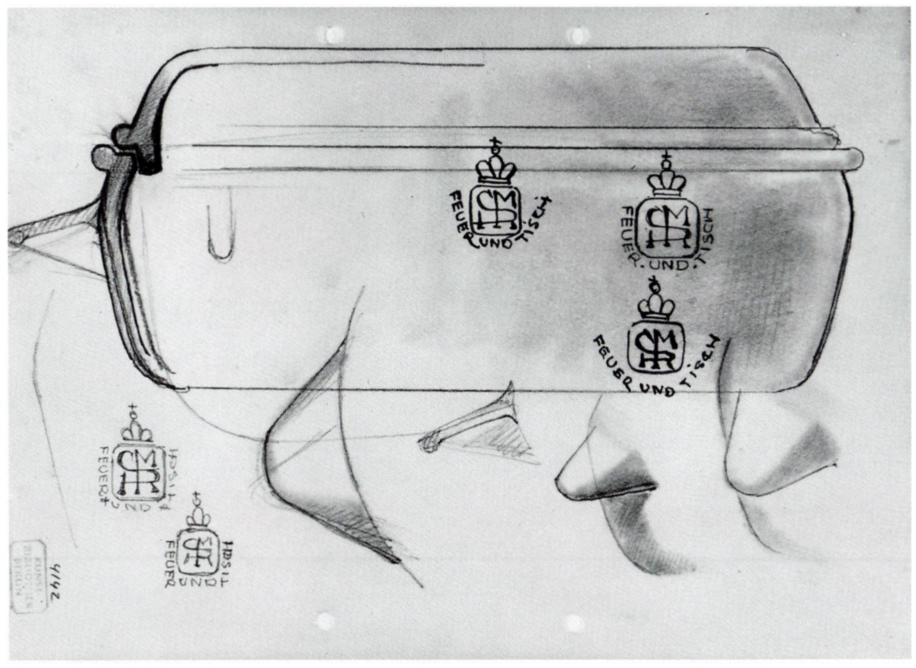

13 Sketch for a heat-resistant porcelain tureen and C. M. Hutschenreuther, Hohenberg, trademark 1944

greatly: "I had often occupied myself with designing cups and other porcelain objects. The factories did not consider my work to be unsuccessful. Yet as to these successes, I was also indifferent to the praise and criticism I received regarding this work, because this Berlin teacup was my secret criterion, pointing out to me tacitly and yet a thousand times more insistently everything that was wrong with my work."[26]

This statement shows the high standards by which Wagenfeld judged his own work and makes it clear why the collaboration with the porcelain industry, which had made unauthorised alterations to his designs and did not produce the quality he expected, gave him little joy. He evidently hoped to work with the Berlin Porcelain Manufactory – an ambition in which he almost succeeded, since he was unofficially offered the position of head of the company in 1948,[27] but was hindered by political circumstances. In 1949, Wagenfeld resettled to work in Stuttgart. Turning his back on Berlin meant that he had to give up his teaching at the Hochschule für Bildende Künste – a job that he had approached with great commitment and enthusiasm.

14 "Porcelain casserole dishes, part of a modern heat-resistant tableware series [...]. Design Prof. Wagenfeld", in: *Die Schaulade,* June 1950. Wagenfeld did not acknowledge the casserole dishes as being his own design

15 "Porcelain milk jugs, heat-resistant, [...]. Design: Prof. Wagenfeld", in: *Die Schaulade,* January 1950. Wagenfeld did not acknowledge the milk jugs as being his own design

There, together with his students, he had developed a set of coffee ware for the catering trade in 1948/49 that was to be manufactured by the State Porcelain Manufactory. In keeping with its purpose, it has a strong body, a far cry from the translucency of the Berlin ware that had so inspired him. Wagenfeld's design is a departure from the full-bellied forms common to hotel ware until that time. Instead he chose a conical form that tapers off towards the bottom – a form that becomes slightly curved in the design of the cups. Strikingly, the handle is an extension of the rim of the mouth and, in the case of the pot, protrudes a little over the body of the vessel. The pourer is designed as a long, drawn down triangular spout; the lid closes flush with the shoulder. The cream jug has two small indented lips for pouring on each side. This solution was important to Wagenfeld as he had noticed on visits to coffee houses "how rarely the small handle on milk jugs [...] is ever used".[28] The austerity of the design points forward to developments in the 1960s. The only thing that had not yet been given any thought was the problem of stackability. The series was never produced.

Wagenfeld took up the striking join between the body of the cups and handles once more in the melamine cabin service produced for Lufthansa in 1955. In 1960, the coffeepot was developed further into a model that seems out of place among Wagenfeld's porcelain designs on account of its severe technoid forms with its smooth lid with no finial and angular handle. It seems rather more in keeping with the spirit of the Hochschule für Gestaltung in Ulm. Wagenfeld had wanted to give the royalties from the service he intended to design around the coffeepot as a gift to the Stedelijk Museum in Amsterdam as the director, Willem Sandberg, was a close friend. On account of the unusual legal circumstances however, the project was realised neither by the Dutch company, Sphinx Céramique, based in Maastricht, nor later by Rosenthal. When Melitta later brought out a similar model, Wagenfeld refrained from pursuing his own design any further.

"Gloriana" for Rosenthal Porzellan/Selb

Wagenfeld's first tableware produced after the war was created once again in collaboration with Rosenthal. Since 1950, Philip Rosenthal jr. had held the position of head of sales and had embraced the challenge of giving the brand a completely new image. He had met Wagenfeld in Darmstadt in April 1952, probably at the Rat für Formgebung

16 Plaster model for porcelain coffee-house tableware, Hochschule für Bildende Künste Berlin, Wagenfeld's class, 1948/49

17 Plaster model for a porcelain coffee pot, planned for Sphinx Céramique/Maastricht, 1960

(Council for Design) and both men appeared to be in agreement on their objectives. In December, Wagenfeld signed a contract as art consultant for the entire porcelain production. Philip Rosenthal evidently had no intention of giving him similar powers as those he had enjoyed at the United Lausitz Glassworks since he also looked around for other designers. Raymond Loewy was of particular interest to him because of his international reputation, yet he soon focussed his gaze on Scandinavia too, which had established a name for itself at the Tenth Milan Triennial in 1954 as a leader in the field of glass and ceramic design.

Künste, once again the body of the vessel swells upwards, merging now into a rounded shoulder whose line is continued in the slightly domed lid. A straight long spout points upwards at a flat angle, the ear-like handle has a wide curve. A striking feature is the finial on the lid, which is in the form of a small loop. It is similar to that found in the *Form 2000* tableware designed in 1952 by Richard Latham, a member of Raymond Loewy's design studio. Yet the handles function in completely different ways, as remarked upon by Bernd Fritz: with Wagenfeld's design the tapered bridge of the loop allows it to be lifted easily between thumb

18 Coffee service *Gloriana*, Rosenthal Porzellan AG, Selb, 1952/53

Wagenfeld's contribution to the "new look"[29] at Rosenthal was the collection entitled *Gloriana.* This went into production in 1953 at the Thomas porcelain factory, part of the Rosenthal group since 1908. It is his first set of fine china to have a delicate relief pattern, consisting here of fine vertical grooves. The form takes up an idea that had already been formulated in the designs for the Bohemia porcelain factory. As in the designs at the Hochschule für bildende

and forefinger meeting in the middle, whilst Latham's design has to be grasped more like a conventional knob on account of the widened bridge in the middle.[30]

Although the company's advertisement maintained "The form has been thought through and designed down to the last detail. [...] All the handles of the hollow pieces can be grasped easily. The interplay of the relief grooves on the cups and saucers is particularly attractive,"[31] Wagen-

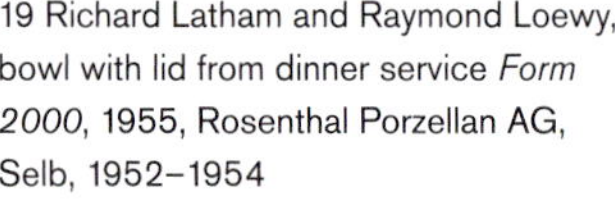

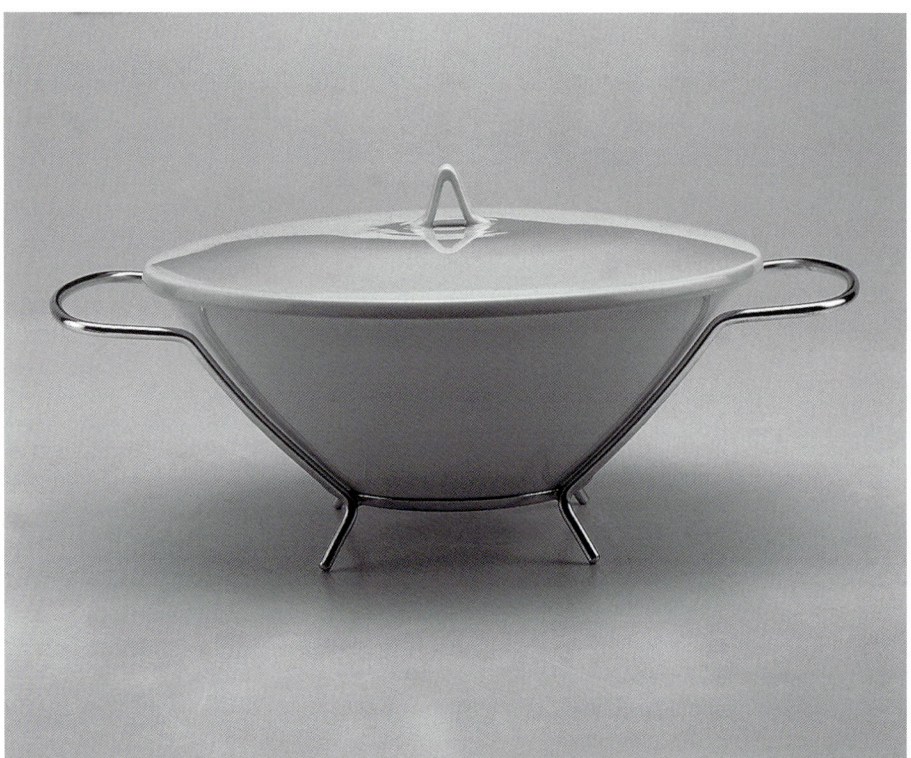

19 Richard Latham and Raymond Loewy, bowl with lid from dinner service *Form 2000*, 1955, Rosenthal Porzellan AG, Selb, 1952–1954

feld was unhappy with the initial execution. In his opinion, it was inadequate, dull and boring since there was no passion for porcelain at the Thomas factory.[32] After Wagenfeld initially gave notice of his contract in March 1955,[33] the collaboration continued at Philip Rosenthal's request but no further services were produced. Neither the plans for the Stedelijk Museum service, nor the reworking of *Daphne*, which Thomas continued to produce for export until 1957, were brought to a satisfactory conclusion. Wagenfeld had been outstripped in the field of porcelain design by his former employee, Heinrich Löffelhardt, whose designs had been awarded numerous international prizes. From 1961 onwards at the latest, Rosenthal was pursuing a different strategy with its *Studio* line, which evidently did not envisage a position for Wagenfeld that met his expectations.

Yet it was here that he was able for the first time, albeit on the sidelines, to fully exploit the beauty of porcelain, its immaculate surfaces and translucency. Since 1952, he had been working on table lamps whose porcelain shades not only served to protect from glare but also to modulate the light through the varying thicknesses of the body of the relief surface – which allowed the light to shine through more in some places and less in others. The shade was supported by three slender silver-plated metal legs, gracefully flared outwards at the bottom. There were also thin-walled bowls with similarly sculpted surfaces that rested, seemingly floating, in a metal framework. The metal parts were manufactured by WMF with whom Wagenfeld had collaborated under contract since 1949.

Parallels with Wagenfeld's combination of porcelain and metal can also be found once again in Latham's concurrent *Form 2000*. Here too the bowl appears almost to float above the table, held by a fine metal frame that also serves the practical purpose of supporting the bowl upright and providing it with handles at the sides without spoiling its shape.

A characteristic of Wagenfeld's work is apparent in his collaboration with Rosenthal that is often overlooked: his delight in decoration, albeit decoration that had to be at one with the form, since "Ornament spoils a piece if it can be removed or added like incidental drapery."[34] Wagenfeld had always resisted subsequent decorations to his designs, not always with success. In Philip Rosenthal he appears to have found the sympathetic ear that he sought in vain with nearly all his other partners. Consequently works were produced which in terms of balance are the best of Wagenfeld's porcelain designs.

In his own special design language Wagenfeld gave form to that which he had admired so greatly in the porcelain produced by the Royal Porcelain Manufactory of Berlin: "The new designs are simple, but they are festive like the early works from the beginnings of porcelain design. Their simplicity is not the 'simplicity of the collective

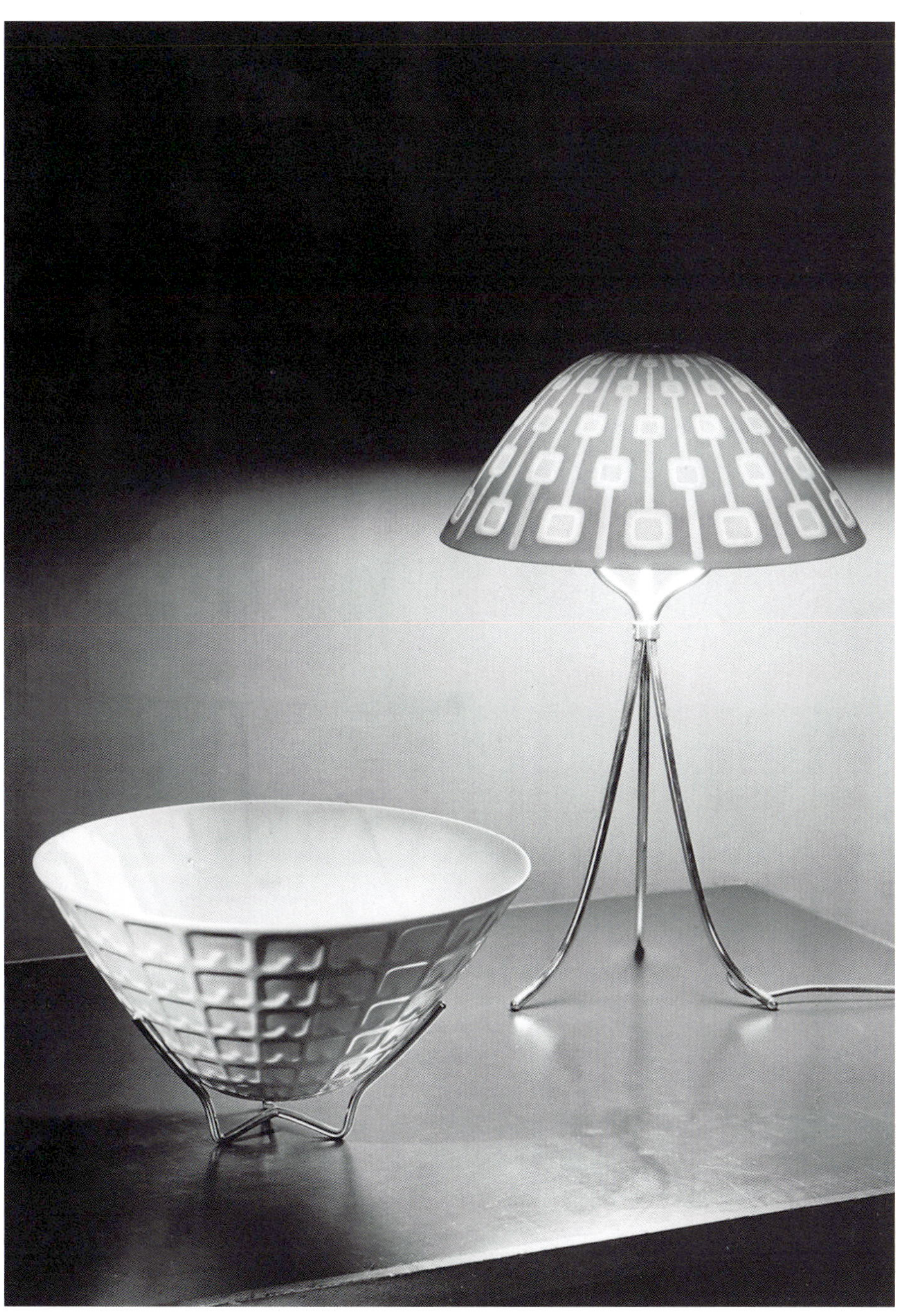

20 Table lamp with china shade and fruit bowl, Rosenthal Porzellan AG, Selb, metal parts: WMF, Geislingen, 1952/53

ideas of the German *volk'* of which some art historians and petit-bourgeois puritans are particularly fond of preaching, rather the comparison leads us to Chinese porcelain and we are reminded of those porcelain pieces in Berlin's Schlossmuseum and the works held at Berlin's Völkerkunde-museum."[35] It was to their perfection that Wagenfeld constantly looked. For him, porcelain was not a field for experimentation, but rather a challenge to create something with the means of his own time that could stand alongside the achievements of the past to which he often so clearly referred.

Notes

1 See Wilhelm Wagenfeld, "Zweck und Sinn der künstlerischen Mitarbeit in Fabriken" (1957), quoted in *Wilhelm Wagenfeld. Vom Bauhaus in die Industrie,* exhibition catalogue, Landesgewerbeamt Baden-Württemberg, Stuttgart 1965, unpaginated.
2 *Kunst und Kunstgewerbe,* Vol. 9, 1928, p. 5, plate 1, quoted in Imke Ristow, *Artur Hennig (1880–1959). Das gestalterische Werk und die Lehrtätigkeit an der Staatlichen Keramischen Fachschule Bunzlau,* Weimar 1999, p. 89.
3 After the famed art school in Halle. See Rita Gründig, "Keramik und Gefässdesign", in: *Burg Giebichenstein. Die hallesche Kunstschule von den Anfängen bis zur Gegenwart,* Staatliche Galerie Moritzburg, Halle, and Badisches Landesmuseum Karlsruhe, Halle 1993, pp. 245–282, here p. 247.
4 Hans-Joachim Beyer and Beatrix Frfr. Wolff Metternich, *Kannenformen der Porzellanmanufaktur Fürstenberg. Stilgeschichtliche Beispiele aus drei Jahrhunderten* (work reports from the Städtisches Museum Braunschweig, 44), Braunschweig 1983 p. 36 f., fig. 34.
5 Klaus Weber, "'Wir alle müssen zum Handwerk zurück!' Die keramische Werkstatt des Bauhauses in Dornburg (1920–1925)", in: *Keramik und Bauhaus,* Bauhaus Archiv Berlin, Berlin 1989, pp. 10–29, here p. 18 f., cat. no. 86 f., 93; *Otto Lindig, der Töpfer,* Museums of the City of Gera, Gera 1990, pp. 15–17, cat. no. 12–14, 17.
6 "Fürstenberg alt und neu", in: *Die Schaulade,* Vol. 10, No. 10, Edition B, 1934, pp. 465–467.
7 *639. Das Fürstenberger Service,* sales brochure, Fürstenberg, no vol. no. (1934).
8 Letter from Wilhelm Wagenfeld to Heinrich König, 15 March 1955, Wilhelm Wagenfeld Stiftung, Bremen.
9 *Deutsche Warenkunde,* publ. Kunstdienst – Berlin, Berlin 1938, product category 01/01 (tableware), issue 6; product category 01/02 (coffee service), issue 9.
10 *Deutsche Warenkunde*, product category 01/02, issue 20.
11 Obituary in: *Die Schaulade,* Vol. 10, No. 1, 1934, p. 35.
12 Marc Cremer-Thursby, *Design der dreissiger und vierziger Jahre in Deutschland – Hermann Gretsch. Architekt und Designer (1895–1950)* (Europäische Hochschulschriften, Series no. XXVII, vol. 226), Frankfurt am Main etc. 1996, pp. 41, 73.
13 In 1938, a set of white tableware for six persons cost 26.65 RM from Arzberg, whereas a similar set in the *639* design from Fürstenberg cost 36.75 RM. Even more expensive still were the ivory and celadon editions at 41.55 RM and 55.95 RM respectively. See *Deutsche Warenkunde,* Berlin 1938, product category 01/01 (tableware), nos. 5, 6.
14 Marc Cremer-Thursby 1996 (see note 12), p. 17.
15 Letter from Wilhelm Wagenfeld to Heinrich König (see note 8).
16 See *Deutsche Warenkunde,* Berlin 1939, product category 01/07 (hotel and canteen ware), issue 4.
17 See Imke Ristow 1999 (see note 2), p. 103 f.
18 Wilhelm Wagenfeld, "Berliner Porzellan", quoted in Wagenfeld, *Wesen und Gestalt der Dinge um uns,* Potsdam 1948, identical reprint, Worpsweder Verlag 1990, p. 46. The essay first appeared in: *neue linie,* Vol. 9, No. 10, 1938, pp. 2, 4, 6, 61.
19 Letter from Director Werner Heckmann to Wilhelm Wagenfeld, 16 December 1943, Wilhelm Wagenfeld Stiftung, Bremen.
20 On the Bohemia porcelain factory see Gabriele Huber, *Die Porzellan-Manufaktur Allach- München GmbH, eine "Wirtschaftsunternehmung" der SS zum Schutz der "deutschen Seele",* Marburg 1992, pp. 35–38, on Wagenfeld's contribution see p. 209 f.
21 Letter from Wilhelm Wagenfeld to Werner Heckmann, 6 January 1944, Wilhelm Wagenfeld Stiftung, Bremen.
22 The Wilhelm Wagenfeld Stiftung in Bremen keeps a series of design sketches connected with the order for C. M. Hutschenreuther and/or Bohemia. Which of these were intended for execution is not apparent.
23 *Die Schaulade,* Vol. 25, No. 6, 1950, p. 209, on the Rosenthal tableware illustrated on the title page of the issue.
24 Letter from Wilhelm Wagenfeld to the porcelain factory C. M. Hutschenreuther, 23 September 1950, Wilhelm Wagenfeld Stiftung, Bremen.
25 Milk jugs illustrated in: *Die Schaulade,* Vol. 25, No. 1, 1950, p. 16; casserole dishes in: *Schaulade* No. 6, p. 212.
26 Wilhelm Wagenfeld, "Von alltäglichen Dingen" (1947), in: Wagenfeld, *Wesen und Gestalt* (see note 18), pp. 35–43, here p. 35 f.
27 Beate Manske, "Biografie Wilhelm Wagenfeld", in: *Wilhelm Wagenfeld: gestern, heute, morgen. Lebenskultur im Alltag,* publ. Wilhelm Wagenfeld Stiftung, Bremen, Bremen 1995, p. 26 f.
28 Quoted in *Wilhelm Wagenfeld. Vom Bauhaus in die Industrie* (see note 1), unpaginated.
29 Hermann Schreiber et al., *Die Rosenthal Story,* Düsseldorf and Vienna 1980, p. 31.
30 Bernd Fritz, *Die Porzellangeschirre des Rosenthal Konzerns 1891–1979,* Stuttgart 1989, p. 73 f.
31 Quoted in Fritz, p. 73.
32 Letter from Wilhelm Wagenfeld to Philip Rosenthal, 12 February 1954, Wilhelm Wagenfeld Stiftung, Bremen.
33 Letter from Wilhelm Wagenfeld to Philip Rosenthal, 3 March 1955, Wilhelm Wagenfeld Stiftung, Bremen.
34 Wilhelm Wagenfeld, "An den Rand geschrieben" (1940), in: *Wesen und Gestalt* (see note 18), p. 24 f., here p. 25.
35 Wilhelm Wagenfeld, "Die Gegenwart in Architektur und Hausrat" (1946), in: *Wesen und Gestalt* (see note 18), pp. 87–121, here p. 102.

Observations on the Drawings of Wilhelm Wagenfeld

Bernd Altenstein

1 Sauce boat and lamps, design sketch, pencil, Bauhochschule Weimar, c.1928

The universal artistic concept of the Renaissance artists, which encompassed the classic disciplines of painting, architecture and sculpture – "disegno" –, became explicit in the wider potential of the discipline of drawing, the most spontaneous and direct, emotional, and also the most abstract way of lending form to thoughts and ideas. For the painters, sculptors and architects – now no longer merely drawing blueprints for the masons on site – their drawings from the first draft to the final details of spatial representation were an instrument for clarifying proportions, measurements and space. And they communicated an illusion of the finished product to their clients. Thus drawing evolved into a universal and increasingly autonomous form of expression.

Drawing as a visual thought process permeates Wilhelm Wagenfeld's work, be it that of his early years of study in Bremen and Hanau or following his period at the Bauhaus school and the Bauhochschule, when his work in conceiving tactile three-dimensional forms for such materials as glass, porcelain and plastic – none of which were processed by himself – inspired at the drawing stage a wealth of formal invention and variations upon it. His drawings overflow with the creative potential of free art in prints and painting, the profession which Wagenfeld originally wanted to follow. However, it is drawing toward the three-dimensional form which mainly characterises his work. Hugo Leven, sculptor and principal of the academy in Hanau, had early recognised Wagenfeld's developing political and social commitment to become a product designer with a sense of social responsibility, a development away from the exuberant expressiveness of his early woodcuts.[1] Consequently Wagenfeld switched to the Bauhaus, where he enrolled in Moholy-Nagy's metal class. As can be seen in Moholy-Nagy's sculptures, the teacher himself was fascinated by the tactile, optical and technical properties of transparent, opaque, smooth, rough, shiny and dull materials and their interplay, their relationships of consonance and tension and the effects these generated. The work in the metal class trained the sensibilities for the perception and analysis of form. Purified form was taken back to basic geometric shapes and their combinations. Wagenfeld's most prominent work from this period is embodied in the table lamp. Drawing then would feature as sketch designs – variations on a theme done with quick strokes of the pencil on a small sheet of paper, sometimes highlighting the outline, sometimes the corporeality of the object – and as working drawings, finding ideas and setting the specifications for the physical prototype.

Wagenfeld's decision to become a designer of industrial products was a logical extension of all that drawing implied. While the aim of every study from the life in Bremen and Hanau had been expressive free drawing and graphics, now a free and open drawing style would initiate the design process. The cone, sphere and cylinder, the stock of solid geometric form in the Bauhaus foundation course, were soon left behind. Wagenfeld's search for a synthesis of geometric clarity and organic individuality was already in evidence in his work from his Bauhochschule period. The repertoire of Bauhaus geometry favoured additive and linear combinations of form. Two-dimensional criteria of proportion determined the shape of an object. Wagenfeld's early experiences with form, however, include its creation out of non-purposive, fundamental solid geometry using the concept of pressure and counter-pressure, a concept which can be observed in nature[2] and which was to become Wagenfeld's dominating form principle for all hollow objects. Even the nudes and portraits he did in Hanau reflect Wagenfeld's attempts to capture his subjects in stereometric analysis as well as in a free line. The recent traditions of Cubism and "Jugendstil" can be seen at work.

The drawing pencil maintains the clarity of the object being drawn. An idea is developed on a piece of paper, the interior and exterior of an object become almost tangible, until they are "arrested" in a spatial representation. One could speak of a thematic time aspect, the drawings charting the development of ideas and the process of creation across the sheet of paper. Although the transparency of a sketched glass can create the illusion of lightness and fragility, Wagenfeld uses it primarily as a stylistic instrument. The drawing paper is conceived as a pictorial space in which the objects – glasses, vases, lamps etc. – appear to float and sway and intersect. The space cannot be clearly defined. There is neither horizon nor base. Red, blue and green drawing pencils, the pressure of the pencil or subtle hatching provide accentuation. The pencil draws the ovals that result from a slightly raised vantage point, connects them to the silhouette of the conceptualised object and has them end in a further oval form, which represents the base, background or an opposing object. Sometimes the lines also flow freely (as in the case of the Hanau portraits) bringing the entire spatiality of the imagined object into the drawing. The paper is filled with large and small shapes, as if viewed from varying distances, or perhaps they are indeed intended to represent objects of varying sizes. Many drawings show the evolution of a family of forms in the compartmentalisation of the silhouettes or serial successions of shapes. Curves are sometimes drawn with tangents in coloured pencil to accentuate the relations of the angles to one another. To certain vase shapes Wagenfeld later adds geometric proportion systems in the tradition of Vitruvius to verify an intuitive sense of harmony. Such characteristics can be seen in his drawings from the 1930s to the 1960s. A further drawing approach is shown in his sketches of designs for door handles, lamp holders and cutlery. In these, his thought processes can be followed again in the repeated cross-sections of shapes, the lines around the shapes and the shading made by the smearing of pencil lines. These sketch designs are composed in such a way that, irrespective of their original purpose, they can be regarded as complete works of art. Wagenfeld was aware of the aesthetic value of such drawings, and he submitted them at exhibitions, along with demonstration drawings created for this purpose.

Designing for the industrial sector often meant a quest for new solutions in the fine detail, not only to meet aesthetic requirements, but also those of manufacturing technologies and practical utility: sockets, spouts and handles, jointed forms, for crossover from one volume to another while simultaneously changing materials. The drawings for such challenges were a fierce battle involving every possible representation technique to achieve satisfactory results. Less in demand here was the expression of free thought, the drawings are rather a running debate on every design proposition appearing on the paper. The repetition of silhouettes, the pressure of the pencil, the emphasis on a particular shape by tracing over it with other pencils, and written annotations are all indications of this.

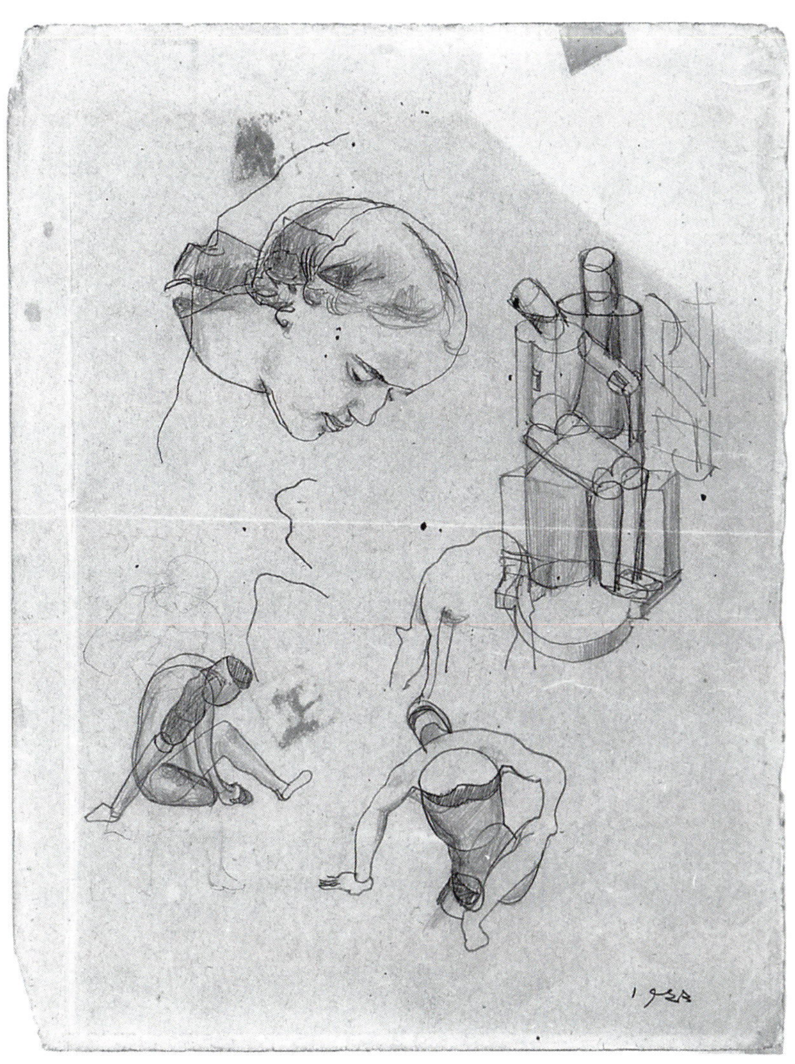

2 Head and figure studies, page from sketchbook, pencil, 1923

Every client wants to be given an idea (early on) of the results to be expected. Be it

Cellini, Dürer or a present-day artist with an order to fill, each one searches for as convincing an image as possible of that which he intends to create. For this reason, over the course of time an extremely labour-intensive culture of model construction and demonstration drawings, and nowadays also virtual animation, has evolved. Not unlike Dürer, who in 1508 prepared a careful ink drawing with light washes for the *All Saints Altarpiece* (completed in 1511) for his patron, Wagenfeld also creates for his an image in his demonstration drawings of the solitary object set off either with vivid colour or with bold strokes of charcoal. The design

3 *Woodcutters,* woodcut, 1923

is elaborated in a statuary and monumental way in these drawings. Demonstration drawings are directed outwards. First draft drawings look inwards towards the workshop and the modeller of the prototype, which is sketched in several variations and then corrected and fine-tuned on many sheets of paper, before appearing anew in convincing modelled form. The working drawings subsequently produced by Wagenfeld are more impersonal, allow the involvement of those working with him and those who share his ideas, and promote the three-dimensional realisation. They constitute an architectural blueprint, illustrating the necessary cross-sections and progressions in wall thickness; proportions are given measurements.

Wagenfeld's drawing, complex and of artistic openness, goes beyond the utilitarian purposes of industrial products; it gives space to the wealth of creative thinking and to the generating of its own world of shapes – richer and more abundant than the sum total of the designs actually adopted for production. The drawings communicate the ideas of the artist and designer facing the challenges of industrialisation and mass production – with an artistic competence quite in the "disegno" tradition and propelled by the motor of Bauhaus design.

Notes

1 Wilhelm Wagenfeld, *Handzeichnungen und Druckgraphik,* published by the Barkenhoff-Stiftung, Worpswede, in collaboration with the Wilhelm Wagenfeld Stiftung, exh. cat. Barkenhoff Worpswede, Worpsweder Verlag 1996, p. 43.
2 Similar studies were done by Karl Blossfeldt in his photographic studies of natural form, in: Karl Blossfeldt, *Urformen der Natur,* Berlin 1928.

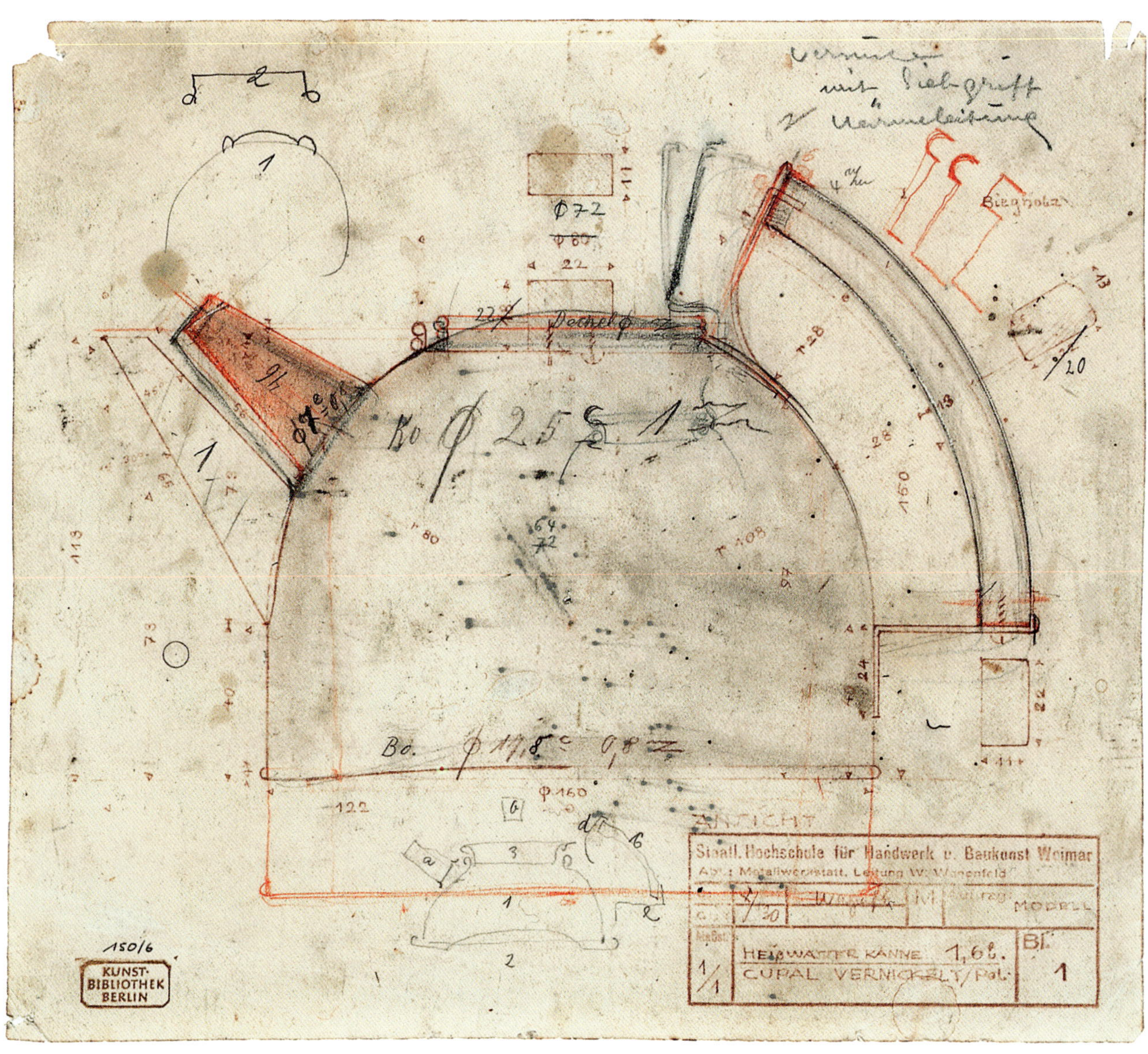

1 Kettle, design sketch for Weimar Bau- und Wohnungskunst GmbH, October 1930

2 Coffee pots, design sketch, circa 1940

3 *Daphne* tea and coffee pots,
design sketch for Rosenthal/Selb,
1937/38

4 *Lobenstein* goblet, design sketch for VLG/Weisswasser, 1936/37

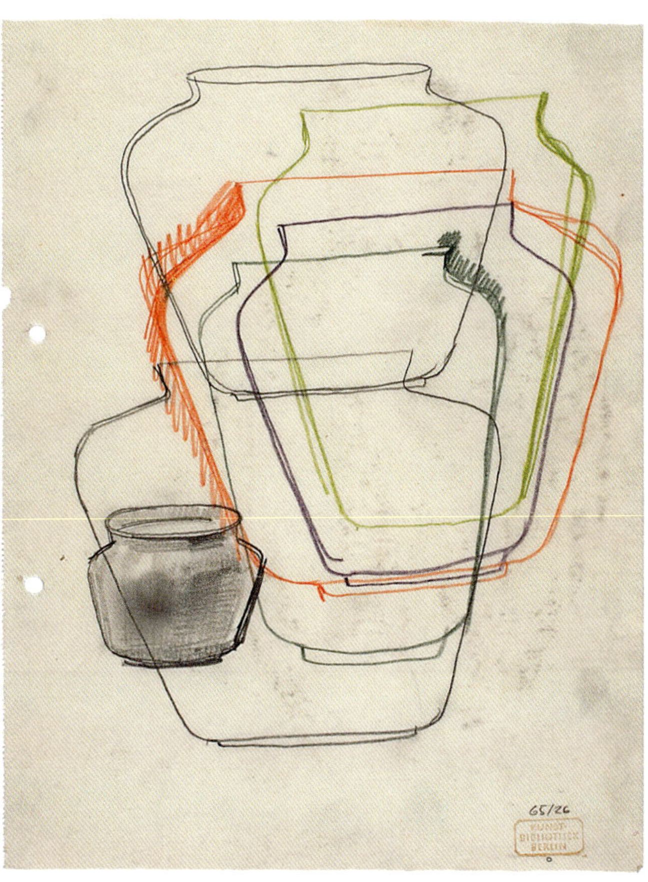

5 Vases, design sketch for VLG/Weisswasser, circa 1938

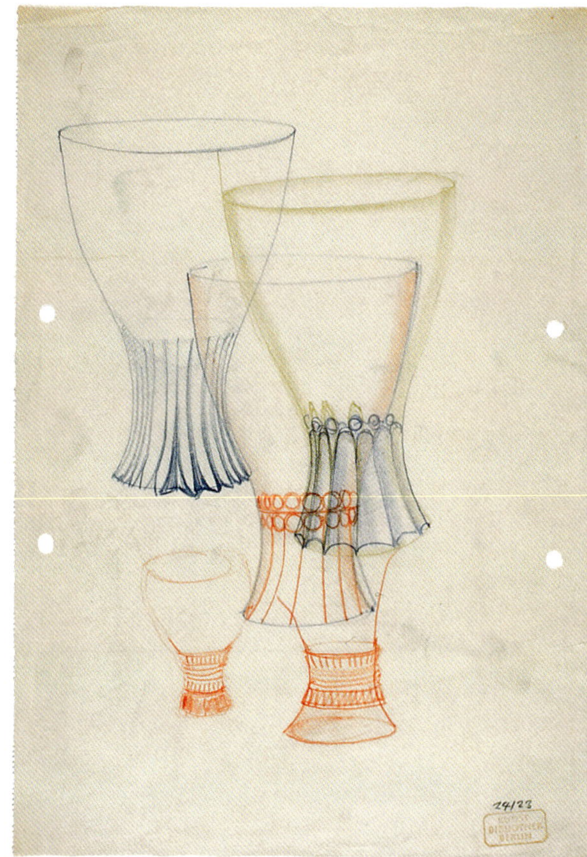

6 Beakers with cut foot, design sketch for VLG/Weisswasser, circa 1939/40

7 Tumblers and spirits glasses, design sketch for VLG/Weisswasser, 1936/38

8 Vases and flasks, design sketch for VLG/Weisswasser, 1935/37

9 Vases and bowls, design sketch for VLG/Weisswasser, 1935/38

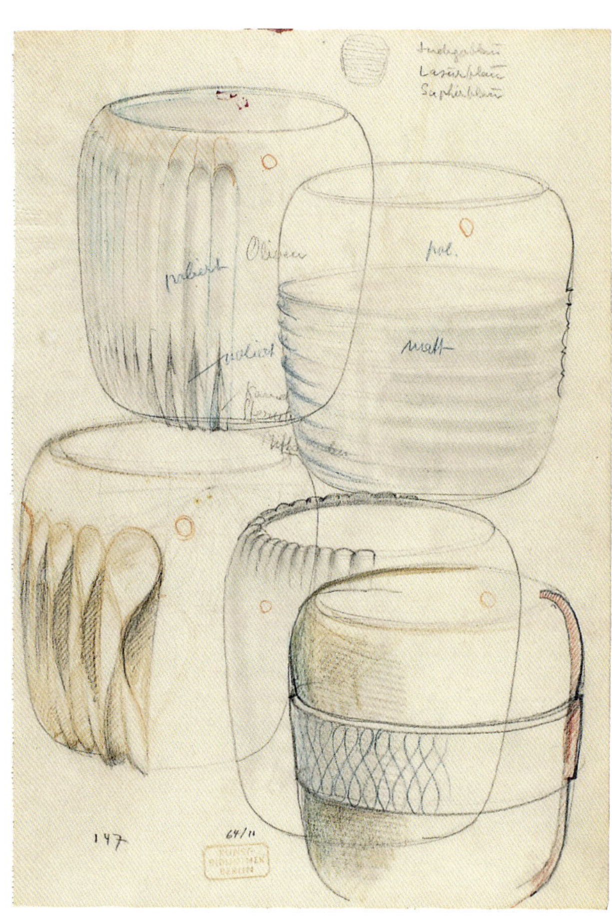

10 Vases with designs for cut patterns, design sketch for VLG/Weisswasser, circa 1936

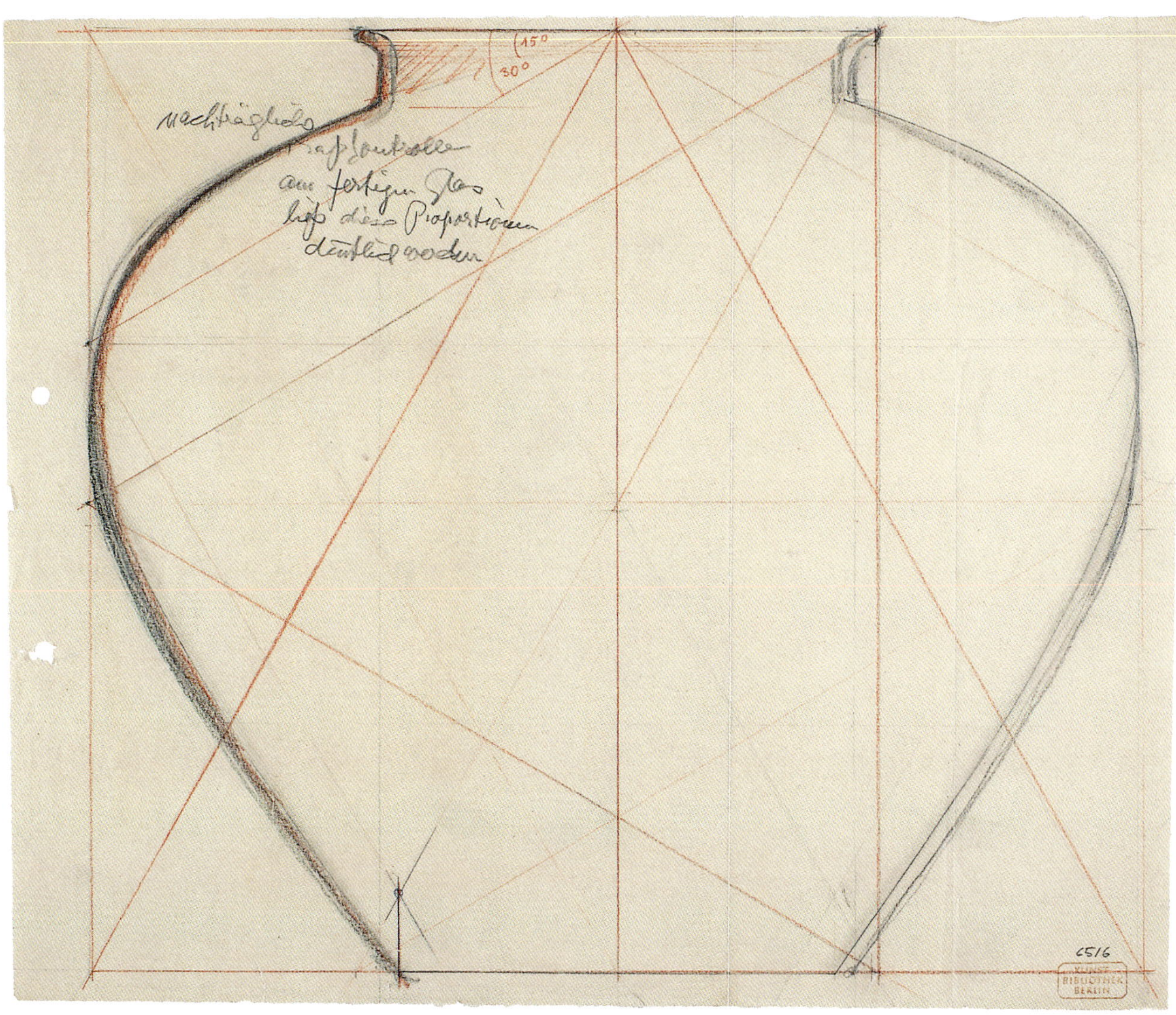

11 “Heart-shaped” vase with proportion studies, design sketch for VLG/Weisswasser, 1935

12 Draft variations on pressed glass bowls, design sketch for VLG/Weisswasser, 1937/38

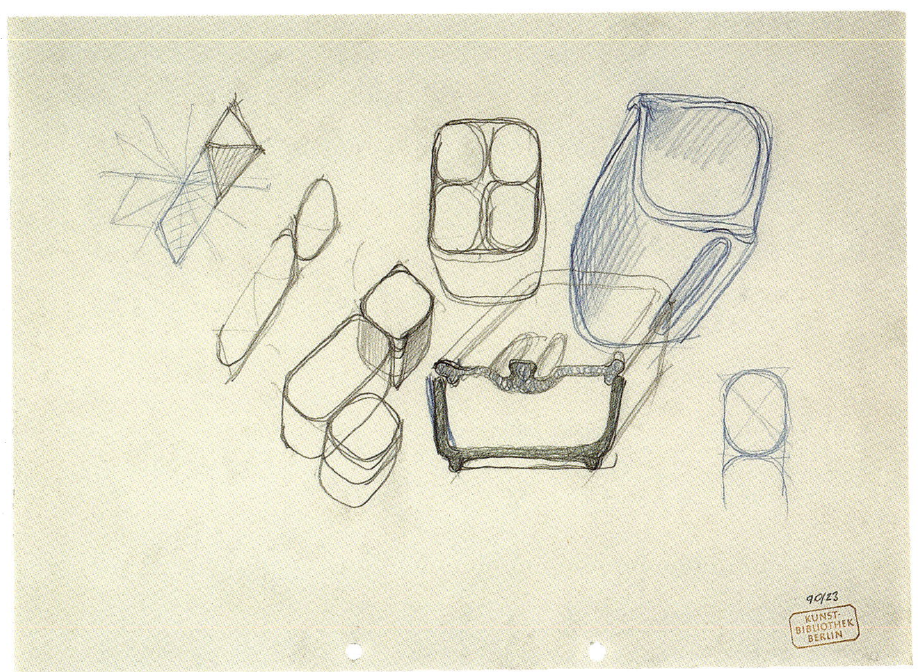

13 *Kubus* food storage set, design sketch for VLG/Weisswasser, 1938

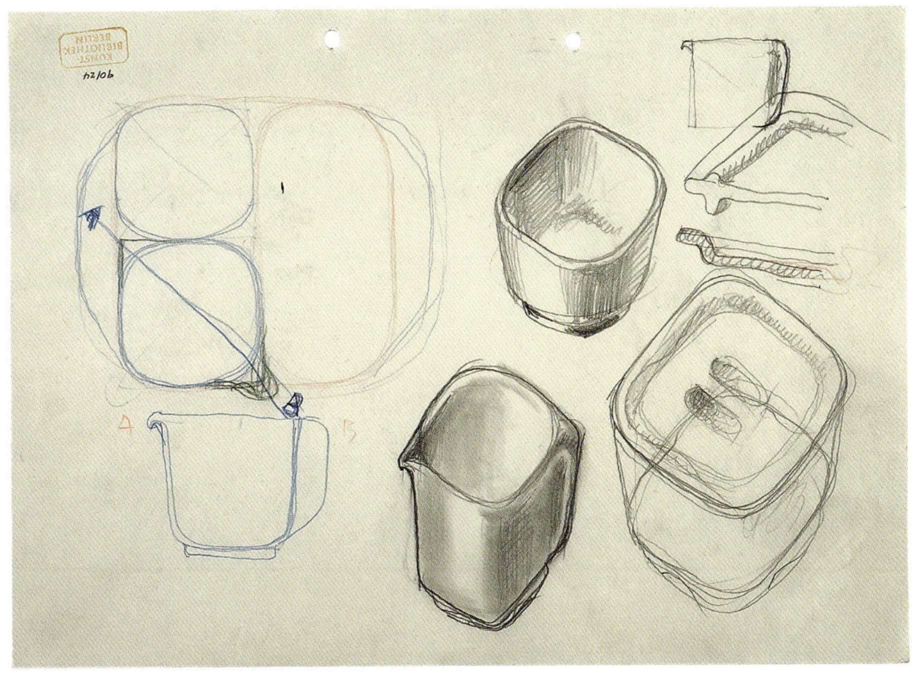

14 *Kubus* food storage set, design sketch for VLG/Weisswasser, 1938

15 Study for cutlery, 1941/42

16 Double casseroles of ovenproof porcelain, design sketch for Hutschenreuther/Hohenberg an der Eger, 21 July 1944

17 *Doria* champagne glasses, design sketch for WMF/Geislingen, 21 April 1961

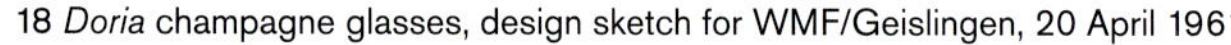

18 *Doria* champagne glasses, design sketch for WMF/Geislingen, 20 April 1961

19 *Ascona* tumblers, design sketch for Peill & Putzler/Düren, 1954

20 *Ascona* drinking glasses, design sketch for Peill & Putzler/Düren, 29 April 1954

21 Vases, design sketch for WMF/Geislingen, circa 1961

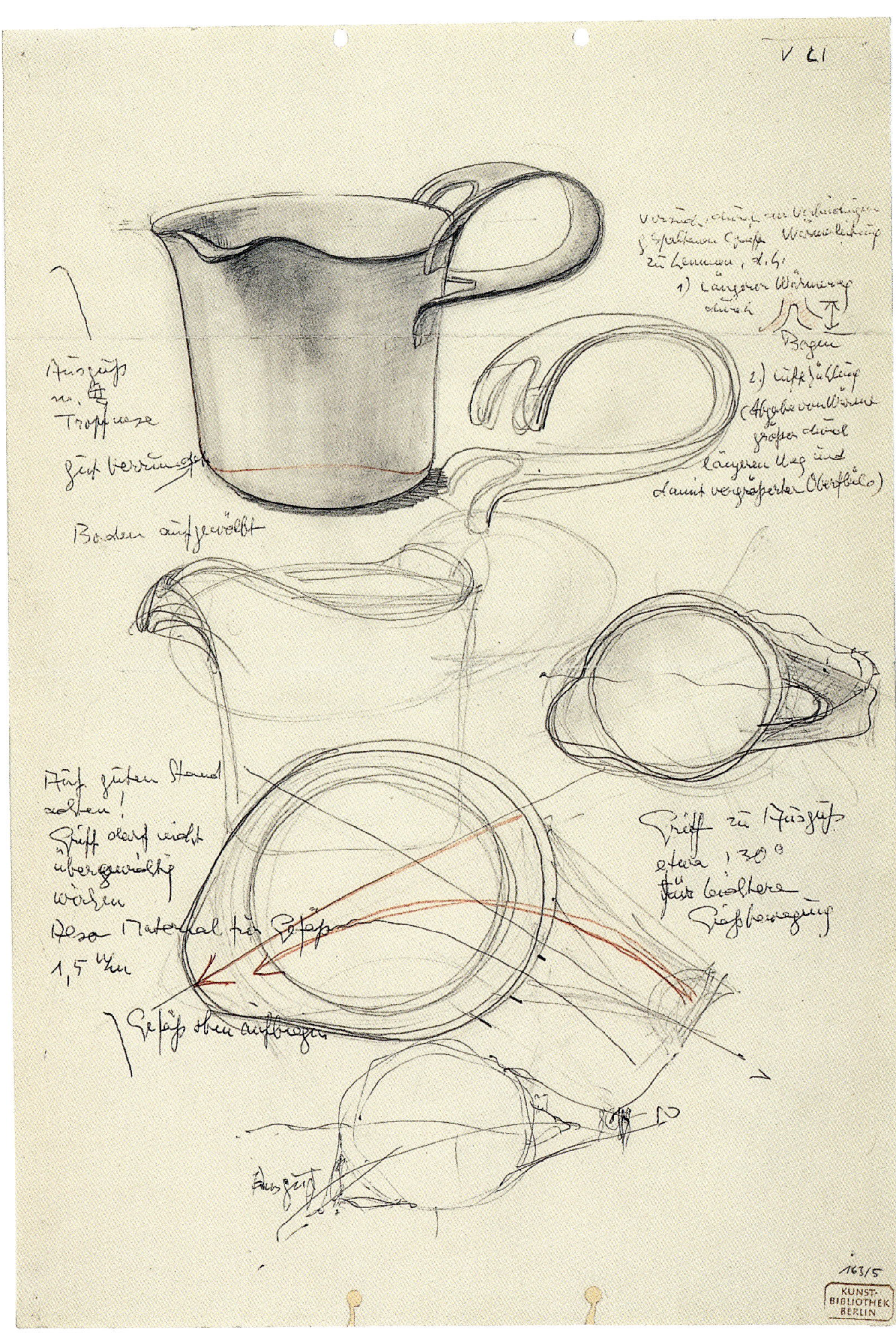

22 Sauce boat, design sketch for WMF/Geislingen, circa 1959

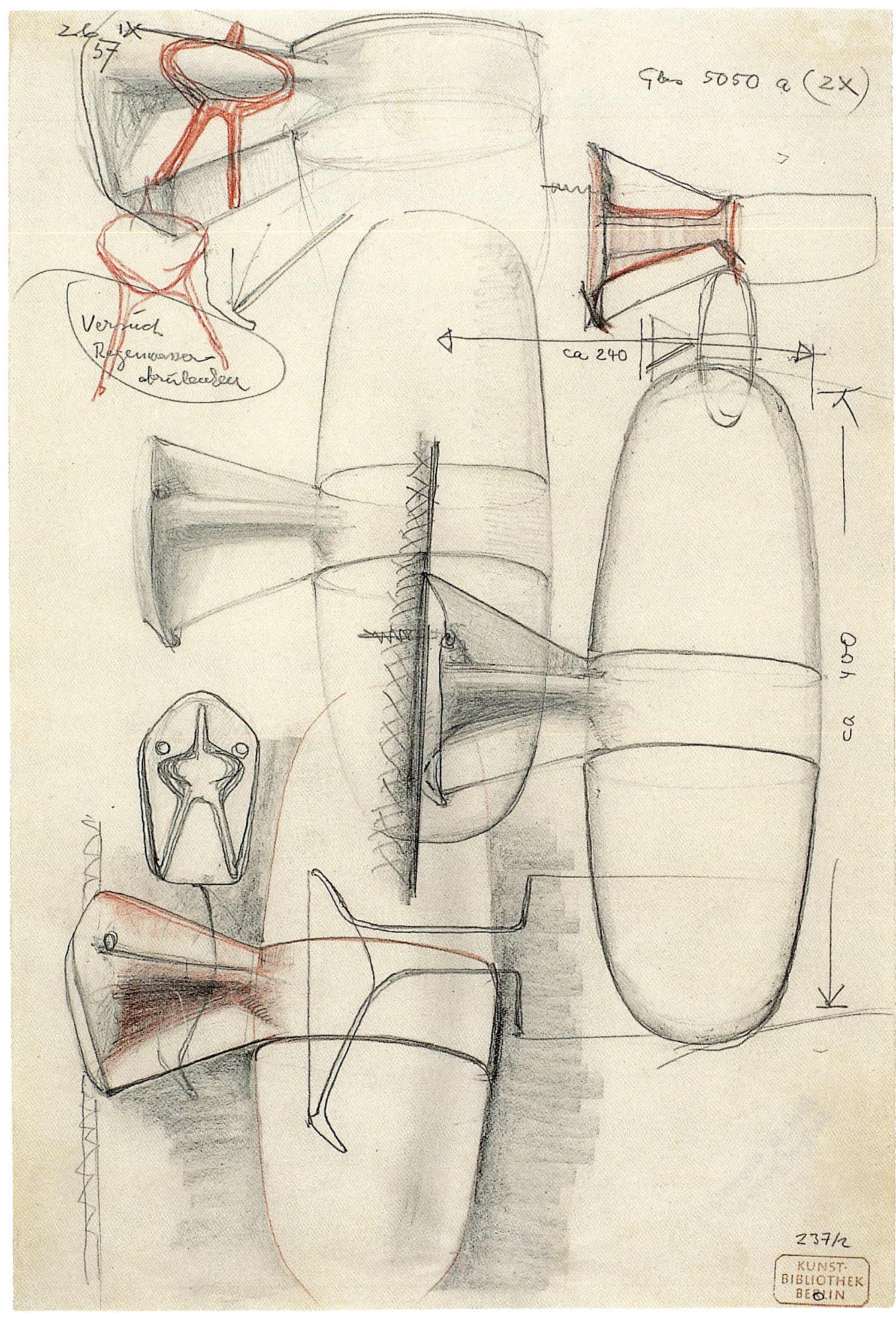

23 Wall light fitting, design sketch for
Lindner/Bamberg, 26 September 1957

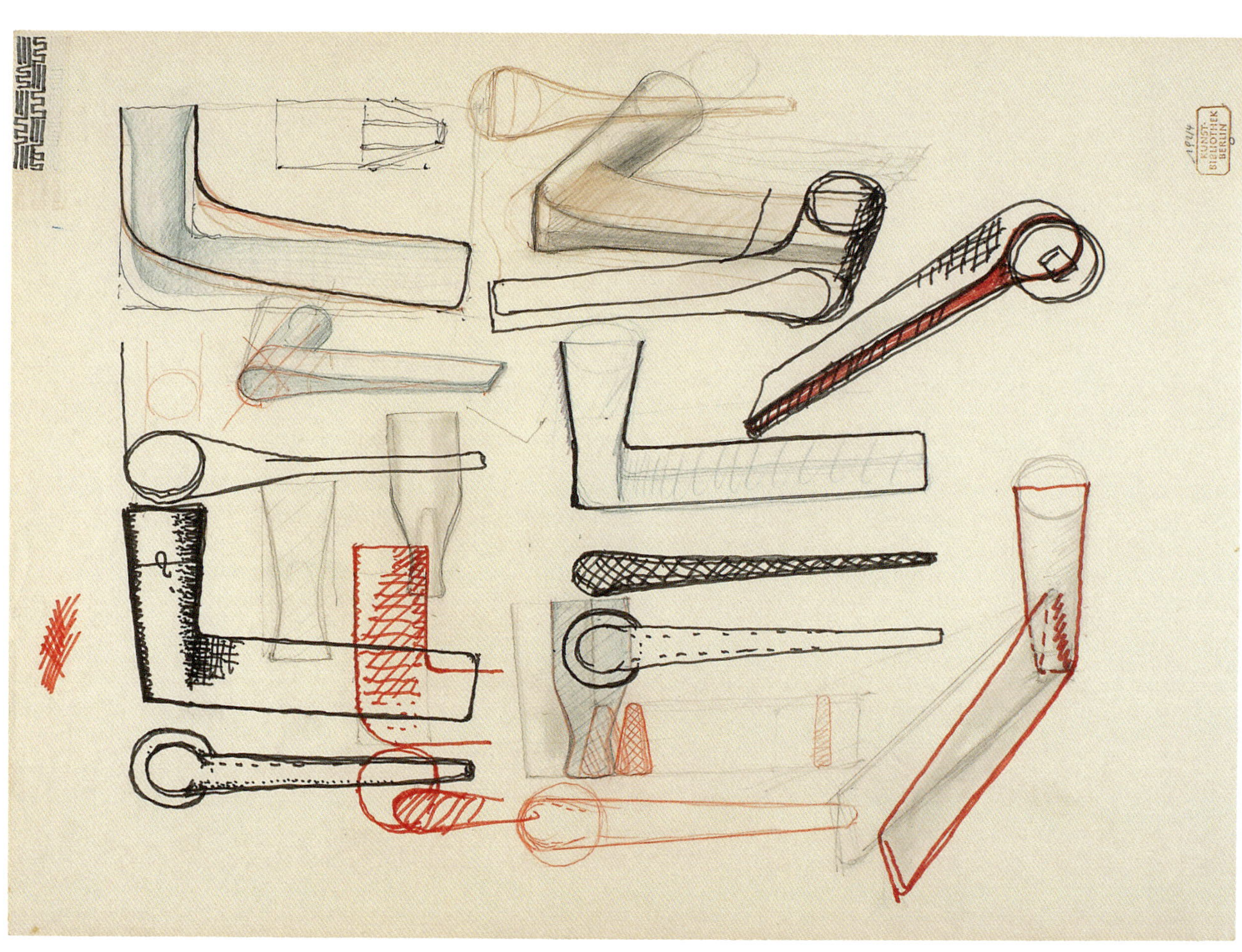

24 Door handles, design sketches for OGRO/Velbert, circa 1965

"No one else went as far"
Wilhelm Wagenfeld and his Position as a Designer in Post-War Germany – a tentative review

Rüdiger Joppien

After the Second World War, with Germany setting about summoning all the creative, formative energy it had to begin the process of the country's reconstruction, Wilhelm Wagenfeld, it seemed, was an ideal proposition. Amongst the industrial designers who had remained in Germany under the National Socialists, he was the most highly regarded; as a designer for firms in the glass and china industries, he not only had some great successes to his name, but was also untainted politically.

For the Schott & Gen./Jena glassworks, beginning in 1931, he had brought an innovative tea set and an altogether new range of heat-resistant glass cooking and baking dishes of elegant design onto the market and had got to grips profoundly with the manufacturing techniques for pressed glass. With the Vereinigte Lausitzer Glaswerke in Weisswasser, Silesia, he had shown that it is possible to take a run-of-the-mill enterprise and, with a newly developed "quality sector", to pitch it into the leading position in the glass industry. He had installed an "artistic laboratory" at the plant and engaged several contemporary designer figures to work as part of it for a while, amongst them artists who were by no means politically amenable to the times, such as Charles Crodel or Ludwig Gies. By the early 1930s, Wagenfeld had already taught at the Staatliche Kunstschule in Berlin and had had a considerable body of writing published. With his silversmith's training, he had come furnished with experience in the metalworking field; as a graduate of the Bauhaus at Weimar (1923–1925) and a member of staff at its successor establishment there, Otto Bartning's Bauhochschule Weimar (1926–1930), he had worked on metal utensils and appliances for the domestic table, but also on table and suspended ceiling lamps and doorknobs and handles. In short, he was probably unmatched by any designer of his generation in the diversity and scope of his activities, not to mention his expertise in matters of commerce and economics. The death in 1950 of Hermann Gretsch,[1] a pioneer of modern design in Germany, like Wagenfeld, but with less teaching, technical and industrial management experience, made Wagenfeld even more of a figurehead of modern design in contemporary perceptions.

Wagenfeld was not the one to capitalise on this position. It would have seemed a logical step to open his own office and to work for industry, certainly there was no lack of offers in that direction. But Wagenfeld was fundamental in everything he did; for him, the important thing was to realise certain premises. His interest lay in practical research, in which he hoped to engage at a German Institute for Industrial Standard Design. The idea was not new: he had propounded it back in Berlin, and now it was to be realised in Stuttgart. Supported by commerce and the state in equal part, it was to serve the development of designs in various product domains, and nurture up and coming generations of designers.[2] Wagenfeld was convinced that he could win over the Württembergische Metallwarenfabrik (WMF) in Geislingen an der Steige as the prime support from the private side and was set to act personally as the intermediary between the factory and the institute. In 1950, he "went public" with a brochure at Gerd Hatje publishers, presenting his comprehensive arguments for this kind of industrial facility.[3] His complaint, also articulated there, was levelled at the low standard of industrial, mass-produced articles. Given their wide dissemination, they were an educational factor. The wider the distribution and more general the nature of an object, the more thought should go into its design and the greater the care that should attend its manufacture. In mass production, Wagenfeld saw an important cultural brief, and it behoved industry to fulfil it.

The correspondence of the years 1948 to 1952 shows how intensely Wagenfeld was pursuing the idea of such an institute; but none would be founded for all that. What was, in fact, inaugurated in 1953, following two years of consultations, was the "Rat für Formgebung" or Council for Design. Its founding principles reflected much of Wagenfeld's educational thinking regarding an ethics of form and of the mass product.

Momentum only came gradually to industrial production at WMF in the post-war period. The priority of essential reconstruction and a public with relatively modest purchasing power still told in the early years. The company entered the 1950s tentatively to say the least, anxious not to put off either its inherited or its new clientele. Wagenfeld's proposals for tableware both flat and pressed glass as well as blown, with a series of new design solutions and experiments in the process. As artistic director, Wagenfeld had been responsible for his own range of glassware. At WMF an entirely different situation pertained. Wagenfeld could only ever (and ever again) make suggestions, propose, appeal; the decisions were invariably made elsewhere. The problem was not the technology, not that the items were not feasible; the problem lay in the half-heartedness with which the company stood behind its modern range or rather beheld it as a risk. Wagenfeld had been used to implementing a matter once it was

1 Egg-cups, butter dish, *Max + Moritz* salt and pepper pots, Cromargan stainless, glass, plastic; WMF/Geislingen, 1954–1957

hollow were only taken up hesitantly, albeit including such pioneering designs as the *Max + Moritz* salt and pepper pots, an egg-cup deep-drawn from a single blank, bread trays and the *Form* cutlery set (series 3600).[4] Only gradually did these and other items lead to the manufacture of a range of stainless steel tableware that would exceed the scope of anything that had gone before.[5]

In the field of glass, too, Wagenfeld rang the changes, aiming at something like a basic stock for the population with only few vase forms and goblet series simple in fashioning and in just two colours. Fundamental though all this may have been, Wagenfeld's role at WMF cannot be compared with the one he had enjoyed before the war at the VLG – the Vereinigte Lausitzer Glaswerke. There, he had been given decision-making powers and was able to try out and implement what he saw fit. In the case of cut or engraved decoration, for example, this meant its application to considered right; now he had to take into account a real effort of persuasion that was still to be engaged in. There was an overriding trend for firms to play safe by seeking reassurance from the market – "the Consumers". Works of quality were slow to assert their place. Thus in the early 1950s, Wagenfeld found himself increasingly fulfilling, in addition to his work as a designer, the rôle of an educator, propagating in his lectures and essays the need for a form for the times, one designed to be beautiful, useful and enduring.

His appeals were directed chiefly at industry, since by the use of the machine, and notably because of that use, he saw it charged with an important cultural job. Wagenfeld argued that new conditions of production were attended by a new responsibility for the producers. Rather than submitting to commerce and mass taste, industry should pursue a long-term concept and place its trust in quality. This was in tune with his own conviction that what was better

2 Double dishes for vegetables,
Cromargan stainless; WMF/Geislingen,
1954

3 Set of *Camillo* drinking glasses, WMF/Geislingen, 1951–1953

4 Set of *Margherita* drinking glasses, WMF/Geislingen, 1951–1953

and durable must ultimately win the upper hand against what was fashionable and period.

Designing something, therefore, was not merely "turning out wrappings"[6] which only defined the outward form, but to explore the essence of a product and its use in human hands. Every object must be defined out of its ability to be employed; it had to serve people and make them aware of their own action, experientially and cognitively.[7] Whether the object that did this was small and by-the-way or a precious item was immaterial. Wagenfeld was not deriding objects of sophisticated taste, but qualifying their significance. The cultural value of an item could not be judged by its social status or its qualities of pomp and circumstance, but only by its design and the degree to which it satisfied its function. That had evidently been Wagenfeld's guiding principle since at least before the war, when he was designing ephemeral mass items such as pressed-glass inkbottles and sophisticated art glass at one and the same time. This cheek-by-jowl or not-only-but-also approach continued to inform the designer's work in the post-war era. Almost concurrently, WMF produced the pair of almost inconspicuous salt and pepper pots and an expansive five-armed candelabrum; a little later, the Rosenthal porcelain factory at Selb was producing a table lamp with relief patterning (see pl. 20, p. 99), while at Bamberg, Lindner's current Wagenfeld design was a series of outside or bathroom lighting fixtures (see plates 17–19, p. 79 f.). For Wagenfeld the issue was always the scrupulousness with which the function of an object had been defined by its design. This was a fundamental precondition especially for economically priced articles for mass consumption;

5 Table candelabrum, brass, silver-plated, WMF/Geislingen, 1952/53

otherwise education toward a conscious relationship with objects could not begin.

Indispensable factors of this care were in his eyes an economy of labour, of the materials and the simplest, most summary form of production conceivable. The last always implied intelligent solutions and these would be the result of long, arduous effort. Objects that commanded respect had always been Wagenfeld's aim in his work. Only utility objects of quality would encourage the production staff's creativity and secure Germany's status as an industrial base in the long term.

Wagenfeld was convinced that a modern approach to industrial production demanded the collaboration of the sales people, the engineers and the artistic consultant. The latter should come with a broad-based affinity for art and culture and an all-round education. The artist as a whimsical genius was not sought at all; Wagenfeld took a well-designed product always to be "the collective achievement of the works" – as a synthesis of all who had a part in the process, not as the product of subjective will.[8]

The prime object of Wagenfeld's considerations was utensils for day-to-day use and making that experience one of beauty – with crockery articles and vessels flat and hollow for supping and dining. The vessel seems to have held the greatest fascination for him, be it as a vase, pitcher, tea or coffee pot or bowl. In this genus he saw the strongest representative of his cultural ideal. There were exemplary precedents of perfection in the utensils of past centuries and civilisations, in which certain types of vessel would appear in variation again and again. Wagenfeld himself owned a collection of old glasses from classical antiquity to the modern period, and it confirmed him in the belief that there were some forms that could not be improved upon. Past experience as a young man are likely to have been prime factors on the way. In 1928, Gustav Friedrich Hartlaub had asked, by way of an exhibition at the Kunsthalle in Mannheim, about "the state of the arts and crafts in the age of the machine" and whether there was such a thing as "Eternal Craft".[9] Two years later (1930), Wolfgang von Wersin dedicated an exhibition to "Eternal Form" at the Neue Sammlung in Munich.[10] It is no coincidence that as debate on the issue of design intensified tangibly to an urgent pitch, both the arts and crafts and anthropological research indicated the existence of simple forms amounting to archetypes, as evinced in vessels of the Stone Age, from ancient Egypt or ancient China. For some, this

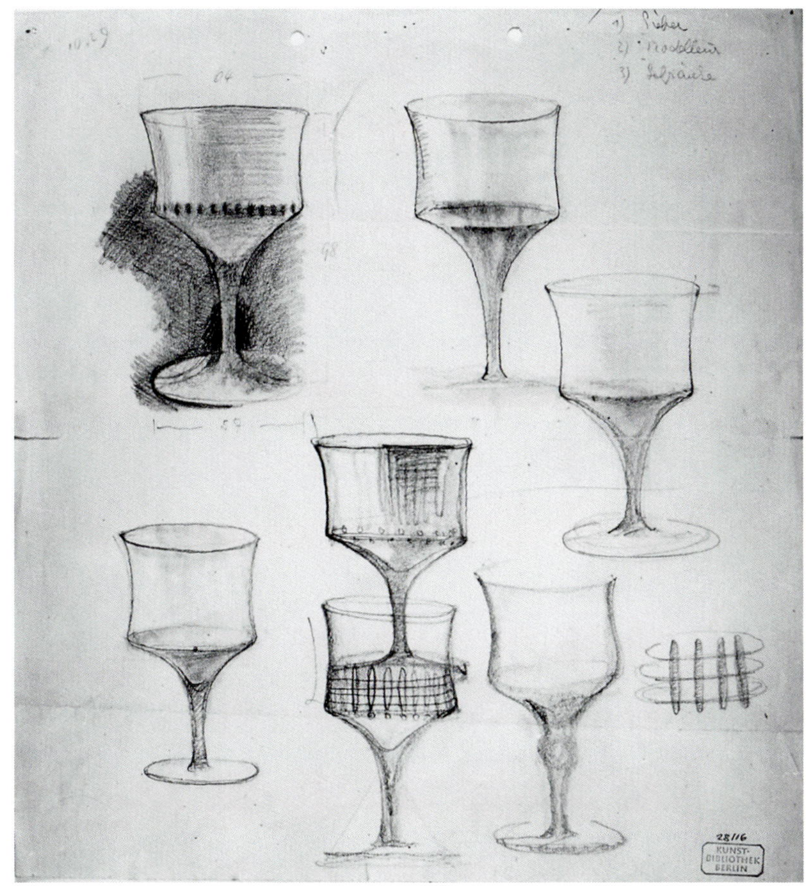

6 Drinking glasses; design sketch, circa 1954

7 Pottery vessel, painted; Persia, 3200 BC, Collection Wilhelm Wagenfeld

8 Beaker-shaped glass, painted with gold and enamel, example of the "Aleppo Group", Syria, mid-13th century

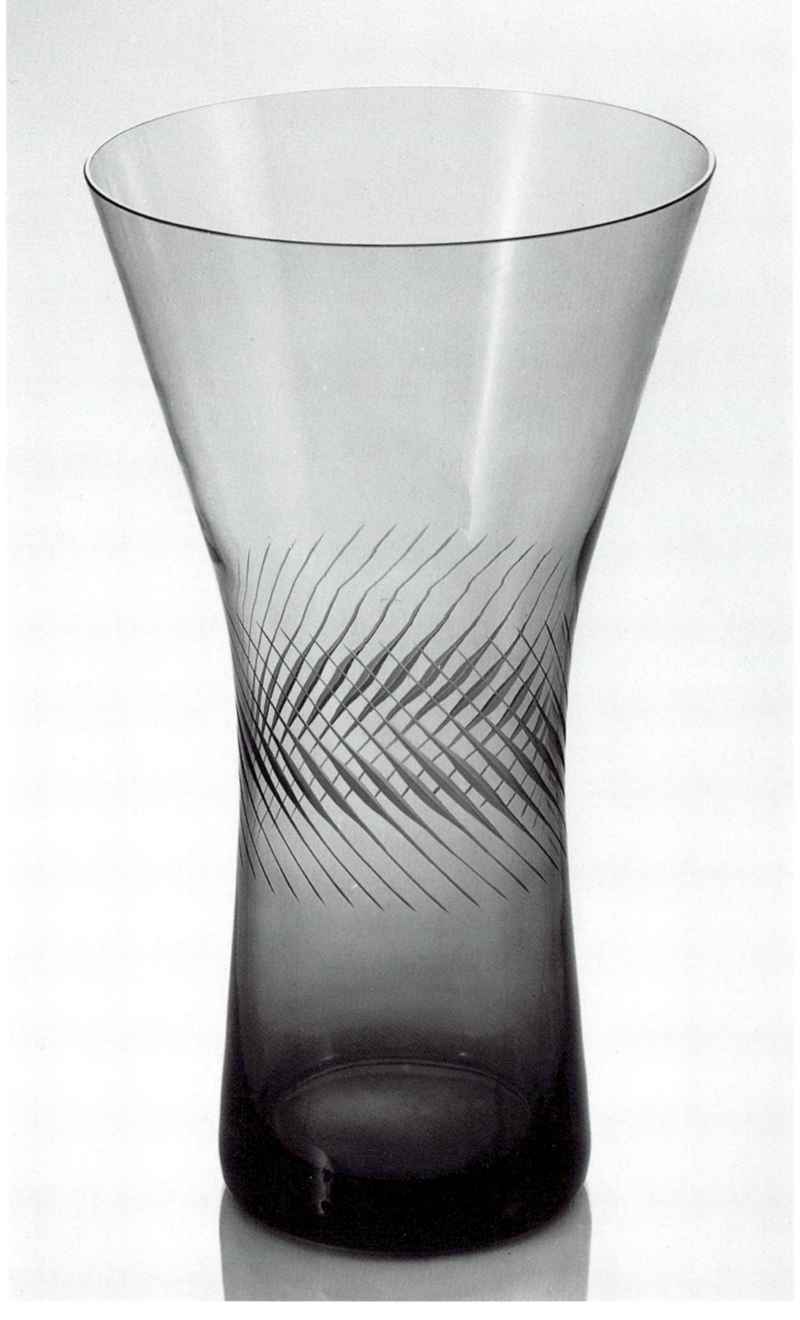

9 Vase, WMF/Geislingen, 1950 (cut pattern 1954)

11 Decanter; glass with applied threads, Venice, 16th century

10 Collared vases, WMF/Geislingen, 1958

12 Vases, WMF/Geislingen, 1950

confirmed the pertinence of "eternal" craft and therein proof for the exemplariness of design conceived of as skilled creative workmanship; for Wagenfeld, the phenomenon posed a different question. How could form that had always been pertinent and could not be improved upon, be realised by 20th-century production methods? Wagenfeld is certain to have been familiar with Walter Dexel's book, *Unbekanntes Handwerksgut* (1935), since Dexel was, for a time, a contributor to the VLG's range of glass.[11] In addition, Wagenfeld's awareness of designs, particularly in glass, from the Near-Eastern civilisations and 16th-century Venetian glass, is conspicuous. Many of his vases and drinking glasses that he designed in the 1930s and early 1950s are essentially based on "ancient" glass types, with a preference for elegant and often elongated bodies; by contrast, the baluster type, with its connotations of the Baroque and a certain folksiness, so frequently met in porcelain pieces of the 1930s, was not to his taste.

In any case, it would have been inappropriate to stop at historical precedents. The circumstances of the times and the conditions of production were different now. The new age took recourse to the machine. It alone was capable of guaranteeing distribution of well-designed utility objects and so generate a much greater educational effectiveness than manual craft with its one-off artefacts ever could.

For the modern industrial product, Wagenfeld called for a standard form, a definitive type. "Industrial forms must be like workmanlike household utensils, that simple and plain for all to see," he had demanded in 1941, elucidating how this applied to machinery: "Machines are tools, like a hammer and tongs. Their place is as much in the workshop as in the factory. Where the machine has destroyed, there man has failed. The industrial product is like what has been hand-made in terms of its own worth." That Wagenfeld was not intoning the Nazis' romantic notions of (art-and-) craft-work with such comments, but, on the contrary, affirming Bauhaus thinking, seems to have gone virtually unnoticed. Market success was on his side; his products told of a strong, self-confident Germany.

It speaks for Wagenfeld's enduring form of modernity that he had no need to reformulate his thinking in democratic post-war Germany. What he demanded as the quality of good design was as up-to-date as the demand that the machine should be employed as a means of producing the best possible mass commodities. These demands could only be met if the artist stepped back and exercised the self-discipline of placing his effort and talent wholly in the service of the matter in hand. "We want to create nothing 'extraordinary' or 'original'," Wagenfeld had stated as long ago as 1937, in his essay of "glass shop-talk" *("Glasfachsimpeleien")*.[13] His designs for WMF well exemplify his earlier dictum. In form they speak the same language as the glasses produced in the 1930s and 1940s for the Vereinigte Lausitzer Glaswerke. The Bauhaus-inspired geometricality that had been the mark of Wagenfeld's metal structures in the 1920s had now ceded to an

13 Otto Lindig, Vase, ceramic with black glaze, Dornburg on Saale, mid-1930s

emphasis of the organic, a characteristic inherent to glass and clay at the outset and patently so in the crafts of glassblowing and pottery on the wheel. Thus the product now was less constructed than a natural, "matter-of-course" form uninfluenced by stylistic posing. It was precisely in this unassuming naturalness and anonymity of a form, thanks to which it was possible to place his vessels next to the best of any period, that Wagenfeld saw the artistic achievement. He preferred the plain and inconspicuous to the conspicuous, the standardised to the individual and the universally valid to the particular. That Wagenfeld should have acknowledged what was normative in the applied crafts reveals his esteem for the old companions at the Bauhaus, such as Marguerite Friedländer and Otto Lindig. They, too, strove for the ideal form.

That was still Wagenfeld's determining approach when, in the early 1950s, he encountered utterly new forms of craft, in particular in hands of the Scandinavians,

14 Gunnel Nyman, *Kapan* Vase; cut glass, Riihimäki glass workshops, Finland, 1947

15 Tapio Wirkkala, *Kantarelli* Vase, glass with ground decoration, Iittala, Finland, 1946

16 Coffeepot and teapot; hotel silver, WMF/Geislingen, 1956–1959

17 Lino Sabattini, *Como* Coffeepot and teapot, silver; Christofle/Paris, France, 1956

Italians and Americans. At the Triennales in Milan, he saw the Finns' highly sculptural, organic, partly cut glass – that of a Tapio Wirkkala or a Gunnel Nyman (whose premature death had already occurred in 1948).[14] Wagenfeld might have been full of admiration for their material technique; but their works were hardly suited to his ideal standard form. In his opinion, the individual piece was being advanced unduly, the individual effect, the unaccustomed contour, the imagination and colour being allowed to displace timeless form. Wagenfeld, too, pursued the organic principle, but he avoided overemphasising the oval or the ellipse

18 Floor Vase, thick coloured glass, WMF/Geislingen, 1950/51

that was characteristic of modernism or "stile nuovo". His stainless steel tableware for WMF is much more reticent in its sculptural, flowing play of forms than could be said of the vessels of a Lino Sabattini, for example. The merry glow of colours in American pottery or Finnish glass equally failed to tempt Wagenfeld to imitate them. His utensils and vessels remained objective and unobtrusively neutral. For the WMF glasses, the only colour he envisaged apart from the clear crystal itself was tourmaline. All additional hot forming and all smelting experiments such as Vicke Lindstrand or Sven Palmquist engaged in at Orrefors, were assiduously avoided. Wagenfeld's vases were wittingly given no sophisticated surface treatment, no concession being made even for the white milky opal glass that the Scandinavians loved to use. It is perhaps not by chance that when WMF appointed Wagenfeld as their artistic adviser, they soon abandoned their art glass sector, no matter that it had existed since the 1920s and that such well-known lines in glass as the *Myra* and *Ikora* had sprung from it. The firm's artistic manager Karl Wiedmann left in 1951 to take up a post as works manager at the Vereinigte Farbglaswerke, Zwiesel. The ceramics workshop, headed by Gerda Conitz and also placed under Wiedmann's supervision, had already been closed down in 1949.[15]

What Wagenfeld had high regard for was Scandinavian design. Like Wagenfeld, the Finn, Kaj Franck, was a typical industrial designer with a marked preference for tableware. His *Kilta* coffee and dinner service, designed in 1948, was among the great designs of its time on an international plane.[16] It differed from German sets, however, in being available in several colours which could be combined freely. A wide variety of colour effects could be attained, all intended to put the user in cheerful mood.

Likewise, Per Lütken, working for the glass workshop at Holmegaard and Denmark's pre-eminent designer in glass in the post-war years, can be compared with Wagenfeld. His *Beaked Vase* with its oviform body, extended neck and asymmetrically drawn mouth is an icon of designing known to this day. The upward splayed lips, which give a flower stalk a slightly tilted hold, were a small extra touch and still functional in conception.[17]

A comparable solution was the *Town and Country* china set of 1946, by Eva Zeisel, who had emigrated to the United States in the late 1930s. Wagenfeld saw her works at an exhibition in Stuttgart in 1951 with the title "Industrie und Handwerk schaffen neues Hausgerät in USA" ("Industry and Handicraft create new Household Utensils in the USA"); but he found her work to be rather a series of "unresolved transitions" between craft and industrial production.[18]

It appears that Wagenfeld was unsettled by asymmetrical designs. He may have discerned a high-handedness in them; asymmetry in his own work is as good as absent. The feature he sought was rather a lightness and gracefulness of the kind he admired in the Viennese exponents and in Josef Hoffmann in particular. But qualities of this kind could grow only out of a sure feeling for one's own time and a sponta-

20 Kaj Franck, *Kilta* table service, stoneware; Arabia Oy/Helsinki, Finland, 1948

19 Per Lütken, Beaked Vase, Model 14405, blown and moulded; Holmegaards Glasvaerker, Denmark, 1952

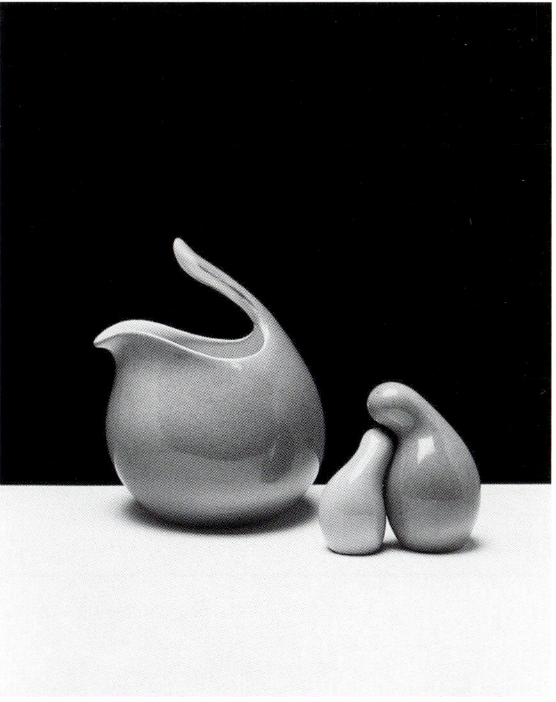

21 Eva Zeisel, *Town and Country* colour-glazed earthenware set; Red Wing Potteries/Minnesota, USA, 1946

neous joy in designing and forming. German design in the early 1950s might have been amenable to the indulgence of a decorative whim here and there and a more fanciful approach in general if living conditions had been different. Unlike her neighbours to the west and in Northern Europe, or in the United States,[19] Germany was smitten with a massive housing shortage, so that households first had to recover in very confined spaces. Utility and usability were paramount and the quality of the necessary items had to be so reliably convincing that they could also tap into sales markets elsewhere.

Industrial Models", the Wagenfeld Workshop, which he founded in 1954.[22] The journal of his one-time collaborator, Heinz G. Pfaender, for the period from September 1954 to March 1957, renders a vivid impression of the sometimes troublesome and laborious work on the models and the continual problems with the production patterns.[23] They comprised a portable radio-record player for Braun/Frankfurt, a stove for Voss/Sarstedt, the *abc* typewriter and a sowing-machine case for Koch's Adler/Bielefeld. It was evidently difficult for the workshop to unite the engineering-style criteria for these objects with a design that

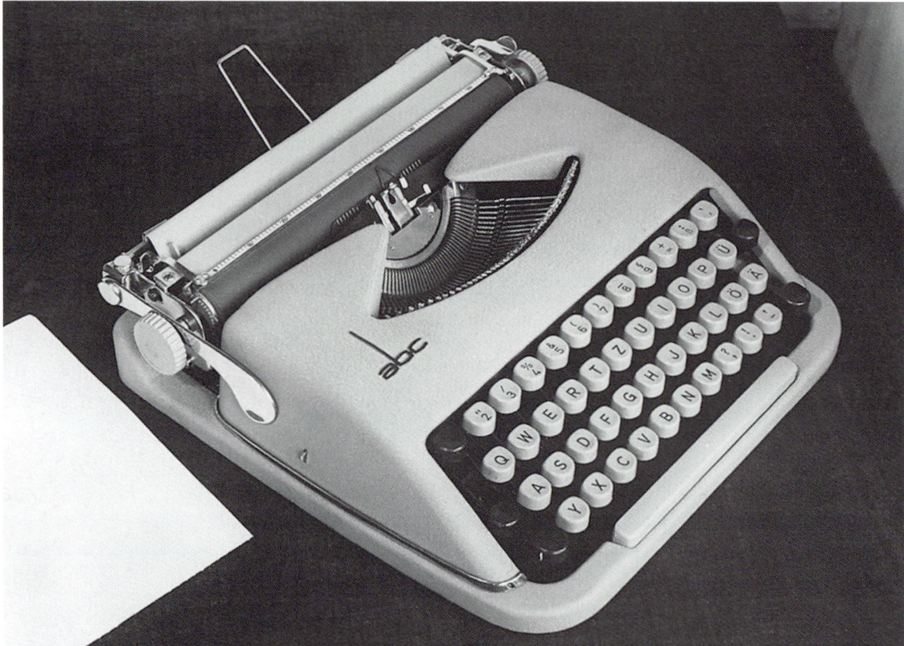

22 *abc* portable typewriter, Koch's Adler/Bielefeld, 1955

Wagenfeld was well aware that technical industrial forms would present designers in future with new design challenges. The Stuttgart exhibition of 1951 on American household utensils already provided a foretaste.

In kitchen equipment, Wagenfeld ascertained that the United States were clearly ahead, in his opinion not least because there, "men handle these things."[20] But he was hesitant to attribute cultural value to such objects too quickly. Thus he wrote in the journal, *Werk* in December 1953, "We will only ever *use* a refrigerator, no matter how useful it is; but a spoon we can use and love, and so too a glass, a chair or a plate. That is probably why utensils and furniture have testified since time immemorial to the spirituality of an epoch – its science and learning, its art and its poetry."[21]

Wagenfeld was sure, notwithstanding, that he had a duty to take up the challenge of new technical apparatus, and it was his declared intention to develop these in the "Experimental and Design Workshop for

Wagenfeld would find satisfactory. While the items did go into production, they failed to enter his œuvre in any significantly idea-generating fashion.[24]

The designer's relation to electric lighting appliances was a deal less fraught. His first experience of the field lay back in the 1920s. Now, from 1952 on, he designed for the workshops of Peill & Putzler, Düren, a series of spherical and teardrop-shaped hanging lamps (see plates 9–14, p. 75 f.), and from 1954, for Lindner, a wide-ranging collection of wall, mirror and outdoor lamps. The hanging lamps of Peill & Putzler have contemporaneous, similar parallels in Scandinavia; but in his ingeniously constructed, material-saving lighting units for Lindner, Wagenfeld created not only beautiful, organic forms, but totally new solutions, innovations in form that would decisively influence lamp design through the 1950s and 1960s (see pl. 20, p. 82)

In plastics, Wagenfeld saw a particularly uncommon challenge. Objects made of this material had already roused his interest at that American utensil exhibition of 1951; the use of plastic was another advance in the USA by which he was highly struck. Contemplating dining set elements made for U. S. airlines, he wrote, "the German plastic products we are familiar with do not stand comparison with these by a long shot."[25] Something had to be done.

Plastics had been in use in Germany in the domestic sphere since the 1930s, and one might ask when the material would be developed and accepted to a stage at which it would supplant traditional materials such as glass and ceramics. Wagenfeld first ventured into plastic articles late in 1954, when he developed almost simultaneously, a portable radio with a built-in record player, the Braun *Combi,* and household objects for the firm of Johannes Buchsteiner at Gingen an der Fils. The *Combi* radio-record player was too hurried a production. Wagenfeld was unhappy with the result, a situation exacerbated when the dyes in the plastics used proved impermanent.[26] Although Wagenfeld went on to design a number of other appliances for Braun, including a record turntable, no collaboration of consequence ensued. The brothers Erwin and Artur Braun, "encouraged and stimulated by Wilhelm Wagenfeld",[27] entered into negotiations with Hans Gugelot of the Hochschule für Gestaltung at Ulm before the year was out and opted for a different, more rectangular and otherwise geometric look to their appliances.

Collaboration with the plastics-processing firm of Buchsteiner proved more fruitful. Out of this partnership came no less than twenty-five products. There was a flight meals set for Deutsche Lufthansa; there were utensils for the table and kitchen, including a salad colander, a watering-can, a set of salad servers and even a child's bathtub. Wagenfeld's expertise with ductile materials such as glass and clay presumably gave him an instant affinity to materials such as melamine resin, acrylic glass, all the objects named being characterised by flowing sculptural expressiveness and dynamic contours. Wagenfeld's activity as a designer for Buchsteiner appears worthy of attention all the more since nobody before him in German design had developed such a wide range of products for plastic.

Compared to that of his contemporaries, Wagenfeld's achievement as a designer is conspicuous not only for the versatility, but also the diversity of his designs. He mapped out some clear major routes for his work in that he concluded exclusive contracts with firms such as WMF, Peill & Putzler, Lindner, Buchsteiner or metal mountings manufacturers OGRO (Otto Grosssteinbeck) of Velbert, but he also sought to supply other producers, for example Voss (domestic heating stoves) or Dietsche of Todtnau (brushes). This approach was in line with Wagenfeld's lifelong receptiveness toward new tasks and his conviction that specialisation was to be avoided. His gift consisted in part of being able to engage with new techniques and manufacturing processes again and again, even if every object required numerous trial series. The burdens these entailed not infrequently taxed the Wagenfeld Workshop to the brink.

23 Lisa Johansson-Pape, hanging lamp, glass, mould-blown, sand-blasted and etched, Stockmann-Orno/Kerava, Finland, 1954

Unlike Wagenfeld, most designers of his time specialised in one material or line of product. Many, hailing from an art and craft or a sculpture background, did not develop as designers for industry until they collaborated with such an enterprise. That was the career of the designer pioneers of the 1920s and 1930s – Wagenfeld's fellows at the Bauhaus, Marguerite Friedländer, Gerhard Marcks, Marianne Brandt, Christian Dell et al. – but also of other artist staff in

24 *Combi* portable radio-record player, plastic, Braun/Frankfurt, 1955

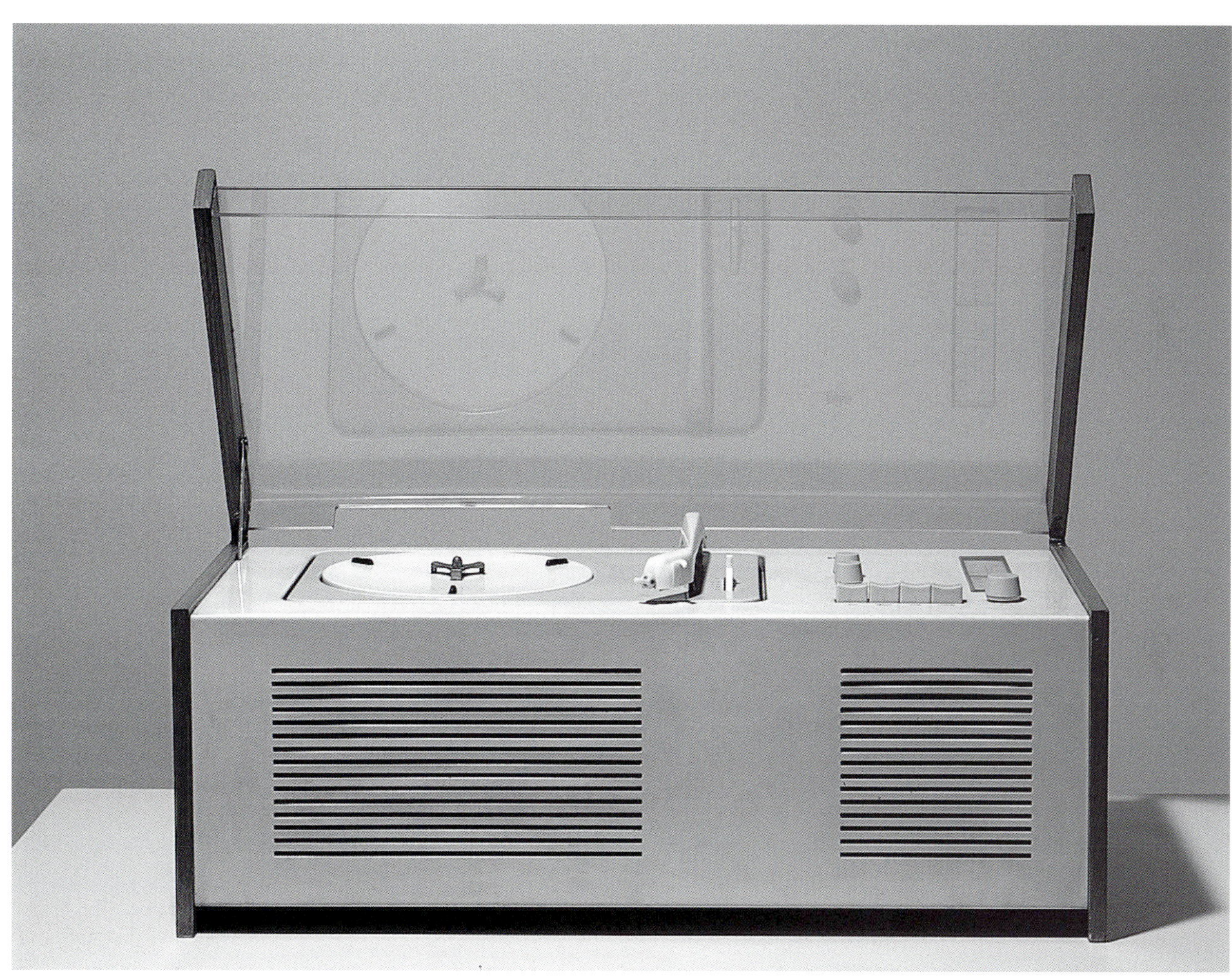

25 Hans Gugelot and Dieter Rams,
Phonosuper "SK 4" radio-record player;
wood, metal sheet, acrylic glass,
Braun/Frankfurt, 1956

26 Lufthansa cabin service; plastic (melamine), Buchsteiner/Gingen, 1955

27 Child's bathtub, plastic, Buchsteiner/Gingen, 1955

28 Door handle, light metal, OGRO/ Velbert, 1966

30 *Staffelstein* set of drinking glasses, pressed and cut foot, Peill & Putzler/ Düren, 1953

29 *Atlanta* 4200 cutlery, silver, WMF/Geislingen, 1955

the china and glass industry such as Trude Petri, Hubert Griemert, Siegmund Schütz or Bruno Mauder. Petri's clear, elegant designs made a lasting impression on Wagenfeld; her *Urbino* service became as much a model for porcelain design in the 1930s as Wagenfeld's range did for Jena glass.

Whereas Petri soon dedicated herself totally to industrial design, Jan Bontjes van Beek, another colleague-in-arms high in Wagenfeld's esteem, was keen to preserve his identity as a ceramist. For the pottery works of Dr. Ungewiss at Dehme, he designed a range of industrial ceramic items, but otherwise made one-off vessels only.

took to the pencil himself. When, just a year later, two of his first series of beakers, *Carina* and *Largo* (1952/53) won awards at the Tenth Milan Triennale, Braun-Feldweg made design an essential part of his work.[28]

Designer Günter Kupetz had completed a sculptor's training when he took charge of a design studio at WMF in 1955, very soon joining forces with his wife Sigrid, Karl Dittert and WMF's in-house designers such as Kurt Radtke and, alongside Wagenfeld, contributing to the company's range of table utensils. Then again, Erich Slany had studied mechanical engineering and specialised, narrowly enough at first, in household

31 Wilhelm Braun-Feldweg, white wine beaker *(Carina* series), Graf Schaffgottsch'sche Josephinenhütte, Schwäbisch Gmünd, 1952/53

32 Trude Petri, *Urbino* tableware service, porcelain, Staatliche Porzellan-Manufaktur (KPM)/Berlin, 1931

Former Bauhaus student Wolfgang Tümpel was working on lamp designs quite early in his career, and in the 1950s also taught industrial design at the Hochschule für Bildende Künste at Hamburg, but remained a silversmith by conviction. By contrast the former gold- and silversmiths Karl Dittert and Peter Raacke steered single-mindedly toward the field of design. Their path was by way of a teaching post at a "Fachhochschule" or technical and applied arts college, where they were given design commissions by industry. Thus, Dittert designed appliances for the hardware industry in Baden-Württemberg (Bruckmann in Heilbronn, WMF etc.), before venturing into other product groups (objects of plastic, furniture) in the early 1970s. A similar course was taken by the trained steel engraver, Wilhelm Braun-Feldweg, who taught product design and production at the Höhere Fachschule für das Edelmetallgewerbe (Higher Technical College for the Precious Metals Trades) in Schwäbisch-Gmünd in the early 1950s and in the process became acquainted with the local glass industry. The consequence of that encounter was that he

appliances before moving on to design capital goods, electrical appliances, tools and machines.

The career of Heinrich Löffelhardt, almost the same age as Wagenfeld, for many years his assistant and sometime friend, is closest to Wagenfeld's from the point of view of his training. By the mid-1930s, he was already a member of Wagenfeld's "artistic laboratory" at Weisswasser. His own career as a designer began in 1953, when he parted ways with Wagenfeld and gave up his post as a member of staff at the Baden-Württemberg Office for Promotion of Trade and Industrie at Stuttgart. From 1954 on, he produced, in rapid succession, designs for baking dishes and sets of goblets for the Schott glassworks at Mainz and their subsidiary, the Vereinigte Farbglaswerke, Zwiesel. Like Wagenfeld, Löffelhardt committed himself to collaboration with only a few companies, all of them from the glass or china sector. Apart from those mentioned, the Gral-Glashütte, Göppingen and the Arzberg and Schönwald porcelain factories were among these. In this field Löffelhardt became a competitor of Wagenfeld's to be reckoned

33 Jan Bontjes van Beek, Vases, stoneware, white industrial glaze, Dr. Ungewiss/Dehme, 1950/53

with, not least because his style of design conspicuously resembled the master's.[29]

To summarise, the career of the freelance designer in early 1950s Germany was fundamentally not pre-set. Most designers had not passed through formal professional training, and found their way to their trade as "cross-over entrants". For them, Wagenfeld was already the authority to quibble with even though he had been the one to awaken any real awareness of the cultural importance of design in the first place. Many young designers, like Günter Kupetz, worked in Wagenfeld's lee, created comparable designs and sought to break the monopoly of his design or the mental set behind it. In 1959 an Association of Industrial Designers, the Verband Deutscher Industrie-Designer (VDID) was founded, and it was, with the exception of Herbert Hirche, exclusively up-and-coming designers like Hans Th. Baumann, Karl Dittert, Günter Kupetz, Peter Raacke, Erich Slany and Arno Votteler who joined it. They shared a striving to carve out a new profile for the designer's profession on a broad base.[30] Accordingly the new body represented both furniture designers and technical design – an indication of the growing significance of new genres of product that were gradually undermining the predominance of household utensils, glass and tableware as design fields.

An important impulse in the growth of this trend emanated from the Hochschule für Gestaltung, the school of design at Ulm. This had been founded in 1953. Its first principal, Max Bill, had also been at the Bauhaus, and he and Wagenfeld held each other in high esteem; but to all appearances they never exchanged thoughts in depth. In part, the school at Ulm was a realisation of Wagenfeld's ideal of an industrial institute that would provide qualified training for young designers; on the other hand, he must also have looked with some misgiving upon its methodology and increasing systematising of design along scientific lines. Like Wagenfeld, Bill accorded artistic considerations a substantial voice in questions of design; but his successors shifted the emphasis to system design. In the young lecturer Hans Gugelot once a collaborator of Bill's, a designer entered Wagenfeld's field of vision whom he valued and who he believed would have a pre-eminent part to play in the development of technical design. Gugelot worked conscientiously; his designs were worked-out and thought-out to the smallest detail, one providing the point of departure for the next. Even though Gugelot showed little interest in decorative goods, in the wherewithal for eating and dining, Wagenfeld was convinced that he had the ability to take design to a new, progressive plane. Gugelot's early success with his designs for radio and phono equipment for Braun AG affirmed Wagenfeld in his view that it must be possible to create products of high quality and, above all, durability equally well in the technical apparatus field. Though the designers at Ulm no longer derived their designs primarily from the craft and technical conditions of industrial production, and though the debate concerning the feasibility of implementing design in commercial enterprises was not a major issue for them, they did concur with Wagenfeld in other matters. Like him, the Ulm designers were opposed to modish design, affectations of style and what he had called "turning out wrappings". In their understanding of what design was, as in his, top priority was given to finding the essence of an object, of its use, as both operation and the service it could provide. The difference lay in the object of these aims – innovative technical apparatus and appliances offering new functional solutions, some as yet unrecognised, to challenges of their own.[31]

In time the school at Ulm exercised an unstoppable fascination at home and abroad, especially the latter; against which Wagenfeld's merits as a designer seemed less spectacular. He had not established an immediately striking style; his achievement having been precisely a look that would be assimilated as natural, a "matter of course". If one were confronted with Wagenfeld's works today, there would be the urge to bring out, to enhance some inherent feature, so "invisible" does his intervention seem, so neutral a mien did his designs adopt. His motto, it must be remembered, was to convince by use, but not to be conspicuous. The countless products under WMF's brand, for whom Wagenfeld worked for more than twenty years, and some items of which are manufactured to this day, are visual documents and a good measure of his unspectacular but all the more enduring influence.

Wagenfeld's achievement as a designer was intimately connected with his commitment to teaching – to his role as a national educator in the widest sense. He campaigned on a wide front for openness toward design. That he must have been a persuasive speaker is attested in the many clients such as Erich Schott or the Braun brothers who came to him on the basis of his lecturing activities. Also, a debate developed around 1950 concerning what contemporary design was achieving and should

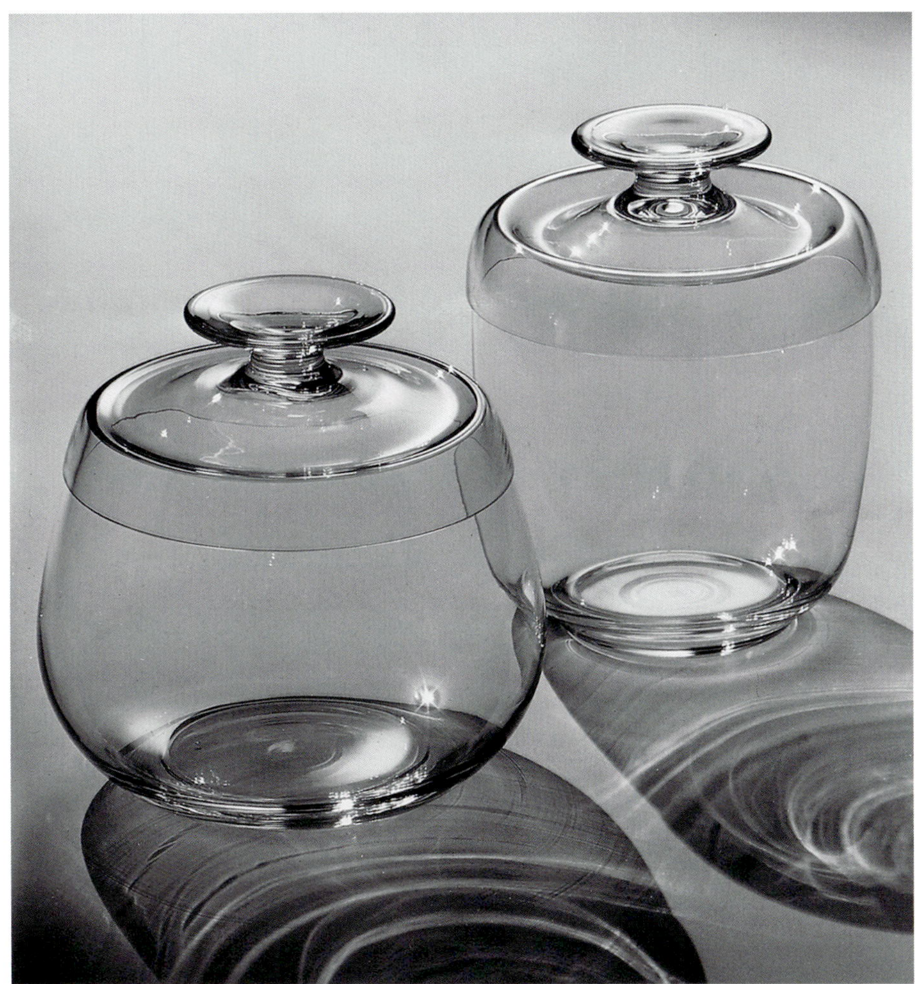

34 Biscuit jars, glass, WMF/Geislingen, 1950

achieve; in this, Wagenfeld's part was decisive. This considered, it remains a particular desideratum that his many lectures and essays, which placed great demands on his time, be gathered as an edition of the collected works.

Wagenfeld received recognition throughout his career. As early as 1939, the Neue Sammlung in Munich organised a special exhibition on his œuvre .[32] Exhibitions in the early 1940s were already highlighting his designs for industrial goods. The Kunsthalle at Mannheim, under curator Walter Passarge, had presented Wagenfeld's activities

For Wagenfeld, this active artistic involvement in industry grew into an internalised conviction that governed everything he did. Occasionally he would tell personally of the many hours, days and weeks he spent with the technicians, modellers and fellow-workers of all kinds in the respective firms. For him there was only joint teamwork and none of the self-seeking artist's solo performance geared to maximum publicity. Wagenfeld's seems an almost anachronistic stance from today's perspective; but there are very tangible signs that his example is being recalled increasingly and what he achieved, admired.

35 *Form* 3600 cutlery set, Cromargan stainless, WMF/Geislingen, production 1952–1969, production resumed 1992

and those of some of his fellows in a show appositely entitled, "Künstler in der Industrie. Vorbildliche Gestaltung industrieller Erzeugnisse" ("Artists in Industry. Exemplary Designs for Industrial Products") in 1941.[33] Passarge could not have been more in tune with Wagenfeld when he opined that the "design of mass-produced goods" had "become a cultural problem of the first order", to which it behoved all, designers, industry and the staff of both to respond.[34]

Sixteen years later, when the Mannheim Kunsthalle mounted one of the first post-war retrospectives of Wagenfeld's work, Passarge wrote an introductory essay and once more underlined "the artist in industry" (1957).[35] Subsequent exhibitions at Munich (1961), Stuttgart (1965) and Cologne (1973) elicited almost identical turns of phrase. The Cologne exhibition of 1973 was entitled "50 years' collaboration in factories" ("50 jahre mitarbeit in fabriken").[36]

It was the future founder of the Bauhaus, Walter Gropius, who, with his great successes as an architect still before him, contributed a remarkable item to the *Jahrbuch des Deutschen Werkbunds* in 1913. Under the heading "The Development of Modern Industrial Architecture" ("Die Entwicklung moderner Industriebaukunst"), his central proposition culminated in the assertion that "[...] facing all industry today [is] the challenge of taking on artistic questions in earnest."[37] Furthermore, "[...] the artist's collaboration is no luxury, no well-meaning bonus, but must become an indispensable constituent in the overall œuvre of modern industry."[38] The architect's principles, including his championing of collaboration between the artist, the business staff and the technician, and his exhortations that the artist should avail himself of the virtues of the machine and comprehend an object's function from within, rather than supplying outward decoration, etc., all read like early versions of the stance Wagenfeld would then represent for a lifetime. There is no doubt that in his essay, Gropius was processing experiences that he had internalised during his time at Peter Behrens's architect's office in Berlin. Today, in view of his work as artistic adviser to the AEG company from 1907 to 1914, Behrens is regarded as the first and most prominent "collaborator in factories".[39] It is only consistent that Gropius should later have felt that Wagenfeld understood him in his aims at the Bauhaus particularly well. In the 1960s, the former wrote to the latter that nobody but he, Wagenfeld, had made the idea of the Bauhaus such a "convincing reality". "No one else went as far."[40] It was a fact that at the Bauhaus Wagenfeld had learnt a crucial lesson that was to govern his whole career. For him, what counted was not artistic vanity, but responsibility toward his fellow human beings.

Notes

This essay is dedicated to the memory of my mother, Käthe Pohl (1919–1999), who taught me during my childhood in the 1950s to take an interest in the things of modern living.
Completion of my contribution was preceded by a number of substantial conversations with Beate Manske of the Wilhelm Wagenfeld Stiftung, Bremen. Her enthusiasm for Wilhelm Wagenfeld proved infectious again and again. Without her wealth of information and suggestions and her willingness to place archive material (letters and literature) at my disposal, this essay could not have been written.

1 Gretsch is regarded as one of the less progressive designers owing to his affinity to the Third Reich. To my knowledge his œuvre has yet to be examined comprehensively. It is said that Wagenfeld held him in no great esteem; but Wagenfeld's companion-in-arms for many years, Heinrich Löffelhardt, acknowledges Gretsch in the *Schriften zur Formgebung* series (vol. 2, 1952) published by the Baden-Württemberg Office for Promotion of Trade and Industry in Stuttgart in 1953. In the course of the 1930s, Gretsch had amassed wide experience in the industrial design field. He worked in a number of sectors of industrial manufacture, among them the glass, stoneware and porcelain industries, for producers of metal utensils and cutlery, for the compression moulding and iron industries and the furniture trade. Gretsch, who had already designed stoves by the mid-1930s, turned after the War to such profane tools as a bread slicer or a vegetable and meat chopping machine. As a trained architect, he was of a practical turn of mind; he evidently lacked Wagenfeld's intellect and vision of underlying principles. On the other hand, they shared many a conviction, such as that of the artist as educator; and Gretsch held that "industrial designers must double as artists, technicians and businessmen, otherwise they will not avoid doing things by halves."

2 A letter Wagenfeld sent from Berlin to Dr. Rudolf Schnellbach, the director of the Landesgewerbemuseum (Museum of Trade and Industry) at Stuttgart (7 March 1949), gives us a good idea of how he envisaged such an institute. The letter discusses Wagenfeld's future role as an official at the Baden-Württemberg Office for Promotion of Trade and Industry and the plan of an "artistic laboratory".

3 *Deutsches Institut für industrielle Standardform*, proposed and elucidated by Wilhelm Wagenfeld, Stuttgart 1950.

4 On Wagenfeld's work for WMF see Beate Manske, "'Fünfzehn Jahre waren nicht vergeblich'. Wilhelm Wagenfelds Mitarbeit in der WMF", in: *Zeitgemäss und zeitbeständig. Industrieformen von Wilhelm Wagenfeld,* ed. Carlo Burschel & Beate Manske, Bremen 1997, pp. 36–47; also the preceding chapt., "Wilhelm Wagenfeld. Notizen, eine Chronologie nicht realisierter Entwürfe", pp. 30–35.

5 On Wagenfeld's significance in the introduction of stainless steel for tableware, see also Klaus Lehmann, "Wie der Edelstahl in die Küche kam", in: *Oikos. Von der Feuerstelle zur Mikrowelle. Hausrat und Wohnen im Wandel,* Design Center Stuttgart and Museum für Gestaltung, Zurich; Giessen 1992, pp. 166–169, where we read, for example, "Like none other, he [Wagenfeld] investigated the properties of the new material and developed from this a design approach that did [it] justice."

6 Wilhelm Wagenfeld, "Industrieerzeugnisse gestalten ist keine Hüllenmacherei", in: *Schweizerische Handelszeitung,* 24 November 1960.

7 Wagenfeld's thoughts on "using" things permeate his whole written œuvre. In 1957, he writes, "Equally the new notion of use leads us every time to new utility goods. So the premise is not the chair, but sitting, not the glass, but drinking, not the pot, but its holding and pouring. Not the lamp, but light and illumination! How sit, how drink, how hold and pour? How light? Where? When? In what surroundings? For which occasions? – is the next question in further deliberations on the purpose and use of things. From considerations about making use of things and our notions of this, come our points of reference for the shape and look of the newly planned artefacts", in: *Zweck und Sinn der künstlerischen Mitarbeit in Fabriken,* typescript, statement of the international "Kongress für Formgebung" (Design Congress) organised by the Rat für Formgebung (Council for Design) at Darmstadt; Darmstadt & Berlin, 14 – 21 September 1957.

8 On Wagenfeld's attitude to teamwork in his workshop, see the quote in Passarge's introduction to the catalogue for the Wagenfeld exhibition at Mannheim in 1957, which states, "[...] in our workshop we play together like a little orchestra", in: *Wilhelm Wagenfeld. Ein Künstler in der Industrie,* exh. cat., Kunsthalle Mannheim, Mannheim 1957, not paginated. In a letter of 30

March 1954 to Dr. Eduard Schalfejew, the president of the Rat für Formgebung, Wagenfeld had expressed his views on a similar topic. "I consciously want to take a different path from that of, say, R. Loewy in the USA, in order to place not so much the design as the achievement of the respective enterprise to the fore." (Copy at the Wilhelm Wagenfeld Stiftung, Bremen). Wagenfeld early came to his conviction of collective achievement. In a lecture to the "Deutsche Glastechnische Gesellschaft" in 1932, he said of this, "For me, one thing is clear. The new household glasses are no longer burdened with the marks of individual design." Or again, "Of the original design, only little may have remained. The design itself, as it were, was smelted down in order to rise again in the form necessitated by the material, by the technical and practical requirements." Compare the greater detail on this in Beate Manske, "Biografie Wilhelm Wagenfeld", in: *Wilhelm Wagenfeld: gestern, heute, morgen. Lebenskultur im Alltag,* publ. by the Wilhelm Wagenfeld Stiftung, Bremen; Bremen 1995, p. 19 f.

9 *Handwerkskunst im Zeitalter der Maschine,* ed. Gustav Friedrich Hartlaub, exh. cat. Städtische Kunsthalle Mannheim; Mannheim 1928.

10 See Fritz Goffitzer (ed.), *"Vom Adel der Form zum reinen Raum". Wolfgang von Wersin zum 80. Geburtstag,* publ. by Österreichischer Werkbund, Linz 1962. In 1930, Wersin ascertained a "stock, independent of the changing times, of some few formal base conceptions or types. [...] It turned out that certain types of vessel constantly recur and are common to almost all civilisations." (p. 31).

11 Wilhelm Dexel, *Unbekanntes Handwerksgut. Gebrauchsgerät in Metall, Glas und Ton aus acht Jahrhunderten deutscher Vergangenheit",* Berlin 1935. Dexel continued his argument in *Hausgerät, das nicht veraltet,* Ravensburg 1937.

12 *Künstler in der Industrie. Vorbildliche Gestaltung industrieller Erzeugnisse,* exh. cat. Städtische Kunsthalle Mannheim; Mannheim 1941, p. 9.

13 Wilhelm Wagenfeld, *Wesen und Gestalt der Dinge um uns,* Potsdam 1948, unaltered reprint, Worpsweder Verlag 1990, p. 62.

14 See Marianne Aav & Nina Stritzler-Levine (eds.), *Finnish Modern Design. Utopian Ideals and Everyday Realities 1930–1997,* The Bard Graduate Center for Studies in the Decorative Arts, New Haven & London 1998, pp. 45, 148 ff.

15 See *WMF. Glas, Keramik, Metall 1925–1950,* ed. Jörg Schwandt, exh. cat. Kunstgewerbemuseum Berlin; Berlin 1980, p. 136 f.

16 On Franck in general, see *Kaj Franck, Designer,* English/Finnish exh. cat. Helsinki Art-Industry Museum, Porvoo et al., 1992. For the *Kilta* design in particular, see Barbara Mundt, *interieur + design 1945–1960 in Deutschland,* Berlin 1993, p. 209 f.

17 See Per Lütken, *Glas ist Leben,* Kopenhagen 1986; on the "beaked vase" see Barbara Mundt 1993 (see note 16), p. 166.

18 Wilhelm Wagenfeld, "Neues Hausgerät in USA", exh. review of "Industrie und Handwerk schaffen neues Hausgerät in USA", Landesgewerbeamt Baden-Württemberg, Stuttgart; Stuttgart 1951, reprinted in: *Baukunst und Wohnform,* vol. 4, no. 5, 1951.

19 Wagenfeld's affinity to lightness and daintiness is also manifest in his assessment of design in the United States. He credited the Americans with an "untroubled ingenious lightness, an obvious joy in experiment." He does add, however, that the Americans possessed an "unconcern which we could never find our way to." Review on the exhibition at Stuttgart (see note 18).

20 Wagenfeld, review of the Stuttgart exhibition.

21 Wilhelm Wagenfeld, "Das Gebrauchsgerät und seine industrielle Formgebung", in: *werk,* vol. 40, no. 12, 1953, p. 412. The view is echoed again in Wagenfeld's essay, "Industriemesse contra Museum", in: *Wilhelm Wagenfeld. Ein Künstler in der Industrie* (see note 8), where he states, "Refrigerator and wireless, car and case of silver cutlery say nothing about the culture of our times. The dissemination of such industrial products bespeaks only the standard of living attained by their purchasers.".

22 Letter from Wilhelm Wagenfeld to Dr. Eduard Schalfejew, 20. March 1954, referring to the plans for his workshop: "Besides lighting appliances, plastics and electrical appliances are to be developed in particular." (Wilhelm Wagenfeld Stiftung, Bremen).

23 Heinz G. Pfaender, *Meine Zeit in der Werkstatt Wagenfeld. Tagebuch 1954–1957,* Hamburg, 1998, and his "Die Werkstatt Wagenfeld aus der Sicht eines Dabeigewesenen", in: *Täglich in der Hand. Industrieformen von Wilhelm Wagenfeld aus sechs Jahrzehnten,* ed. Beate Manske & Gudrun Scholz, Worpsweder Verlag 1987, pp. 250–254.

24 Wagenfeld went on to design a number of different items for Braun, such as the *Smoothy* for the American market; he was also involved in the development of diverse products, an electric shaver, a flash unit and a Multimix. Information on this is contained in a letter from Wagenfeld to Erwin Braun, 19 July 1956 (carbon copy at Wilhelm Wagenfeld Stiftung, Bremen). Even so, no long-term contracts, which Wagenfeld would have dearly obtained, for example for kitchen equipment, ensued. Wagenfeld was anticipating a signal from Braun and did not want to bind himself to another firm during these negotiations. He realised other projects with thermostats for Jakob Schwenk GmbH, Stuttgart, and with models for a syllabic typewriter for Alpina, Kaufbeuren; but these technical instruments were rather the exception to the rule in his wide-ranging œuvre of designs.

25 Wilhelm Wagenfeld 1951 (see note 18).

26 Letter from Wilhelm Wagenfeld to Erwin Braun, 29 August 1955, in: Heinz G. Pfaender 1998 (see note 23), p. 45 f.

27 Fritz Eichler, "Realisationen am Beispiel: Braun AG", in: *System-Design. Bahnbrecher: Hans Gugelot 1920–1965,* ed. Hans Wichmann, exh. cat. Neue Sammlung, Munich; Munich 1984, p. 22.

28 Braun-Feldweg's design approach was more given to geometrical lines. The difference is shown in a striking juxtaposition of two vases by Braun-Feldweg and Wagenfeld in Barbara Mundt (1993; see note 16), cat. nos. 271, 272. On Braun-Feldweg's glasses see Peter Schmitt, "Braun-Feldwegs Beitrag zum Glasdesign der fünfziger und sechziger Jahre", in: *Form und Industrie. Wilhelm Braun-Feldweg,* ed. Siegfried Gronert, Frankfurt am Main 1998, pp. 26–47.

29 Literature on Löffelhardt is scant; but see the leaflet, *In memoriam Heinrich Löffelhardt,* publ. by the Badisches Landesmuseum Karlsruhe; Karlsruhe 1980.

30 See Christian Marquart, *Industriekultur – Industriedesign. Ein Stück deutscher Wirtschafts- und Designgeschichte: Die Gründung des Verbands Deutscher Industrie-Designer,* publ. by Design Center Stuttgart; Berlin (no vol. no.; circa 1993), with biographical sections on the designers mentioned in the main text.

31 Gugelot distinguished several stages in the designer's work. The first dealt with the "firm's production range", the second with the analysis of the planned product, the third with the design, the fourth with the selection, the fifth consisted of "the calculation and adapting the product to the

requirements of the plant and the manufacturing standards", the sixth with model-making. See Gugelot's talk at the Slade School of Fine Arts, London, in: Hans Wichmann 1984 (see note 27), pp. 51 f.

32 *Wilhelm Wagenfeld,* exh. cat. Neue Sammlung des Bayerischen Nationalmuseums, Munich; Munich 1939.

33 *Künstler in der Industrie* (see note 12). The exhibition showed works by Carl Crodel, Hermann Gretsch, Margret Hildebrand, Josef Hoffmann, Heinz Löffelhardt, Adolf Loos, Bruno Mauder, Richard L. F. Schulz, Leo Schumacher, Wilhelm Wagenfeld, Siegmund von Weech and Wolfgang von Wersin. The exhibits consisted entirely of utensils for the domestic table, textiles and fashionable accessories; there were no technical instruments.

34 *Künstler in der Industrie*, p. 3.

35 *Wilhelm Wagenfeld. Ein Künstler in der Industrie* (see note 8).

36 *wilhelm wagenfeld. 30 jahre künstlerische mitarbeit in der industrie,* exh. cat. Neue Sammlung, Munich; Munich 1961; *Wilhelm Wagenfeld. Vom Bauhaus in die Industrie. Ein Querschnitt durch vier Jahrzehnte künstlerischer Mitarbeit in der Industrie,* Landesgewerbeamt Baden-Württemberg, Stuttgart; Stuttgart 1965; *wilhelm wagenfeld. 50 jahre mitarbeit in fabriken,* exh. cat. Kunstgewerbemuseum der Stadt Köln, Cologne 1973.

37 "Die Kunst in Industrie und Handel", in: *Jahrbuch des Deutschen Werkbundes,* 1913, p. 17.

38 "Die Kunst in Industrie und Handel", p. 18.

39 Tilmann Buddensieg & Henning Rogge, *Industriekultur. Peter Behrens und die AEG 1907–1914,* Berlin 1979.

40 Letter from Walter Gropius to Wilhelm Wagenfeld, 21 June 1964, printed in: *Täglich in der Hand* (see note 23), p. 63.

Wilhelm Wagenfeld at the WMF

His "artistic collaboration in the factory" in the light of economic aspects

Carlo Burschel/Heinz Scheiffele

The designs created by Wilhelm Wagenfeld for WMF Württembergische Metallwarenfabrik/Geislingen an der Steige span the years from 1949 to 1975. In 1997, they stood on centre stage at a major exhibition which was carried out in the secretariat of the German Federal Environment Foundation, the Deutsche Bundesstiftung Umwelt[1] in Osnabrück in collaboration with the Wilhelm Wagenfeld Stiftung, Bremen. Europe's largest environmental foundation lauded Wagenfeld's designs for WMF as shining examples of "lasting design"[2], thereby drawing an important connection between his life's work and the challenges facing industrial design today. The exhibition proved that Wagenfeld's design maxims – even if under different social and economic conditions – were very forward-looking, especially in his demands for the sustained development of industrial design. The study of Wilhelm Wagenfeld's life work therefore always remains a challenge and an inspiration for future thinking in industrial design, past the historiographic merits of doing his œuvre justice as a "classic" of German industrial design.

In addition to Wagenfeld's designs for the Lausitz Glassworks/Weisswasser (VLG), in recent years researchers have begun to focus more on his work for WMF.[3] At first glance numerous parallels can be drawn between Wagenfeld's collaboration with the respective firms. When one looks more closely, however, it is the differences which are of greater significance for evaluating his WMF designs.

For a proper analysis it is helpful to reconstruct the creative process of Wagenfeld's WMF designs in the light of the firm's operation. An industrial management viewpoint is apt to focus, structure and describe the economic, technological and organisational conditions of artistic collaboration in industry at a time of general economic difficulties.

Only when one takes these aspects into consideration is a particular mark of quality in Wagenfeld's work revealed: the potential of its inherent virtues for a state of industrial design characterised typically by the ecological challenges it faces.

Thus, Wagenfeld had always had the longevity of his designs in mind; very early in his career he had anticipated and warned against the undesirable trend towards a "throw-away" society. Long before anyone spoke of environmental protection, he formulated the criteria for "environmentally-friendly" products and production processes based on his ideas about the social and cultural responsibility of manufacturers and designers.

Wagenfeld's comprehensive way of thinking, which can be evaluated in the context of the creation of a new job description, finds its expression in the definition of "artistic collaboration in industry".[4] This collaboration meant a fundamental joint responsibility that did not end with the artistic concept (drawing) or the development of a model and its variations, but also applied to (mass) production and the distribution of the product.

In the language of today's environmentalists one would say that Wagenfeld, in his lifetime, was already taking such factors into consideration as the "product life cycle" of his designs, long before the term or the circumstances to which it became a response, could possibly have had any real significance for industrial design. A good example of this are his Cromargan designs for WMF, which were distinguished by their simplified production process and economical use of materials.

The Company History of WMF

At the start of Professor Wagenfeld's collaboration with WMF, the company could already look back on a long history that was essentially marked by the upheaval of the two world wars.[5] However, the details of the history of WMF, already described elsewhere, are of less interest here[6] than exclusively the aspects that had a lasting effect on the company into the 1950s. In July of 1953 WMF celebrated the one-hundredth anniversary of its founding. On this occasion, the commemorative publication *Geformtes Metall Gestaltetes Glas* was issued, in which there was particular emphasis on the company's collaboration with Professor Wagenfeld. In the special issue of the *WMF-Mitteilungen* newsletter[7] (August 1953) the works chronicle was divided up into the eras of Daniel Straub (1853–1880), Carl Haegele (1881–1897), Hans Schauffler & Direktorium (1898–1923) and Hugo Debach (1927–1939); Wagenfeld worked together with WMF during the era of Arthur Burkhardt, which began in 1951 and lasted until 1970.

As early as 1927 WMF introduced stainless steel products to the market under the name "Cromargan" (V2A steel), but it was not until after the war that these became a synonym for WMF, thanks primarily to Wagenfeld's designs. In the same year Debach founded the "Neue Kunstgewerbliche Abteilung" (NKA; the New Craft Section), which, after many years of experiments, produced small but high-quality collections of art glass (*Unika*, *Ikora*, *Myra* and *Lavaluna* glassware), ceramics and metal objects (*Ikora* metal).[8] The knowledge gained in the NKA were also put to good use in mass production, although the quality of these serial products was not to be compared with that of the NKA objects. There were also freelance designers working for the NKA, among them Richard Riemerschmid and Paul Haustein. Fritz August Breuhaus de Groot designed a metal and lamp collection for WMF which was then sold under his name. The "Breuhaus Collection" showed definite parallels to the early "Wagenfeld Collection". Relatively independent of the rest of the (mass) production at WMF (in particular cutlery, hollowware, glass, hotel and canteen dishes and Silit (i.e., enamelled steel) dishes, a small, exclusive selection for a demanding clientele was produced, which WMF used to enhance the company image in suitable publications. These products were more often to be seen in exhibitions and at trade fairs than in everyday use by large segments of the population. In the early post-war years, this practice may have been a precedent for WMF's dealings with Wagenfeld's works, although the fact has to be borne in mind that, while WMF originally desired Wagenfeld's increased artistic influence on their production programme, in the end it could not be afforded due to the financial situation in the company at that time.

The following retraces Wagenfeld's collaboration with WMF – his longest working relationship with any one company – with particular reference to the managerial context, for example by retracing also the channels through which decisions were made. Economical and organisational developments at WMF, which underwent fundamental changes on several occasions over the long period of Wagenfeld's employment there, are also examined.

Collaboration between Wilhelm Wagenfeld and WMF in the 1950s

The collaboration between Wilhelm Wagenfeld and WMF began in 1949. Wagenfeld, who at that time also held a post as expert for industrial design at the Württemberg Office for Promotion of Trade and Industry in Stuttgart,[9] found himself in the employ of a company heavily damaged by the war. The contact to WMF had come through Dr. Wolfgang Weber whom Wilhelm Wagenfeld knew from conferences of the Deutschen Glastechnischen Gesellschaft in the 1940s. In a letter of 28 October 1948, Weber renewed contact to Wagenfeld in Berlin, then not only teaching as a professor at the Hochschule für Bildende Künste but also head of the faculty for standardisation at

„WIR DREI"

sagte Dr. Arthur Burkhardt, Vorsitzer des Vorstandes der WMF (links) zu Inge und Günter, „bilden den Vorstand unseres Werkes und tragen die oberste Verantwortung gegenüber der Belegschaft, unseren Kunden, den Käufern unserer Erzeugnisse, den Aktionären und der Öffentlichkeit. Mein Kollege, Herr Direktor Dr. Ohr (rechts), ist der erste Kaufmann des Betriebes und Herr Direktor Seizer, hier neben mir, ist unser Techniker. Es ist nicht leicht, uns gleichzeitig zu erreichen. Aber wir haben uns hier für einige Minuten zusammengefunden, um Sie beide als Repräsentanten der Käufer unserer Waren und der 10000 Besucher, denen wir in den letzten beiden Jahren unser Werk gezeigt haben, zu begrüßen. So sind Sie sogar im doppelten Sinn ein ‚Jubiläums-Brautpaar' geworden. Wenn Sie jetzt Ihren eigenen Hausstand gründen, dann werden Sie sicherlich vieles von dem, was wir herstellen, in Ihrer eigenen Wohnung haben und es gerne benutzen. Hoffentlich haben Sie Freude daran, und vielleicht denken Sie bisweilen an all die Menschen, die Sie hier in unserem großen Werk an der Arbeit gesehen haben, an einer Arbeit, die jeden Tag und Jahr für Jahr für Sie, unsere Kunden, geleistet wird."

1 The Board of WMF (left to right: Dr. Arthur Burkhardt, Dr. Otto Seizer, Dr. Helmut Ohr) with the newlyweds "Inge and Günter", from: *Jubiläumsfestschrift,* 1953

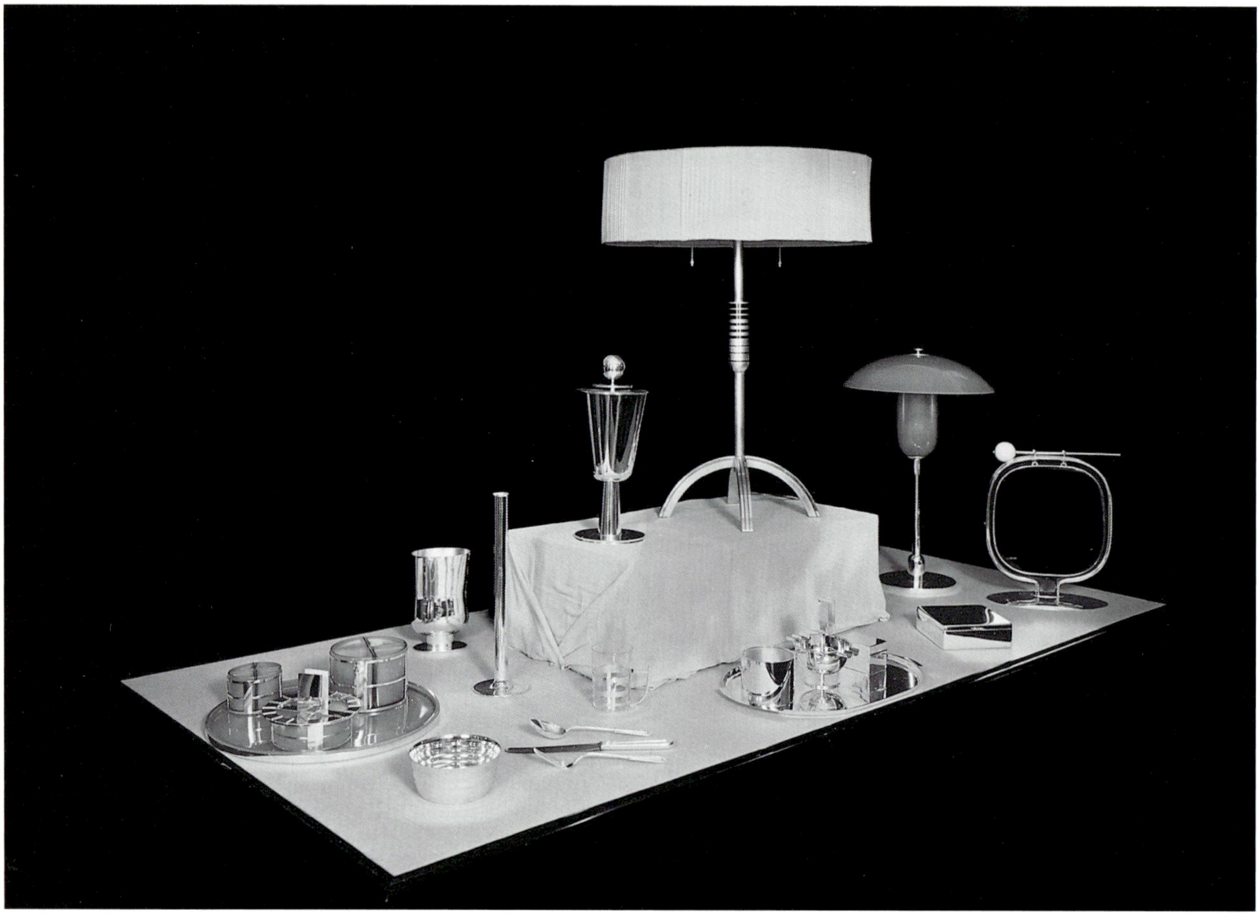

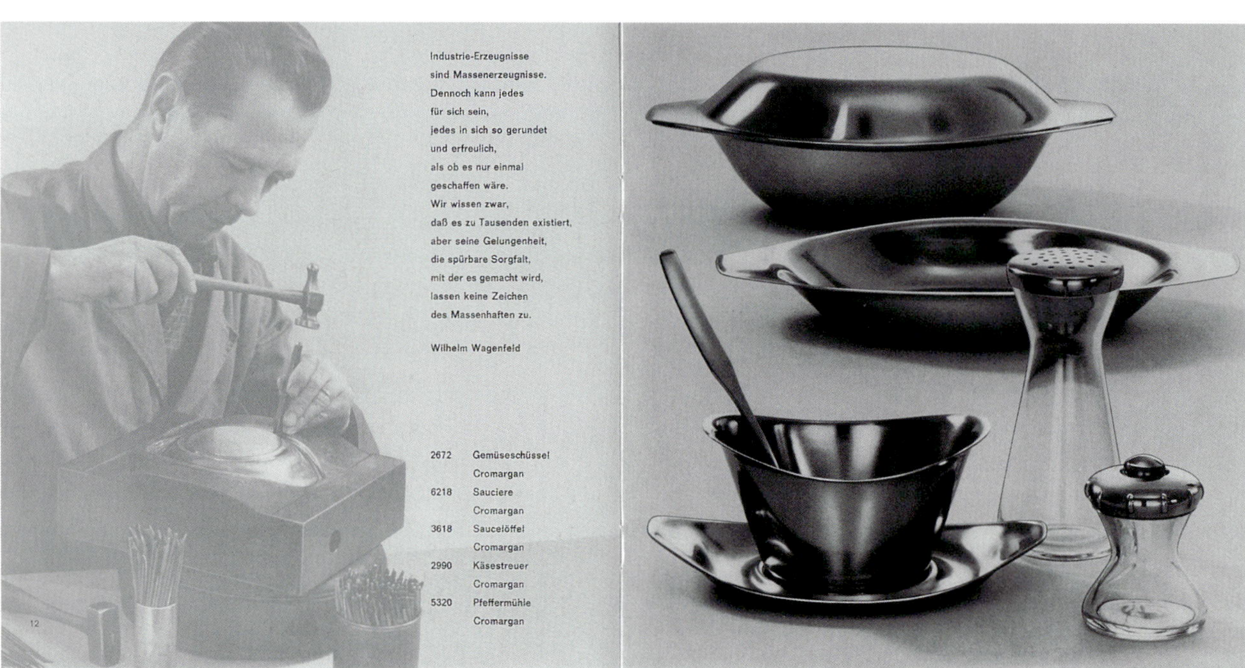
Industrie-Erzeugnisse
sind Massenerzeugnisse.
Dennoch kann jedes
für sich sein,
jedes in sich so gerundet
und erfreulich,
als ob es nur einmal
geschaffen wäre.
Wir wissen zwar,
daß es zu Tausenden existiert,
aber seine Gelungenheit,
die spürbare Sorgfalt,
mit der es gemacht wird,
lassen keine Zeichen
des Massenhaften zu.
Wilhelm Wagenfeld
2672 Gemüseschüssel
Cromargan
6218 Sauciere
Cromargan
3618 Saucelöffel
Cromargan
2990 Käsestreuer
Cromargan
5320 Pfeffermühle
Cromargan
12

2 Selection from the collection of Breuhaus de Groot, WMF stand at the Leipzig Grassimesse, 1928

3 Double spread of a brochure from 1964 which aimed at "elevated taste"

the institute for structural engineering at the German Academy of Sciences. At this point, furthermore, Wagenfeld still had a contract with the former VLG (later named Oberlausitz Glassworks, OLG) and "was working on interesting pressed glass concepts for the Sendlinger Optische Werke and also on a new porcelain service."[10] The first meeting between Weber and Wagenfeld took place in January 1949[11], and in a letter from the Board of the WMF from 29 March 1949, Wagenfeld was offered a one-year consultancy contract with the relevant licensing conditions. This and all later contracts contained a preamble which neatly summarised the way Wagenfeld envisaged his collaboration with WMF. The preamble of the contract from the year 1953 is quoted here as a case in point.

"1. The contracting parties have on 26 April/9 May 1949 entered into a contract which, based on the extension of 3 June 1950 was officially valid until 30 September 1950. The parties are in agreement that the contract relations are tacitly extended until 31 March 1953. The new contract shall go into effect on 1 April 1953.

2. The purpose of the contract is the artistic promotion of WMF products by Wagenfeld in every area of production. Wagenfeld's primary responsibility is to develop a special sector of high-quality products in collaboration with other departments of the WMF, whereby Wagenfeld is allocated the responsibility for artistic aspects and shall also assume artistic management for this sector. This special sector is to include not only Wagenfeld's designs, but can also, at any given time, be expanded to include work by other artistic designers of repute who are recommended by him."[12]

This preamble reads like a description of what Wilhelm Wagenfeld had meant by "artistic employee in the factory". It also makes clear just how much Wagenfeld carried over from his experiences at the VLG into his idea of the collaboration with WMF. The central passage of the contract is that he was promised the "artistic management" of the quality sector. But the experiences he had with the realisation of his designs up to 1953 were anything but encouraging. "You cannot believe, could scarcely believe, how lonely my work in Geislingen often is, when everything I do is criticised, and nothing or almost nothing is carried out, while the folders are full to bursting with objects finalised to the last detail for glass and metal and one attempt after the other is made for new and unknown objects, and only a few vases and jars of mine that you know from Geislingen have made it to the shops and again and again there have been secret variations of my work made – to satisfy the 'middle-class taste' of dealers and travelling salesmen."[13]

The reasons for this behaviour of the WMF can be traced primarily to the economic situation in the company at the beginning of the 1950s, which is briefly outlined below. The WMF, in particular Wagenfeld's direct contact partners – Professor Dr. Arthur Burkhardt, who later became Chairman of Board and Dr. Wolfgang Weber, director in charge of "new product acquisition"[14] –practised what appears from today's vantage-point to have been a "wait and see" strategy. On the one hand Wagenfeld was given specific commissions to develop new products, intended to bind him to the company, and on the other hand, it was common knowledge (until c. 1953) that expensive investments in "tools" were a financial impossibility. This also explains why, with the exception of the *Form* 3600 cutlery,[15] the first designs by Wagenfeld were only realised by WMF if their production involved relatively low investments. For the first vases, only inexpensive wooden moulds were needed (it was not until later that glassmaking

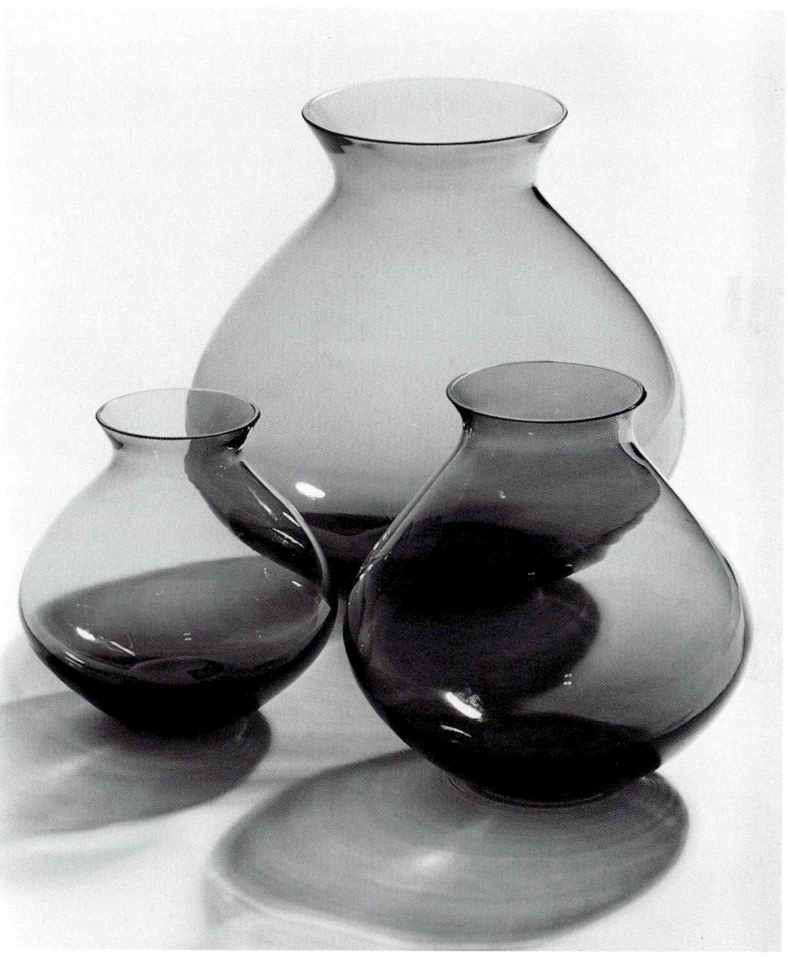

4 Vase samples, early 1950s, not manufactured in series, WMF/Geislingen

5 Display window of the WMF outlet in Stuttgart, 1949. Here new samples were tested before the decision about including them in the production programme was made (lower row, the second vase from the left was not included)

6 Typical display window of a customer of WMF, from: *WMF-Mitteilungen*, 1953

IN DIE HOLZFORM EINGEBLASEN

wird hier eine große Glasvase. Denkbar einfach sind die Werkzeuge: die wie in alten Zeiten aus Holz gearbeitete kugelförmige Fassung und die Glasmacherpfeife — das ist eigentlich alles. Formgefühl und handwerkliche Kunst sind die entscheidenden Zugaben. Ein ursprünglicher Schöpfungsvorgang spielt sich jedesmal ab, wenn aus dem zusammengeschmolzenen Gemenge von Quarz, Pottasche, Kalk und anderen Chemikalien rund um die glühenden Öfen der Glashütte tausenderlei Formen geblasen werden. Dampf und Rauch steigen in dichten Wolken hoch empor. Wenn sie sich verzogen haben, ist das gläserne Gefäß geboren, dessen Entstehung uns immer neu wie ein Wunder erscheint.

7 Blowing glass into the wooden mould, for a floor vase by Wagenfeld
from: *Jubiläumsfestschrift,* 1953

Wir stellen auch Glas her

Für manche unserer Abnehmer wird diese Überschrift etwas seltsam erscheinen. Viele haben unsere Hüttenanlage in Geislingen zwar schon gesehen, aber immer wieder begegnet man der erstaunten Frage: „Was – die WMF stellt auch Glas her?" Viele meinen auch, die WMF beziehe ihr Glas von irgendeiner fremden Hütte. Deswegen möchten wir hier einmal ganz klar ausprechen: Wir haben auf unserem Werksgelände in Geislingen eine sehr bedeutende Glashüttenanlage, und zwar nicht erst seit kurzer Zeit, sondern schon seit dem Jahre 1883. Die WMF-Hütte ist damit die älteste der heute im Betrieb befindlichen Glashütten in Württemberg. Sie vertritt nicht nur eine bedeutende Tradition, sondern hat in den letzten Jahren beachtliche Neuschöpfungen herausgebracht. Wurde früher mehr die Herstellung ausgefallener dekorativer Stücke gepflegt, so beschäftigt sich die WMF-Hütte heute neben der Produktion von Montagegläsern für unsere Hohlwaren, vorwiegend mit der Gestaltung von schönem, zweckmäßigem und preiswertem Gebrauchsglas.

Ganz bewußt gebrauchen wir die Markenbezeichnung „WMF-Glas", die manchem zunächst widersinnig erscheinen mag, da das Zeichen WMF nur auf „Metallwaren" hindeutet. Aber wir wollen mit der Kennzeichnung „WMF-Glas" zum Ausdruck bringen.

8 Glass production at WMF in the 1950s,
from: *WMF-Mitteilungen,* 1955

9 Confectionery jars, silver plate, WMF/Geislingen, 1951/53

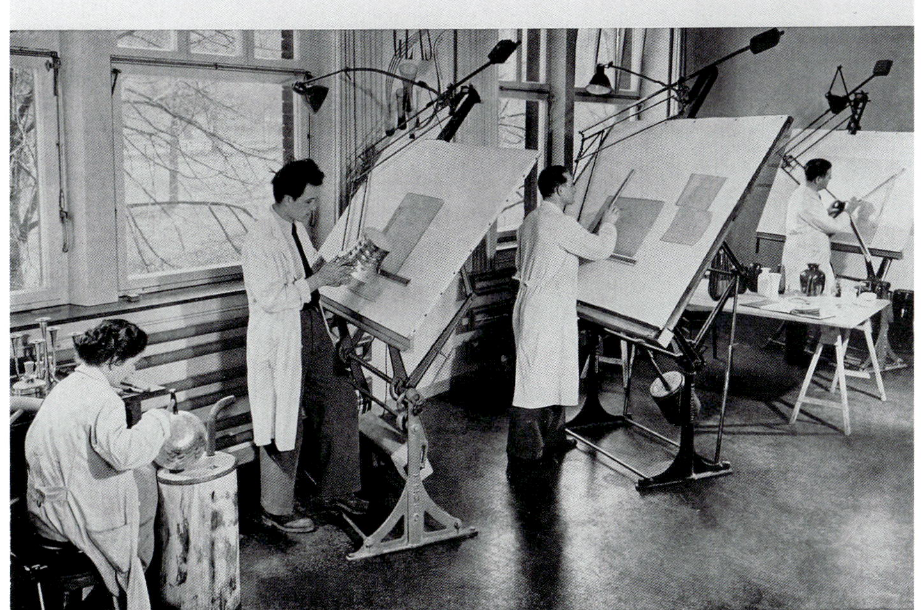

EIN BLICK IN WAGENFELDS ATELIER

Gläser und Vasen, von Professor Wagenfeld entworfen und in seinem Atelier gezeichnet und modelliert, setzen sich auch beim Publikum immer mehr durch und sind typisch für den Teil des WMF-Produktionsprogramms, der sich konsequent um neue, künstlerisch einwandfreie Formen bemüht.

21

10 Wilhelm Wagenfeld's atelier at WMF/Geislingen, from: *Jubiläumsfestschrift,* 1953

moulds were made of metal), and the two silver-plated confectionery jars (in small numbers) could also be manufactured on the spinning lathe with low tooling expenditure. A further characteristic of Wagenfeld's initial period of collaboration with WMF was that he regularly worked in a studio set up specially for him in the works, in other words, he was personally present. This proximity to the company should in no way be underestimated, as it made it possible for him to attend more intensively to his duties as artistic manager of the so-called "quality sector". The establishment of his own workshop in Stuttgart, therefore, had a considerable effect on Wagenfeld's later co-operation with WMF.

The causes for the strained financial circumstances at WMF in the early post-war years can be briefly outlined as follows. During the war WMF had completely stopped their conventional production and almost exclusively produced goods for the wartime economy. The capitulation had left the status and ownership of the company's assets unclear, most of the plant buildings were heavily damaged, many of the "Niederlagen" – WMF's own retail outlets – were destroyed, the export orders had come to a complete standstill and the foreign investors had been lost. Some of the management staff were imprisoned, and it was not until after the monetary reform that the company could begin to prepare for production suitable to peacetime requirements. After 1949 the continued existence of WMF was in no way certain. After some initial progress was made and investments had been made to restore destroyed or dismantled machine parks and company outlets, WMF again suffered a severe economic crisis in the business year 1951/52, due to the rise in raw material prices caused by the war in Korea. Consequently, in the period between 1949 and 1952 there could be no thought of investing in tools for new products. The first profits towards the end of the 1940s came from the stores of finished and semi-finished products, which WMF had always kept in good quantity. It was not until 1953 that the company could record a more positive economic development, which was essentially due to the enormous need to replace many goods for everyday use which had been destroyed in the war. A clear sign that WMF was rebuilding the company, evident to all, was in the construction of an exhibition building which was opened in 1956. The interior of the building was decorated in such as way as to illustrate the confidence and positive image of the WMF in the Burkhardt era. This was where the entire product range of the company was displayed and groups of visitors were greeted.[16]

The first statement made by WMF in the post-war period was through the annual report[17] for the years 1944 and 1945 as well as the annual reports for the years 1946, 1947 and 1948 – marking what was termed the "Reichsmark cut-off". These documents, each consisting of but a few pages, give us very little information about the financial situation of WMF: "The financial statement has not yet been prepared for the year 1946, which has now also come to an end. Therefore, no information can be given about the results. On the other hand, we are happy to be able to report a rise in profits and improved production. In the present circumstances a longer-term forecast is completely out of the question." The annual report (published in 1947) named as members of the Board Dr. Arthur Burkhardt, Otto Clausnizer and Dr. Wolfgang Weber. "Due to the monetary reform, from 20 June 1948 there have been fundamental changes to the asset structure and the liquidity of the company, and it will not be possible to assess the effects these changes will have until later on. [...] As of the end of July 1946 the following members of the Board stepped down: Dr. Arthur Burkhardt, Otto Clausnizer and Dr. Wolfgang Weber. [...] The current Board members are: Director Dr. Arthur Burkhardt and Director Hans Haase." The next annual report, for the year 1948/49, was not issued until 1951 and contained the initial Deutschmark balance sheet. On the Board now were Dr. Arthur Burkhardt, Dr. Helmut Ohr and Otto Seizer (industrialist Arno Geyer resigned in September 1946). The initial Deutschmark balance sheet for WMF showed an accumulated annual loss of 131 998.77 DM and total assets of approximately 26 million DM.[18] In the same

11 Facade of WMF's new exhibition building, Geislingen, 1956

12 The exhibition hall of the building, opened in 1956, symbolising the new modern image of the WMF at this time

year the annual report for 1950 was published, which showed profits of 326 465.67 DM with around the same total assets. In the business year 1951, profits rose to 423 953.06 DM. This and the previous year were characterised by high investments, essentially for modernising the machine park (1951: 3.15 M. DM, 1950: 1.76 M. DM). For the first time, the annual report for the anniversary year 1953 contained several photos which showed the new plant building and WMF products. There were also several excellently placed illustrations of the *Form* 3600 cutlery and several vases by Wagenfeld.

1959 that the next catalogue for glass products was issued, and in it most of the designs in the field of vases and drinking glasses were by Wagenfeld. Generally it can be said that glassware for WMF had always been merely an additional sideline and particularly in the early years – due to high energy and wage costs – only gradually picked up.

For the economic consolidation of WMF in the mid-1950s, in addition to the turnover from cutlery (silver, silver plate), Cromargan products (including cutlery made of Cromargan) were particularly important. The general need to replace goods for

13 Shelves in the WMF exhibition hall with glass designs by Wilhelm Wagenfeld

The first WMF product catalogue and brochure[19] from the period between 1949 and 1951 carried on smoothly from the 1940s and were proof of WMF's attempts to sell off what little inventory remained. It was not until the end of 1951 that WMF also began to adjust their advertising measures to the new market conditions. In the early 1950s, however, only a few special brochures on product designs by Wagenfeld were printed. With a product range of around 4000 articles, Wagenfeld's works were not advertised with special focus, but rather "sprinkled" loosely through the pamphlets: The only exception was the glass department of WMF. The first catalogue, published in 1949, had some expense lavished on the production, yet contained only designs from the 1940s. The next glass catalogue from 1951 had several pages (amongst others the cover page) given to a comprehensive collection of vases and glasses by Wagenfeld. It was not until

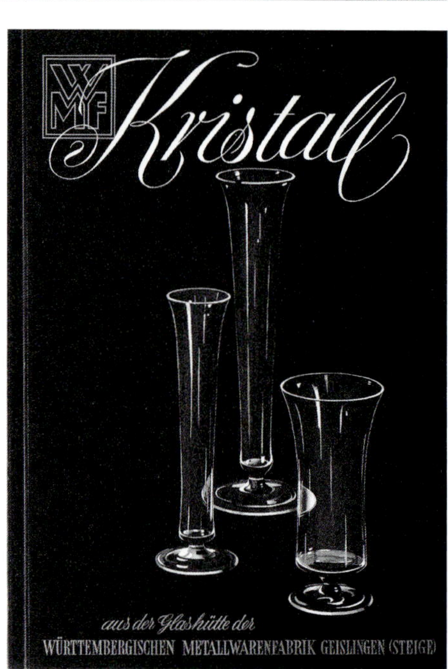

14 Cover from the WMF glass catalogue from 1951

15 Suggestion for a "Wagenfeld display window", from: *WMF-Mitteilungen,* 1954

everyday use, already mentioned above, lasted into the 1960s.

The Founding of the Wagenfeld Workshop in 1954

A critical turn in the collaboration between Wagenfeld and the WMF came with the founding of the Wagenfeld workshop in Stuttgart in 1954.[20] The details of the founding of the workshop need not be elucidated here. However, several aspects which are outlined here were to be of central importance for the continued collaboration with WMF.

For Wagenfeld the WMF did not at this time represent a reliable partner. But as he was dependent upon the royalty payments, which were again dependent upon the turnover from his designs, he was at that time forced – for economic reasons as well – to react to the many inquiries from the consumer goods industry (e.g. Peill & Putzler/Düren). It therefore also became clear that the capacity of the workshop, which had been founded against all odds, was in no way set up exclusively for carrying out development work for WMF – nor could it ever be. In retrospect, the following economically-relevant aspects can be ascertained: to the extent Wagenfeld organised his design work himself through the founding of his workshop and built up further working capacity for the consumer goods industry, he effectively reduced – in response to the unclear behaviour of WMF towards him – the capacity that could be available for the company it had been created to serve. "You promised us – as duly provided for in the contract which was drawn up between us – that you would, in future, be able to maintain a sufficient capacity in your atelier so that the planned objectives, which we outline below, can be achieved in a reasonable amount of time for us."[21] By 1954 even the WMF had gradually overcome the difficult post-war years; improvements also became discernible in the way it organised the acquisition of new products. With the founding of his workshop, however, Wilhelm Wagenfeld spent much less time at WMF, although the company still provided him with his own atelier there – beside the design atelier of Dipl.-Ing. Kurt Mayer. Not hard to imagine how difficult the artistic management of the quality sector became to Wagenfeld who must have been regarded increasingly as a "freelancer". The work force at WMF consisted mostly of employees who had been with the company for a very long time and who had known each other before and during the war.

Although Wilhelm Wagenfeld had been offering his suggestions for new products independently since the beginning of the 1950s, due to the higher degree of internal organisation at WMF from early in 1953, this was no longer possible. The committee for the creation of new products was a firmly-rooted body, which consisted of Board members and Dr. Weber, Dipl.-Ing. Kurt Mayer (head of the WMF atelier), sales representatives and other management staff of WMF. In this committee it was determined which new products should be developed, and the proposed developments were then released for production, sent

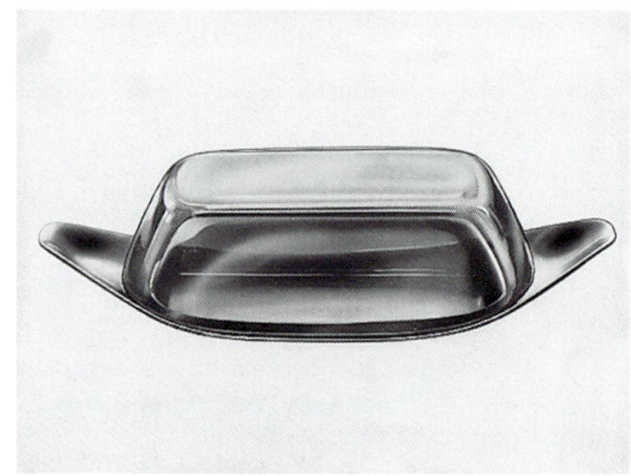

16 Butter dish, Cromargan/plastic, WMF/Geislingen, 1955/57

back for re-working or rejected outright. The influence wielded by the sales representatives and the managers of the company shops on the decisions as to the acceptance of new products in the WMF production programme was extraordinarily powerful.

In comparison to Wagenfeld's collaboration with the VLG, there was yet another important difference. His contact partner at the VLG had been Dr. Mey, whose influence as Chairman of the Board was incomparably stronger than that of Professor Burkhardt and Dr. Weber at WMF. Nevertheless in the 1950s, besides his well-known vases of tourmaline glass, Wagenfeld was able to achieve very high sales, especially in the Cromargan sector, for example with the serving plates or the butter dish of Cromargan or the *Max + Moritz* salt and pepper shakers, some of which are still in production today and which have become a synonym for WMF. Last but not least of course the *Form* 3600 cutlery deserves mention, which was sold in Cromargan, in solid silver (800) and silver plate, as well as the comprehensive hotel silver service.

Wilhelm Wagenfeld's Collaboration with WMF in the 1960s and 1970s

At the beginning of the 1960s, WMF could no longer be compared with the WMF of the 1950s. The network of outlets had been

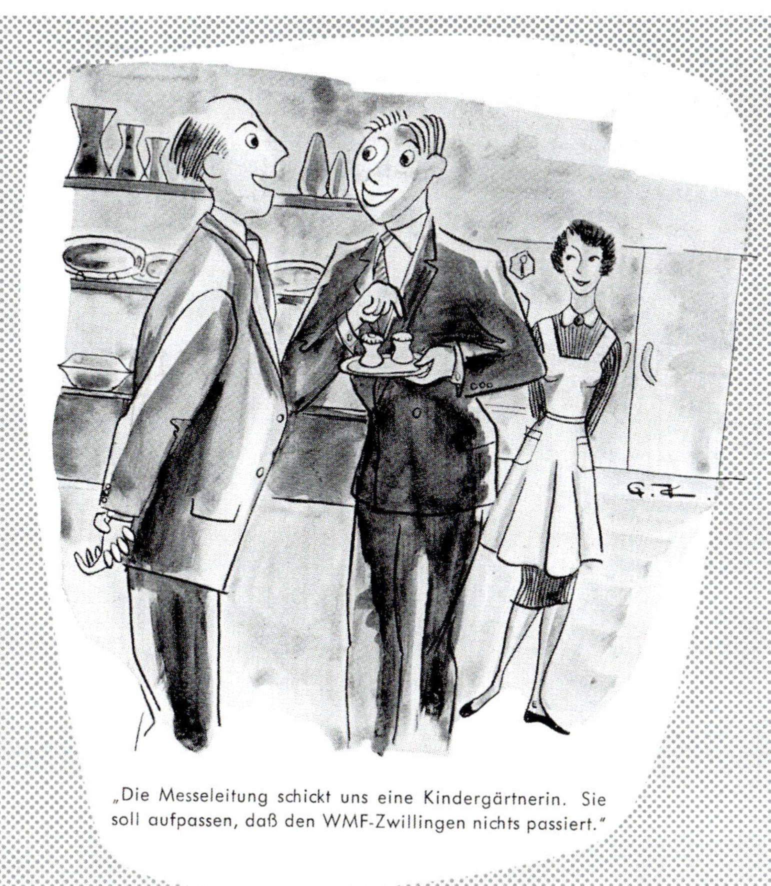

G.K.
„Die Messeleitung schickt uns eine Kindergärtnerin. Sie soll aufpassen, daß den WMF-Zwillingen nichts passiert."

17 Advertisement for salt shaker and pepper mill (twins), cartoon by Günter Kupetz, from: *WMF-Mitteilungen,* 1957

18 *Max + Moritz* salt and pepper shakers and pepper mill, WMF/Geislingen, 1952/54 and 1954

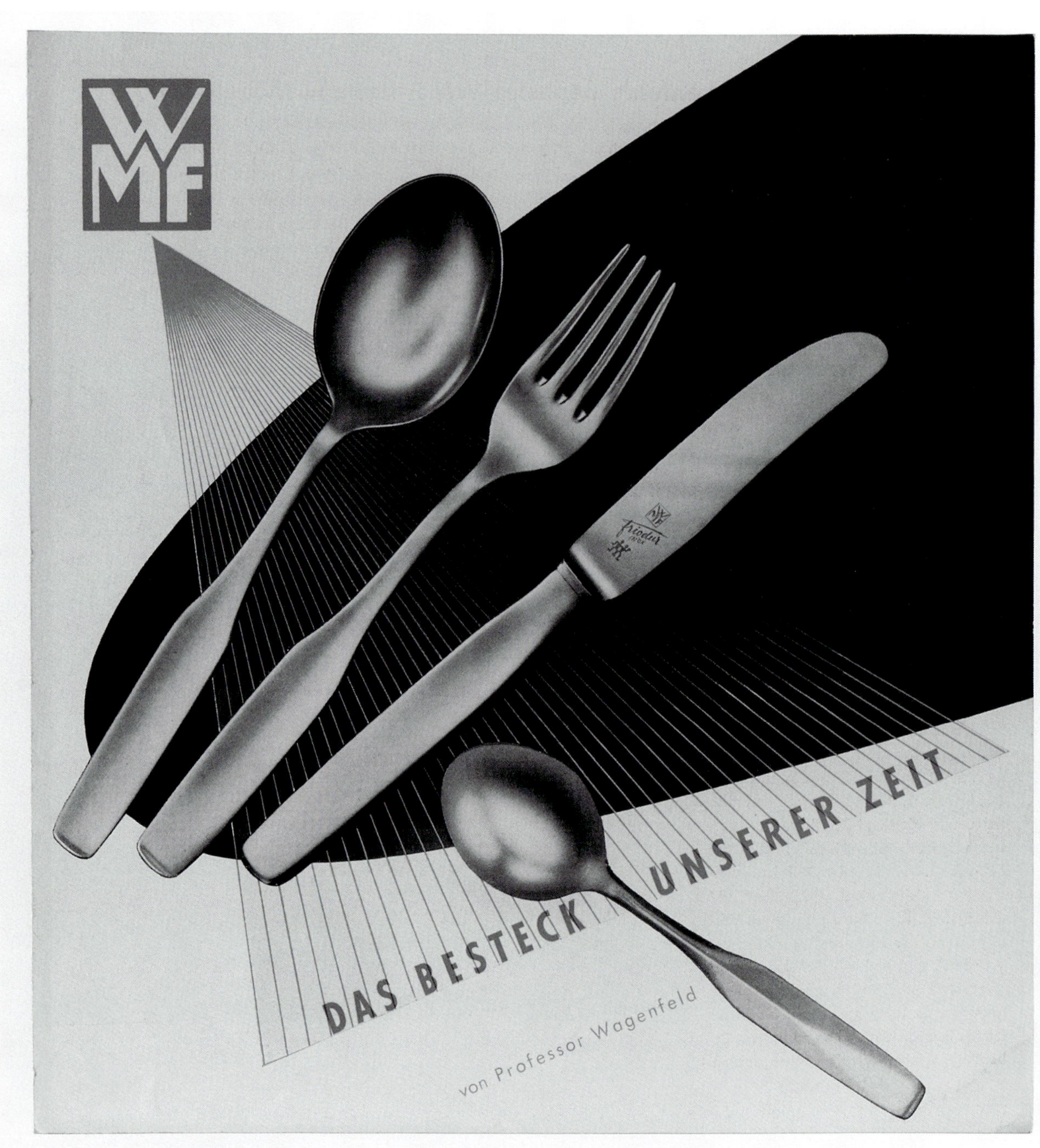

19 Cover page of a brochure on Wagenfeld *Form* 3600 cutlery, 1953

modernised and was again completely "intact"; WMF had succeeded in reinstating its name as a quality-conscious cutlery manufacturer in wide circles of the population. Towards the end of the 1950s WMF continued their winning streak with Cromargan, which encompassed not only cutlery but also their hollowware production. In addition to the in-company design atelier under the management of Kurt Meyer, Sigrid and Günter Kupetz, Dipl.-Ing. Kurt Radtke and Karl Dittert, among others, also worked for the company. In the 1960s the WMF product range included around 6000 different products, but only a fraction of these could be counted as part of the quality sector that Wagenfeld was aiming for. A constant source of irritation for Wagenfeld was also the copies of his designs he observed issuing repeatedly from within the company. In 1963, Wagenfeld wrote to Director Werner Weidner: "[...] 13 years have gone by and unfortunately I have not been able to contribute much to the general shifting of production to a level that corresponds both to the high quality of execution of the WMF products and to the mentality of the firm, to which it owes its reputation – that is to say the attitude of producing solid, dependable and enduring products, so to offer the purchaser of WMF products something of real use."[22]

From the 1960s, in addition to other Wagenfeld's designs, the *WMF 61* vase [23] and *Doria* drinking glass series deserve special mention. The vase series embodies a completely new type and in the 1960s there was no precedent like it in terms of design and serial differentiation. The vases were sold in tourmaline glass and clear glass[24] and were reproduced by Schott/Zwiesel in 1998. A further focal point of Wagenfeld's design work for WMF during these years was the designs for Cromargan, the technological possibilities of forming and processing this material having been considerably advanced. Thus the heavy and expensive hotel silverware (heavy silver-plated alpaca) was entirely replaced by the production of lighter-weight hotel dishes of Cromargan towards the end of the 1960s. It was now technically possible to offer utensils made of silver-plated Cromargan.[25] The serving platters (four different sizes) made of Cromargan were designed by Wagenfeld in such a way that the complicated and expensive welding of decorative trim and handles was no longer necessary; instead, the handles were hollowed flange extensions of the plate itself. Material savings, low production costs and classic design were especially noticeable features of this successful design. Several different jelly jars and a mustard pot also belonged to the category. The lid of the jar was attached inside its mouth by means of a spring ring, and the hinge of the lid cut and formed out of its handle without any material wastage. This concept, still convincing today, combined low production costs and simple production processes with durability and longevity, as the individual parts of the jars could be purchased separately if they needed replacing, and guaranteed perfect material separation for disposal.

Encouraged by the rapidly rising sales figures of his products, Wagenfeld made an unusual attempt to expand decisively the basis for the company's production of high-quality ware: in 1962 the Board approved the formation of an external "artistic council", which was to classify the entire annual production of WMF according to criteria which would be agreed upon.[26] This step, extremely unorthodox for a company, was evidently a subject of fierce debate amongst the members of the Board. It was only after long negotiations that Wagenfeld's proposed committee was finally constituted in January 1963; its members included Willem Sandberg, Director of the Stedelijk Museum in Amsterdam, art critic Wilhelm Rotzler from Zurich and architect Norbert Gutmann from London. In September of that year the first evaluation was presented, which was compared with WMF's profit and loss figures by the marketing department.

The result was so positive that even the firm was surprised. 79 percent of the entire collection was classified as flawless, and these articles accounted for 83 percent of sales. The sense of surprise at WMF was not least "because it was frequently argued in the house that the poorer articles, i.e. what the average girl (Group 3) wants, played a dominant role in turnover figures and quantity sold".[27]

Despite this entirely encouraging result, the Board still clearly had reservations towards independent experts, who were not necessarily sworn to secrecy, because Wagenfeld, with great disappointment, himself made the recommendation to Arthur Burkhardt to dissolve the artistic council in the autumn of 1964. Thus WMF's venture to surrender itself to a critical and design-oriented public and have the confidence to expand their own top product range remained nothing more than an episode.

In 1966 there was a break in the collaboration between WMF and Wilhelm Wagenfeld. As the extremely high sales figures for the Cromargan designs incurred royalty payments in proportion, the firm was not willing to extend the existing contract

20 Display window of the WMF outlet in Ludwigshafen in the 1950s with focus on the Wagenfeld designs.

21 Sales room of the WMF outlet in Stuttgart (the floor vase on the right in the picture is a Wagenfeld design)

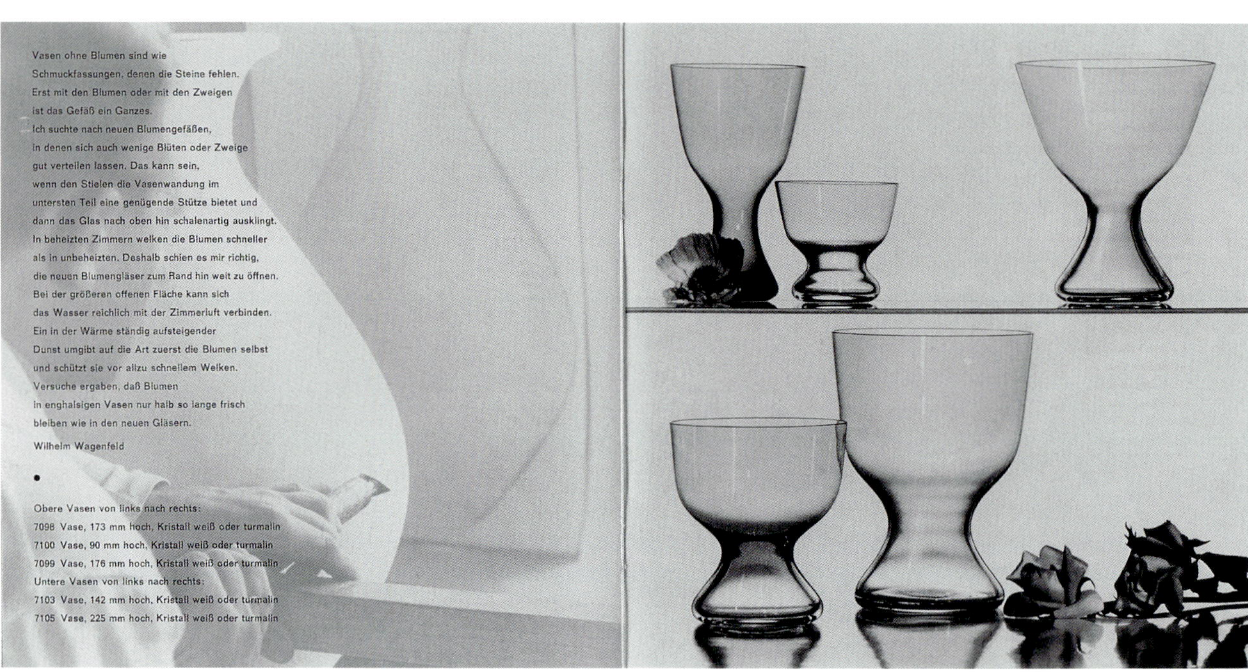

Vasen ohne Blumen sind wie
Schmuckfassungen, denen die Steine fehlen.
Erst mit den Blumen oder mit den Zweigen
ist das Gefäß ein Ganzes.
Ich suchte nach neuen Blumengefäßen,
in denen sich auch wenige Blüten oder Zweige
gut verteilen lassen. Das kann sein,
wenn den Stielen die Vasenwandung im
untersten Teil eine genügende Stütze bietet und
dann das Glas nach oben hin schalenartig ausklingt.
In beheizten Zimmern welken die Blumen schneller
als in unbeheizten. Deshalb schien es mir richtig,
die neuen Blumengläser zum Rand hin weit zu öffnen.
Bei der größeren offenen Fläche kann sich
das Wasser reichlich mit der Zimmerluft verbinden.
Ein in der Wärme ständig aufsteigender
Dunst umgibt auf die Art zuerst die Blumen selbst
und schützt sie vor allzu schnellem Welken.
Versuche ergaben, daß Blumen
in enghalsigen Vasen nur halb so lange frisch
bleiben wie in den neuen Gläsern.

Wilhelm Wagenfeld

•

Obere Vasen von links nach rechts:
7098 Vase, 173 mm hoch, Kristall weiß oder turmalin
7100 Vase, 90 mm hoch, Kristall weiß oder turmalin
7099 Vase, 176 mm hoch, Kristall weiß oder turmalin
Untere Vasen von links nach rechts:
7103 Vase, 142 mm hoch, Kristall weiß oder turmalin
7105 Vase, 225 mm hoch, Kristall weiß oder turmalin

22 Double spread from a WMF brochure from 1964, showing Wagenfeld's vase series of 1961

23 Roast platters, Cromargan, WMF/Geislingen, 1953/54

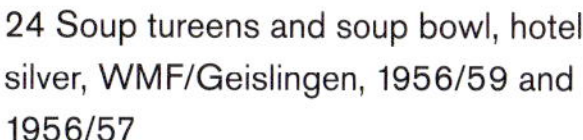

24 Soup tureens and soup bowl, hotel silver, WMF/Geislingen, 1956/59 and 1956/57

25 Preserve jars, glass/ Cromargan, WMF/Geislingen, 1964/67

with the same wording. 16 787 of the cream service with tray (543.01)[28] were sold between 1964 and 1967; 208 610 condiment dishes (529.01) between 1969 and 1979; 987 656 serving platters (524.02) between 1970 and 1979; and 1 626 206 butter dishes (509.01) between 1969 and 1979 (in the Cromargan version).[29]

WMF listed the royalty payments as "remuneration" for work done by Professor Wagenfeld, without noticing that he also financed the running costs of his workshop with this money and that lengthy experimental and developmental procedures often resulted in high expenses. It is easy to

26 Cream set with tray, Cromargan or silver, WMF/Geislingen, 1954

27 Child's cup, Cromargan or silver, WMF/Geislingen, 1953/54, from 1973 sold as "camping cups"

imagine that the in-company WMF atelier managed by Kurt Mayer could, at first glance, be run more efficiently and, more importantly, at less expense. After long contract negotiations, a new contract between the WMF and Wagenfeld was completed in 1970.

However, the consumer goods market underwent some drastic changes at this time. The need to replace goods, so prevalent in the post-war years, had more or less been met and the country began to change in many areas of society. The cultural upheavals caused by the changes which would later be identified with the "generation of 1968" became noticeable. In the glass sector, people tired of smoked glass and so WMF became "colourful". Quick turnover from short-lived gift articles gained in significance.

With the end of the Burkhardt era (1970), WMF switched over most of its production to such articles. From around 1968 the company began to undergo gradual changes. Numerous employees who had been with the company for many years left, and "Beate and Felix",[30] new advertising protagonists, were introduced into the WMF's advertising strategy. Once again, a new WMF was required, this time a "young" WMF, a far cry from the serious efforts to get a new start in the consumer goods industry in the early post-war years. The younger generation was discovered as a new target group, "free" and "easy" consumers who wanted to enjoy life. As for efforts to link up to international design trends, i.e. to win over renowned designers for the firm's quality sector, in the 1960s none seemed to be under way at WMF. WMF also ceded its loyalty custom to jewellers (cutlery, silver-plated hollowware) and hardware stores (Cromargan, Silit dishes) and with its *tischfein* brand, acquired wholesale clients from among the department stores. The life-long connection between the consumer and the company ("Ein Leben lang mit WMF") was yesterday's news; today's was quick sales with rapidly-changing new products.

By the end of the 1960s, Wagenfeld's collaboration with WMF was practically at an end. Many of his developments, for example for a complete set of cutlery designed and thought out to the last detail, were categorically rejected by the new Board.[31] A set of serving tongs from 1975 was integrated into the production in 1977 as Wagenfeld's last design for WMF. Chairman of the Board Dr. Wilfried P. Bromm wrote about this design: "I am glad that, once again, a product has been created that is perfect in design and flawless in function."[32]

From 1965 more and more of Wagenfeld's designs were taken out of the WMF programme. By the end of the 1960s, almost the entire programme of Wagenfeld's tourmaline glasses was replaced by modern colourful glasses (amongst others by Cari Zalloni and Erich Jachmann). At the beginning of the 1970s the "rustic craze" was also noticeable in the WMF assortment: increasing numbers of "nostalgic" brass articles and wrought-iron ornaments were sold. In the glass sector, the *Eichenhof* series was produced, which was an imitation of old, cheap Waldglas. Many of the WMF glasses from this time have thankfully been forgotten. They even went so far as to offer a floor vase made of Waldglas in the form of a milk churn.

At the same time, there were increasing disputes between Wagenfeld and the WMF about the changed production of his designs, which were not discussed with him and which he had in no way agreed to. This applied in particular to a large number of colour variations of his vases. Several designs of Wagenfeld's, however, managed

28 First post-war issue of the *WMF-Mitteilungen*, cover page, September, 1952

DIE GABEL
WMF 3/73
WMF-Mitteilungen für den Fachhandel

IN FRANKFURT AUS DER TAUFE GEHOBEN:

Das neue Verkaufen mit WMF

Umsatzplussystem in aller Munde

Die große Neuheit dieses Herbstes war nicht ein einzelnes Produkt. Gesprächsthema Nr. 1 war nicht ein einzelner heißer Tip.

In aller Munde war vielmehr ein ganzes, erstmals geschlossen angebotenes Verkaufssystem. WMF präsentierte den Besuchern ihres Standes die Summe ihrer Erfahrungen auf dem sich rasch verändernden Geschenkartikelmarkt.

Was der Lebensmitteleinzelhandel seit Jahren vorexerziert: exaktes Marketing im Ladengeschäft, bietet jetzt auch WMF ihren Einzelhandelskunden an.

Lesen, mehr noch: gebrauchen Sie die Fibel, die wir dieser GABEL vorausgeschickt haben. Und lesen Sie in diesem Heft, um was es uns dabei geht; um was es Ihnen dabei gehen muß.

Den Besuch auf dem Messestand der WMF in Frankfurt nutzten weit über 1000 Einzelhandelskunden zur Teilnahme an einem „Sehausschreiben". Die Gewinner der Warenschecks über 5000 bzw. 1000 DM werden wir Ihnen in der nächsten Gabel nennen.

Neue Formel für einen alten Bekannten

Auch Cromargan ist 18/10

Seitdem es die Euronorm 88/71 gibt, glaubt mancher Anbieter auf dem Markt, mit der neuen Bezeichnung „18/10" einen besseren Stahl als Cromargan vorweisen zu können.

Mitnichten. Alle unsere Chromnickelstähle fallen nach der neuen Norm unter die Bezeichnung 18/10. Die alte Formel 18/8 werden wir daher künftig nicht mehr verwenden.

Sie tauschten Erfahrungen freimütig aus

WMF diskutierte Vertriebsprobleme mit Einzelhändlern und Fachpresse

An der diesjährigen 2. Reisevertretertagung der WMF nahmen erstmals Gäste teil. Mehrere Einzelhändler ergriffen das Wort zum neuen WMF-Umsatzplussystem.

Man tauschte Erfahrungen aus. Man sprach selbstkritisch und anregend. Die Fachpresse erlebte diese Begegnung in aller Ausführlichkeit mit.

29 At the beginning of the 1970s *WMF-Mitteilungen* received a new title and a new image

30 Sales room of a WMF outlet, 1975

to remain in the WMF assortment and are able to achieve high turnover figures even today.

Just how much Wagenfeld's relationship with WMF had changed could be clearly seen in the preamble of the contract which he completed with the then Board of Directors on 17 May 1970:

"The contracting parties have been working together since the spring of 1949. In the long years of this co-operation, Wagenfeld has always been able, in mutual team work, to create a significant group of high-quality products which have not only brought WMF business benefits but also earned the firm a name as a leader in the domain of forward-looking product development. In honouring this special achievement and in the hope of successfully continuing this collaboration in the future, both contracting parties wish to substitute for the contract terminated with effect from 31 December 1966, the following contract to take effect on 1 January 1970.

Wagenfeld shall work for WMF in the capacity of a freelance employee as stipulated in the provisions of this contract [...]."[33]

The former artistic manager of a quality sector, under contract to contribute to the developmental process of the entire product range, had now become a "freelancer" of the WMF. Compared to the preamble of the 1953 contract, this one made sobering reading. What had begun as a joint responsibility of both designer and plant for the artistic creation of high-quality products under the banner of a new beginning, had become at WMF a "business as usual" set-up in a turnover market increasingly difficult and full of unsettling crises. At this point the function of the industrial designer, increasingly instrumentalised by the business sector during these years, was revealed as that of a pure "turnover enhancer". For a long time now the important thing had no longer been the introduction of new products as long-term constituents in the product range, intended to define and enhance the company's image. Quick turnover with rapidly changing new products now characterised the turnover policy of WMF and the entire sector.

Résumé

In the time of Wagenfeld's collaboration with the WMF three entirely different "companies" can be determined:

1. The WMF of the post-war years (the early 1950s),
2. The consolidated, quality-conscious WMF (mid-1950s to 1960s),
3. The WMF as "gift article wholesaler" (1970s).

When Wilhelm Wagenfeld came to Stuttgart, his past success at the VLG meant that in working for WMF, he could expect to exercise a widespread influence on a traditional, quality-conscious cutlery and glass manufacturer. Due to the firm's size, his work could also be expected to have a far-reaching national and international influence. Because of the WMF's financial difficulties in the post-war years, but perhaps also due to a myopic "Swabian mentality" there or simply a low willingness to take risks, Wagenfeld's efforts to assume a fundamental influence on the production programme of the WMF failed. His biggest supporters, Chairman of the Board Professor Dr. Arthur Burkhardt and Director Dr. Wolfgang Weber, despite their managing functions in an enterprise of this size, were dependent on the long-term employees in many internal company matters. The foundation of the Wagenfeld workshop in 1954 meant an expansion of the general working possibilities for Wagenfeld on the one hand, but a restriction of his capacities for WMF on the other, as the company had not proven to be a loyal and reliable partner and he had therefore entered into successful cooperation with other companies. Independent of this situation Wagenfeld was regularly and conspicuously featured in the publications of the company. The end of the 1950s to the beginning of the 1960s was the most fruitful time in Wagenfeld's work for WMF. The company owed it not least to its collaboration with Wilhelm Wagenfeld that it was able to build up an image as a businesslike manufacturer of high quality products, Wagenfeld's designs being esteemed in wide sections of the population. By the end of the 1960s, partly due to changed market conditions (increasing foreign competition), the company had completely changed its image and become a "gift article wholesaler" where the tenets of Wagenfeld's design approach could no longer really find a place. Despite this development, the WMF repeatedly produced and sold special Wagenfeld lines.

From the mid- 1950s to the mid-1960s, however, Wagenfeld was able to realise his ideas with one of the biggest metal-processing manufacturers of cutlery and hollowware and glass besides, and he created a comprehensive assortment of products which became well known far beyond the Germany's borders.

Notes

Our special thanks go to Ms. Beate Manske M. A., managing director of the Wilhelm Wagenfeld Stiftung, Bremen, for her far-reaching professional and editorial support and not least for her good-natured patience with the authors. To Mrs Erika Wagenfeld we should like to express our heartfelt gratitude for her helpful tips and her interest in our work.

1 The interest from the foundation capital (over 3000 million DM) is used to promote innovative ecological projects. The trustees of the environmental foundation are appointed by the German federal government; the foundation capital is derived from the privatisation proceeds of Salzgitter AG.

2 "Lasting design" alludes to the model of "sustainable development" for the Earth; in Rio in 1992, over 170 countries pledged to meet this goal on all levels of society/market economy with "Agenda 21". Compare German Bundestag (publ.), *Abschlußbericht der Enquete-Kommission "Schutz des Menschen and der Umwelt" des 13. Bundestages: Konzept Nachhaltigkeit. Vom Leitbild zur Umsetzung* (Zur Sache), 98, 4, Bonn 1998.

3 Compare also the catalogue raisonné of WMF designs by Wilhelm Wagenfeld in: Carlo Burschel and Beate Manske (eds.), *Zeitgemäß and zeitbeständig. Industrieformen von Wilhelm Wagenfeld,* Bremen 1997, 2nd edition, Bremen 1999.

4 See Wilhelm Wagenfeld's definitive *Wesen and Gestalt der Dinge um uns,* Potsdam 1948, unchanged reprint Worpsweder Verlag 1990.

5 For the company history of the WMF AG, see: *WMF-Mitteilungen,* vol. 3/4, 1953, p. 6–11; WMF AG (publ.), *Geformtes Metall Gestaltetes Glas,* Geislingen an der Steige 1953; *WMF Geschäftsbericht 1978 (125 Jahre WMF)* and Jörg Schwandt, *WMF. Glas, Keramik, Metall 1925–1950,* Berlin 1980. Also illuminating is the novel by Rudolf Baumgardt, *Das silberne Band,* Darmstadt 1953. Originally planned as a commemorative publication of the WMF (the book mentioned in the text, *Geformtes Metall Gestaltetes Glas* was then published by the WMF after all), it describes the history of the WMF. The names of the characters were altered; a "translation" of these names can be found in: *WMF-Spiegel,* no. 2/3, 1954, p. 18.

6 Compare also the illuminating dissertation by Volker Hecht, *Die Württembergische Metallwarenfabrik Geislingen/Steige 1853–1945. Geschäftspolitik and Unternehmensentwicklung,* St. Katharinen 1995, and the work by Annette Denhardt, of great interest to collectors, *Das Metallwarendesign der Württembergischen Metallwarenfabrik (WMF) zwischen 1900 and 1930,* thesis, Münster 1990, Hamburg 1993.

7 In addition to around ten different brochures each year, from September 1952 WMF published the painstakingly produced *WMF-Mitteilungen* (for trade customers such as jewellers, goldsmiths etc.) and from July 1953 the similar *WMF-Nachrichten* (for customers such as hardware shops etc., primarily for the Cromargan programme and the Silit dishes). In the 1960s the publications were merged and at the beginning of the 1970s, in much simpler form, renamed *Die Gabel* which is still being issued to this day. The employee journal *WMF-Spiegel* is also still in print today. Additionally published at larger intervals are the comprehensive product catalogues of the WMF, which in the 1950s and 1960s were divided into the various categories (Cromargan, glass, cutlery, silver-plated hollowware etc.) and which were only intended for trade customers.

8 For more on production methods of the NKA see Annette Denhardt 1993 (see note 6), p. 112 ff.

9 Wilhelm Wagenfeld resigned this position in 1950. His successor was Heinrich Löffelhardt.

10 Letter from Wilhelm Wagenfeld to Dr. Wolfgang Weber, 11 December 1948, Wilhelm Wagenfeld Stiftung, Bremen.

11 Letter from Wilhelm Wagenfeld to Dr. Wolfgang Weber, 18 December 1948, Wilhelm Wagenfeld Stiftung, Bremen.

12 Preamble from the contract with WMF AG of 13 June 1953; this contract was in effect until 31 December 1955 and was then extended by a period of one year if not terminated by one of the contracting parties with a three-month notice period. With the letter of 27 September 1966 this contract (including the addendum of 22 June 1962) was terminated by the WMF and then extended at a later date with changes to the contract. Excerpt from the licence contract, archives of the Wilhelm Wagenfeld Stiftung, Bremen.

13 Letter from Wilhelm Wagenfeld to Gordon Fraser, 14 January 1952, Wilhelm Wagenfeld Stiftung, Bremen. Quoted by Beate Manske, "'Fünfzehn Jahre waren nicht vergeblich'. Wilhelm Wagenfelds Mitarbeit in der WMF", in: *Zeitgemäß und zeitbeständig* (see note 3), p. 39.

14 During the war Dr. Weber was a member of the Board of the WMF. After the war he was no longer on the Board, but managed the (albeit central) department for the acquisition of new products. Today, his position would be comparable to that of a department head, although he retained the title of "Director".

15 Even this only began being produced after importer Gordon Fraser had ensured prospects of satisfactory sales figures in the USA.

16 See *WMF-Mitteilungen,* no. 2/3, 1956.

17 For the details summarised here, see the annual reports of the WMF of 25 July 1947, 9 November 1949 and from 1950 to 1953.

18 Annual profits of the WMF AG: 48 M. DM (1956); 65 M. DM (1959); 116 M. DM (1962); 120 M. DM (1965); 125 M. DM (168); 152 M. DM (1970); 147 M. DM (1971); 175 M. DM (1972). Compare the annual reports of the WMF AG from these years; the figures are rounded off. The WMF annual report for 1998 showed assets of 744 M. DM (company assets, shares of the WMF AG: 580 M. DM).

19 Brochures and product catalogues of the WMF AG from the years 1949 to 1975, source: Wilhelm Wagenfeld Stiftung, Bremen, and two private collections.

20 Heinz G. Pfaender's *Meine Zeit in der Werkstatt Wagenfeld. Tagebuch 1954–1957,* Hamburg 1998, is highly illustrative of this time.

21 Letter from the WMF to Wilhelm Wagenfeld, 29 July 1959, Wilhelm Wagenfeld Stiftung, Bremen.

22 Letter from Wilhelm Wagenfeld to Director Werner Weidner, 7 October 1963, Wilhelm Wagenfeld Stiftung, Bremen.

23 Between 1964 and 1969 58 546 vases from the "WMF 61" vase series were sold. Compare letter from Dr. Wilfried P. Bromm to Wilhelm Wagenfeld, 14 December 1970, Wilhelm Wagenfeld Stiftung, Bremen. On the enclosed sales statistics Wagenfeld made the note: "for WMF too noble".

24 Compare Carlo Burschel, "Serielle Handwerkskunst aus der Fabrik – zu den Vasenentwürfen 'WMF 61' von Wilhelm Wagenfeld", in: *Design + Design,* no. 45, 1999, p. 12–14.

25 Cromargan, the V2A steel from Krupp, could not be silver-plated before. Moreover, the production of Cromargan hollowware was considerably more difficult than that of hollowware made of nickel silver (Alpaca). For more on the technological details of metalworking in this period, compare Wilhelm Braun-Feldweg, *Metall. Werkformen and Arbeitsweisen,* Ravensburg 1950.

26 The following information about the work of the artistic council of the WMF was gleaned from the private correspondence of Wilhelm Wagenfeld; copies in the Wilhelm Wagenfeld Stiftung, Bremen.

27 In-company memo "Begutachtung der WMF-Kollektion" from 9 November 1963, copy in the Wilhelm Wagenfeld Stiftung, Bremen.

28 The catalogue raisonné numbers of the Cromargan designs correspond to the WMF cat. raisonné, in: *Zeitgemäß and zeitbeständig* (see note 3).

29 For a comparison, some sales figures for glass designs by Wagenfeld (on the catalogue raisonné numbers, see note 3): pressed glass ashtray (500.11) between 1964 and 1967: 13 818 pcs., vase (449.01) between 1964 and 1967: 4351 pcs., vase (465.02) between 1964 and 1967: 6309 pcs. and of the silver-plated cocktail shaker (559.01) between 1964 and 1967: 1233 pcs.

30 "Beate & Felix" were deployed by the WMF as protagonists in an advertising campaign aimed at the young and carefree consumer. The younger generation was expected to provide the turnover that could no longer be expected from the previous WMF target group ("A life long with WMF"). The competition from cheaper (and usually inferior quality) metal goods from other countries, combined with the fact that the demand for restocking depleted households had been largely satisfied, had led to a drastic decline in turnover.

31 Compare *Zeitgemäß und zeitbeständig* (see note 3), p. 95.

32 Letter from Dr. Wilfried P. Bromm to Wilhelm Wagenfeld, 24 June 1975, Wilhelm Wagenfeld Stiftung, Bremen.

33 Compare preamble of Wagenfeld's licence contract with the WMF, 17 May 1970, Wilhelm Wagenfeld Stiftung, Bremen

Wilhelm Wagenfeld Today

Volker Albus

1 *Mario* beer glasses and tray, Cromargan stainless steel, WMF/Geislingen, 1952/53

If one should leaf through catalogues or books that contain information on Wilhelm Wagenfeld's œuvre today and try to pinpoint characteristics that betray the period in which they were made, generations past, then it is only in the rarest of cases that the works themselves will provide a clue; their outward appearance usually does not betray a particular decade and its stylistic predilections.

It is in contemporaneous photographs that first leads are to be found – in an unwavering and absolutely unspectacular objectivity, compositions whose one aim is to do justice to the features of the subject, and above all, the ever rarer medium of black-and-white. All this is pure 1920s or 1930s; it is the lucid aesthetics of classical object photography. No soft-focus lens, no expressive shadows, no "image"-larded settings, nothing of that tendency. Glasses or pieces of porcelain are placed more or less at the centre of the composition and mostly shown from a slightly elevated vantage-point, enhancing the delicate material qualities and making the whole body of the object visible.

Where there are "settings" for the glasses, cutlery, china and lamps, this is another hint that the articles were created, as it were, before our time; most staged contexts are of the "set table" kind, invoked by the arrangement of individual product groups. True, today's all too clamouring-bright colour supplements call us daily to new "table-spread impressions", but it could hardly be said that their stagecraft is governed by sober functionality or restrained festivity, as once it was. This has ceded to wholehearted and copious celebration of the pleasures of life, status or some major seasonal event.– In short, they simulate various contexts for our respectable parlour-game, wished-for, intended, created, "designed" – never used.

Meanwhile, consumer attitudes to the table and to eating have also changed. Certain vessels associated with specific dishes or out-of-the-ordinary forms of preparation are gradually disappearing to the furthermost shelves in the cupboard. One need only mention escargot pans, sauce-boats, soup tureens or the stalwart coffee-pot in all its variations – all still valued utensils, but which no longer accord to today's conventions and the notions of a "post-modern" culture of the table as derived from them.

Looking at the photographs issued for the various corporate catalogues elicits equally associative attributions of period; here, too it is patently the connections specific to eating habits or conventions which locate all the individual-portion jugs, vegetable dishes or the salt stick beaker unmistakably in the 1950s.

This is not to say that Wagenfeld's works, such as his vases and tableware, absorbed none of the feel of their time; but on the whole, any period contexts in these groups of work are more likely to be gleaned from the manner of day-to-day use one can still read out of them than in their looks in the first instance and above all, not because they embody any ideologies of form, let alone fashions.

This contrasts with a host of designs which not even this social/behavioural angle of contemplation will help to date – all the less since they are still available on the market today or because anyone today would be glad to have them in their home or because they survive in very like form as the current common type. These are the vessels, glasses or cutlery that represent something of a standard, a fundamental,

2 Set table: *Camillo* glasses; *Form 3600* cutlery, bread dish, Cromargan; candlestick, brass, silver-plated, WMF/Geislingen. *Gloriana* dining service, Rosenthal/Selb; 1952/53

3 Hotel silverware: teapot, cream jug and sugar bowl, tray, WMF/Geislingen, 1957/59

4 *Camillo* glasses, *Form 3600* cutlery, tray, Cromargan, WMF/Geislingen, 1952/53

5 Vases, WMF/Geislingen, 1950

6 Escargot pan, tongs and fork, Cromargan, WMF/Geislingen, 1959–1965

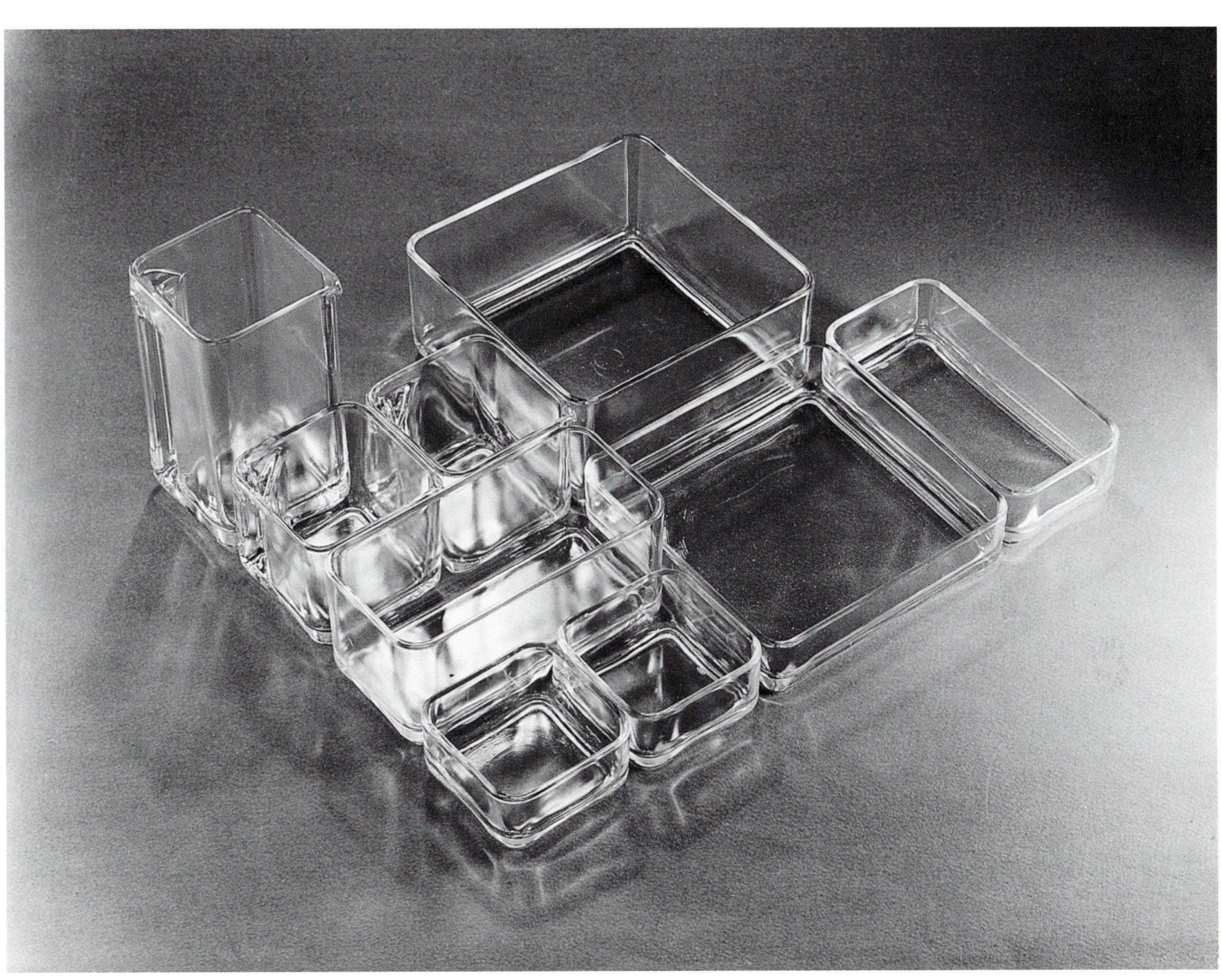

7 *Kubus* storage ware, pressed glass,
VLG/Weisswasser, 1938

complex solution to a design problem. Even the notion of a "standard" is misleading, since it overemphasises the functional, or again the fulfilment of a function and thence, crucially, the qualities of objective utility.

There is no doubt that a number of Wagenfeld's creations are prime examples of functionality superbly resolved; suffice it to highlight the *Kubus* set of glassware of 1938, which, thanks to its rectangular, modular design and the material used, pressed glass, constitutes an ideal solution to everyday problems of domestic food storage which it would be hard to better. Yet to stereotype his work with that criterion alone would be to over-simplify and de-emotionalise both it and our understanding of objects in their own right. It would desiccate our relation to objects, foods and drink, in short, the environment as it affects our sense of well-being. It would also deny Wagenfeld's most likely primary aim, to do justice and indeed cultivate this sensuality of the whole complex that lies between an object and an action – "for the purpose of domestic things [is] defined by their being used [...], which is how we sense and feel them more essentially than and before we think about them, [so] the practical needs must be satisfied and the utilitarian aspects concealed in such a way that this is not the first thing people notice [...], because anything that has been designed or formed is only genuinely satisfying if it is freely accessible to our senses and we can assimilate it inwardly for no logical reason, purely through our sensibility."[1]

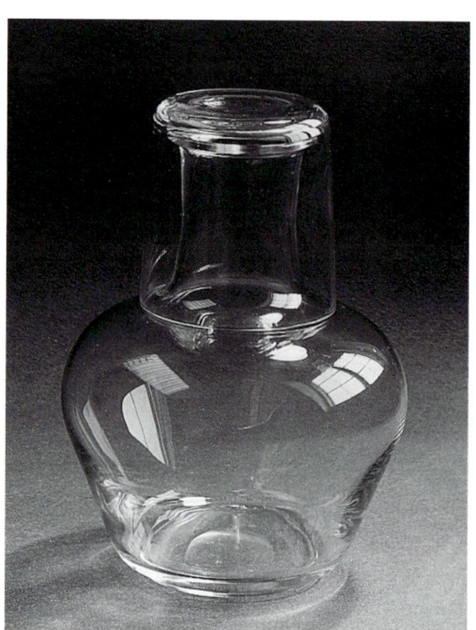

8 *Tiefenbronn* drinking glass set, VLG/Weisswasser, 1938

9 *Basel* tumbler-top decanter, VLG/Weisswasser, 1939

To retrace all Wagenfeld's works that illustrate, and satisfy, this tenet, would take up too much space here. Certainly the *Form 3600* cutlery service is among them, designed for WMF and again available as an "edition"; certainly, too, all the glass goblets for the VLG Glassworks at Weisswasser from the 1930s, the bowls and plates from the same period, the ale and wine mugs, the *Basel* tumbler-top decanter, the lidded bowl for the Schott & Gen. Glassworks at Jena; and most certainly of all, the tea service dating from 1930–34, again designed for Schott & Gen. Here is an instance of that rare sense of a "pure feeling for [its] purpose" that makes any further explanation superfluous.

I still recall quite clearly my own feelings when a friend first poured me some tea in these superb cups. Never, before or since, did I enjoy this drink in so pure, immediate a state, so liberated of all ceramic, decorative and "practical" material.
The glass seemed to me as if evanesced, at most the transparent presence of material conveyed a subtle caressing, a kind of crystalline fixing of the aromatic elixir.
No cups these, they could not be less like profane vessels; rather they were "instruments" to render the enjoyment of this drink more immediate, chiming the subtleties of its taste.

What design factors had made and still make for this rare experience? Apart from the problems supposedly inherent in the production technology, the artistic design choices made would seem to be crucial, if not to say obvious, candidates.
The cups are of glass, very thin glass at that, and their shape corresponds to a gently flattened segment of a sphere. In principle, that sums it up.

But what precise observation, what an all-embracing knowledge, what a subtle sensitivity toward this drink, to our manner of drinking and our own notions of the drink, lie behind these so apt and only seemingly so

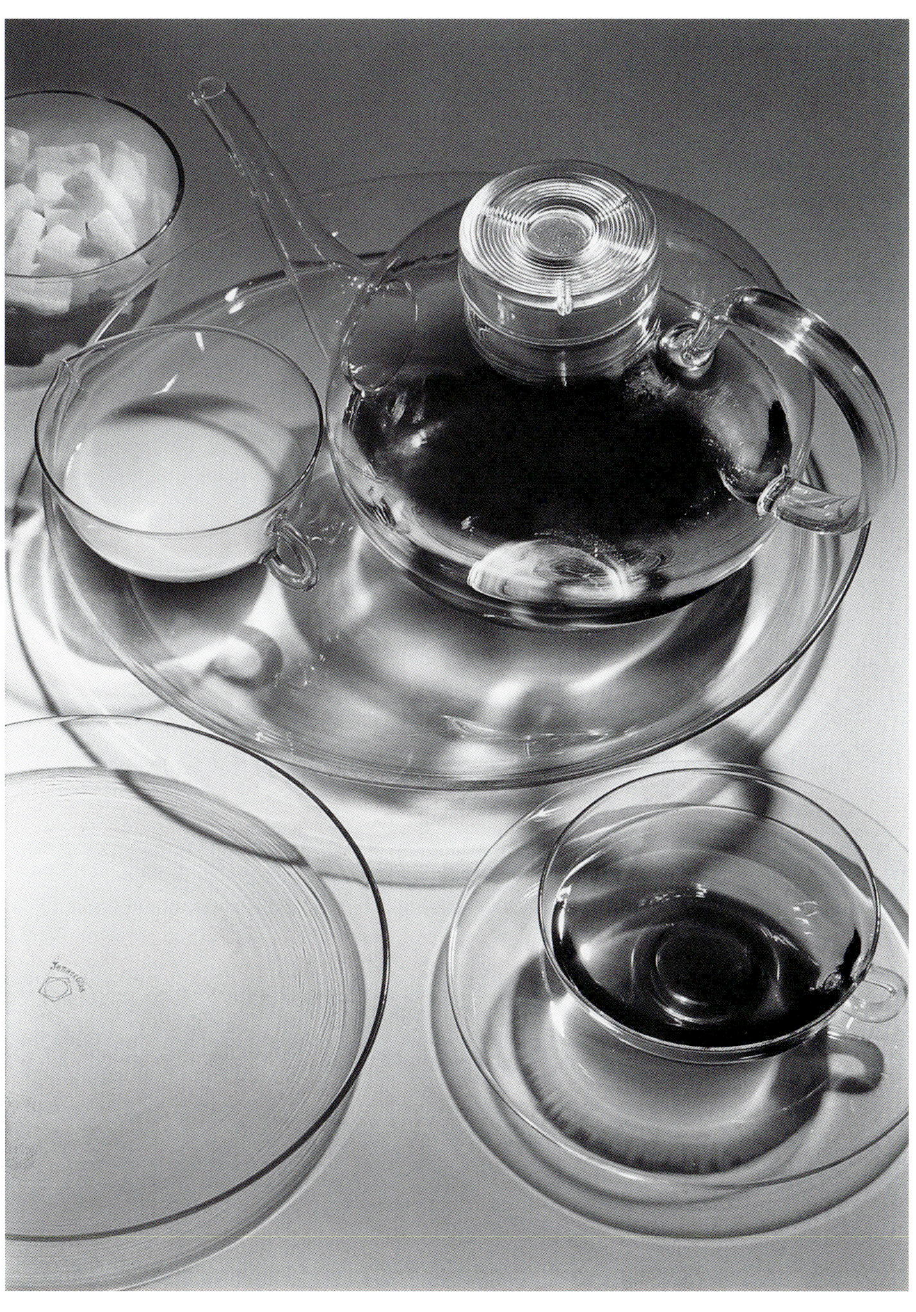

10 Tea set, Schott & Gen./Jena, 1931

11, 12 Jasper Morrison, door mountings, metal, FSB/Brakel, 1989

obvious choices. What a welter of "socially" moulded associations, what an arsenal of purely "practical" considerations must have been overcome here in order to arrive at a composition so expressive of the "essence" of tea-drinking? We can only guess. In design history there have not been many creations which, beyond satisfying the whole gamut of criteria of function, have also been apt to "restore the capacity of an object to relate to man".[2] Arne Jacobsen's *Ant Chair* (model 3100, 1952), a number of Hans Gugelot's designs for Braun, especially his electric shaver, the *Sixtant* (with Gerd Alfred Müller, 1961/62), some of the designs of Charles and Ray Eames or, to cite an example from our own times, Jasper Morrison's range of handles for FSB (1989), can be considered exceptions.

When ideal solutions like these are so few and far between (I really cannot conceive of a better articulated aim so fittingly realised than that explicit in these works), one cannot help wondering whether such a stance, such an approach today is even noticed, or, in view of the primarily mercantile rule of the corporate sales divisions, not even considered, an anachronism. Recent developments and those of the 1980s in particular, however, show this same fabric of the way object and man relate forming one of the focal points in the designs of today's leading protagonists. Though, at first glance, it would seem against all better judgement to see the slightest hint of correspondence between, say, Ron Arad, Ettore Sottsass or Philippe Starck on the one hand and Wilhelm Wagenfeld on the other, it is worth noting that it is the way we respond to things – to shelves, chairs or even the notorious lemon squeezer – that constitutes the essential impetus behind these designers' much-discussed work. The only problem with these products is the paradox that the same aspect is far too often ill-appreciated and mostly overlooked altogether, even to the extent that its opposite – an expressive, "designery" touch – claims disproportionate attention. It has to be said that the disproportion is cultivated and therefore to be accounted for by the designers themselves.

However fashionable we may find Starck's *Juicy Salif* lemon squeezer, the fact remains that its design, seemingly so eccentric, is derived causally from a precise analysis of a sequence of actions, the pressing of a fruit and the associated aim of pouring the juice thus gained into a glass. Much the same applies to Ron Arad's *Rolling-Volume* armchairs, those seating sculptures modulated from steel sheet and made for rocking and lounging, that is, active sitting; or to Ettore Sottsass' Memphis icon, the free-standing *Carlton* shelf unit with compartments arranged in a manner more promising of "disorder" and in fact primarily an acknowledgement of our ordering principles, which are not always aligned strictly on the rectangular.

Yet there is no need to strip an artefact of all its concentrated "lifestyle" (Starck) of this kind, of exaggerated, permeating or perfected moulding of expressive, sculptural (Arad) or ideal/conceptual quality (Sottsass) before we can ascertain its essential "sense of purpose", the ever-continuing quest for the "essence and form" of a utensil to be designed, of a piece of tableware or furniture and the concomitant modernity of Wagenfeld's design principles. In fact, the turn away from such primarily conceptually determined demonstrations of design in recent years has revealed a kind of rebirth of enlightened design culture. It has given rise consistently to products which can justifiably be seen in quite close proximity to Wagenfeld. The *FNP* shelf unit designed by Axel Kufus in 1989 comes to mind; so do various pieces by Konstantin Grcic. Thus the *FNP* shelves fulfil to a T every criterion that might be distilled from an objective consideration of the species. Its concentrated structure (it consists of only three basic elements) allows it, firstly, to be put up with ease; secondly, the compartment proportions of three units high to two wide correspond to the usual cross-section of book formats. The material, both for the sides and (loose) shelves, is MDF (medium-density fibreboard) – the perfect match for paper and cardboard. This places Axel Kufus's

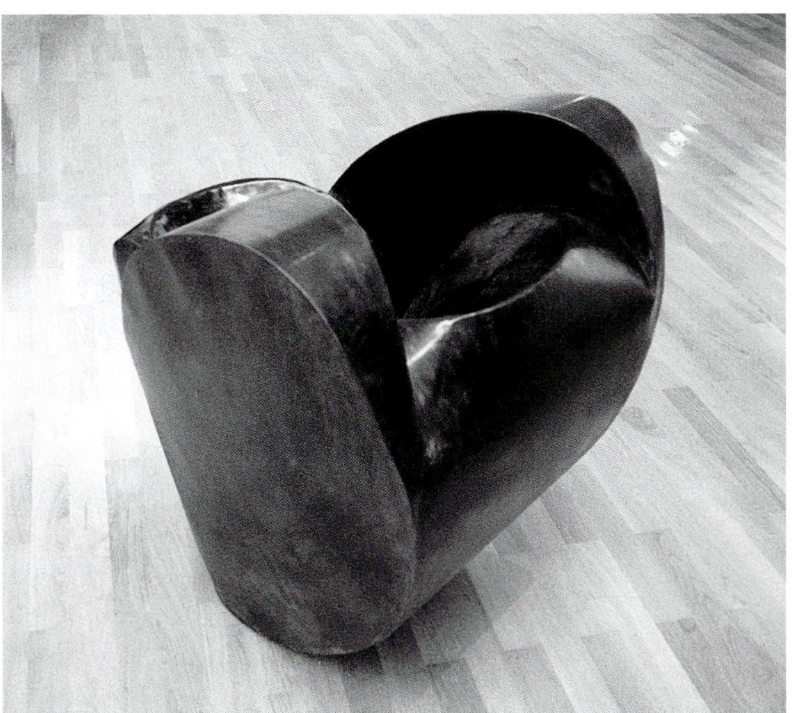

13 Ron Arad, *Rolling Volume* armchair, steel, polished, small-scale production run, 1988/89

14 Axel Kufus, *FNP* shelves, MDF, Nils Holger Moormann/Aschau, Chiemgau, 1989

shelves among the family of furniture guided in every sense and exclusively by its purpose and our notions of that purpose. It seems almost as if we had to wait for the appearance of this particular instance to articulate the definitive ideal vocabulary of mutually attuned function, construction and material constitution. Three or four other shelf systems that satisfy all our demands excellently readily come to mind; but the majority, under closer examination, place the constructional ambitions of their creators to the fore. This is the case in Dieter Rams's *606* shelf system for Vitsoe, in Haller's *USM* system and in the *Syntax* system presented last year at Milan by Vieler (designer Achim Heine). None of these systems conveys the essence of its shelfness first and foremost; pride of place goes to the ingenuity at play.

A solution of the same kind of complexity as Axel Kufus achieved in the *FNP* shelves is Konstantin Grcic's in his pair of ashtrays for the Nymhenburger Porzellanmanufaktur. These are two bowls of strictly geometric shape. One, conceived for a cigar, corresponds to a rectangle; the other, for two cigars, a square. Like the basic shapes, the depressions in both bowls are clearly defined. The rectangular version is reminiscent of an extended, extremely shallow roof in the negative. The square bowl, by contrast, might have been moulded after a picture frame. The even, wide rim is bevelled slightly inward; the interior surface itself is kept perfectly plane. But the essential distinguishing feature of these two ashtrays consists of a trestle-like bridge (or in the second case, two) with a semicircular recess mid-way, which complements the edge of the bowl to form a defined rest for the cigar. That now no longer has to be the subject of a balancing-act on the rim, now broader, now narrower, of the ashtray, and it can no longer tip in one or the other direction – neither into the mass of dead ash, nor onto the table. The cigar is as if borne up on a litter, celebrated as befits a token of individual luxury. The shape of the bowls, the thin forming of the porcelain shell and its whiteness, the entire composition of the design, all underscores this impression. These bowls, worked to a fineness, are more like a neutral backdrop than a receptacle for ashes. They form to all intents and purposes a platform, a kind of stage to attune us visually to facets of this stimulant that we experience only through the sense of taste.

What greater common factor can we discern out of the designs of Grcic and Kufus on the one hand and Wagenfeld on the other? The concept of a "standard" is wholly inadequate, as we have seen; to speak of "timelessness" captures the seminal quality of all these works rather better. – With Wagenfeld's work in mind, their immortality is substantiated not only by the fact that these utensils – plates, glasses and vessels – could conceivably appear as part of some product line at any time in the present (the same applies, in a converse sense to Wagenfeld's, to the *FNP* shelves and the two ashtrays; they could pass convincingly as products of the 1920s or 1930s). More essential to both is that they show that such a thought is not based on any nostalgic reminiscence or even a chance flavour of the month, but only on the purposive design of these objects, on the way we treat and think of the books and stimulants and fine foods connected with this service, these shelves or ashtrays. The implication then, of course, is that the design of these creations is not just timeless but enduringly modern.

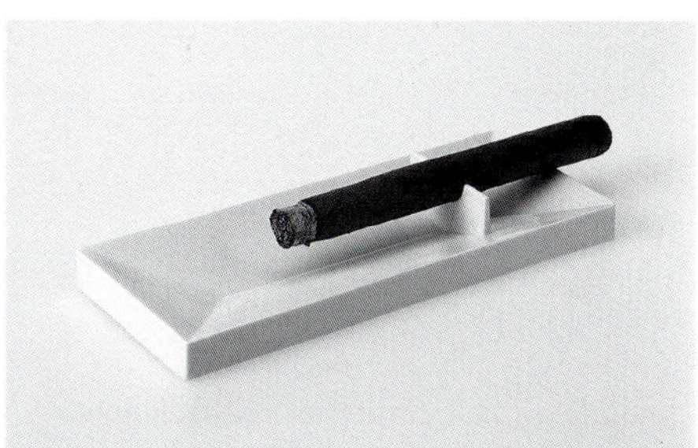

15 Konstantin Grcic, ashtray, Porzellan-Manufaktur Nymphenburg/Munich, 1999

Notes

1 Wilhelm Wagenfeld, "Das Gebrauchsgerät und seine industrielle Formgebung" (1953), lecture at the Kunstgewerbemuseum Zürich, quoted from Lisa Hockemeyer, "Hässlichkeit verkauft sich schlecht", in: *Zeitgemäss und zeitbeständig,* eds. Carlo Burschel and Beate Manske, Bremen 1997, p. 26
2 Wagenfeld, as note 1, p. 23.

Wilhelm Wagenfeld, Biography

Beate Manske

1 Wilhelm Wagenfeld with his sisters, about 1914

15 April 1900
Wilhelm Wagenfeld is born in Walle, Bremen, the son of Heinrich Wilhelm Wagenfeld and his wife Elisabeth, née Wichmann, at Vollmersstrasse 52. Two sisters, Anna and Auguste, follow in 1902 and 1904 respectively. His father, a committed social democrat, is a spokesman for the transport workers in the docks.

1914–1919
Apprenticeship at the drawing-office of the Bremen silverware factory of Koch & Bergfeld; spends the following year in employment as an industrial draughtsman. From 1916 to 1919, also attends the school of arts and crafts in Bremen. His imagination is caught by Expressionist art and literature; first pieces of graphic art. As a member of the Socialist Youth movement, he campaigns for an end to the First World War.

1919–1922
With the recommendations of his masters, Wagenfeld obtains a grant to the academy of drawing at Hanau and the affiliated technical college for precious metals, which he leaves as both a "Meisterschüler" of painter Reinhold Ewald and a trained silversmith. Takes part in competitions for religious implements and jewellery. His prints and drawings are sold through Alfred Flechtheim's gallery in Frankfurt am Main.

2 Work place in the workshop, Koch & Bergfeld, pen and ink drawing, 16 December 1916

1922–1923
Active in Bremen and Worpswede. Installs a workshop at the "Haus im Schluh"; prints and drawings (including woodcuts and etchings), but also designs for metalwork and jewellery. Friendship with Heinrich Vogeler and Bernhard Hoetger.

1923–1925
Metal workshop at the Staatliches Bauhaus, supervised by László Moholy-Nagy and Christian Dell. 1924 Final apprentices' examination before the Weimar crafts guild as a silversmith and engraver, submitting as his prentice work a silver "fat/lean" sauce boat. Designs the "Bauhaus Lamp".

Right column:
3 Wagenfeld in his garret at Hanau; self-portrait, pencil drawing, 1920

1925
Marries Else Heinrich; her son, Michael (b. 1921) is given Wagenfeld's surname. Johann is born to them in 1926, Heinrich in 1928.

1926
Member of the Deutscher Werkbund.

1926–1930
Assistant in the metal workshop at the Staatliche Bauhochschule Weimar, the successor to the Bauhaus; appointed head of metal workshop, 1928. Designs for metal appliances and a series of table and ceiling lamps; from 1929 on, practical collaboration with industry. Begins his lively journalistic career. His circle of friends includes Otto Lindig, Theodor Bogler, Ludwig Hirschfeld-Mack, Hinnerk Scheper, Bernd Bernson and his wife (the translator of Moholy-Nagy's writings).

4 Wagenfeld (1st row, 4th from r.), at the Bauhaus party at the Ilmschlösschen near Weimar, 19 November 1924

1930
The National Socialists close the Bauhochschule. Work by the metal workshop is exhibited in Schwäbisch-Gmünd. Wagenfeld begins work as a freelance with designs for metal appliances and lamps, sometimes in collaboration with the Jenaer Glassworks (individual commissions). Under commission from the Ministry of Economics, supports the glass-blowing trade (cottage industry) in the Thuringian Forest. Co-operation with the jewellery manufacturers Ottmar Zieher, Schwäbisch Gmünd, begins.

From 1931
Artistic collaboration in big industry – contract for heat-resistant household glassware with the Schott & Gen. glassworks of Jena.
Individual commissions for porcelain works (Service *639* for Fürstenberg, Weser, 1934, and the *Daphne* service for Rosenthal AG, Selb, 1938).

1931–1935
Teaches at the Staatliche Kunsthochschule Grunewaldstrasse, Berlin (appointed Professor, 1935). Meets Ludwig Mies van der Rohe and Lilly Reich.

1932
Member of the Deutsche Glastechnische Gesellschaft.

1933
Walter Gropius, Martin Wagner and Wagenfeld protest against the Nazi "Gleichschaltung" of the Deutscher Werkbund.

5 Wagenfeld at the Hotel Kempinski, Berlin, 1933

1935
Wagenfeld terminates the binding agreement with the Jenaer Glassworks, but continues to work on individual commissions (until 1937).
Takes over artistic management of the Vereinigte Lausitzer Glaswerke (VLG) at Weisswasser in Upper Lusatia – the largest glassworks in Europe. Strong social commitment at the plant. The introduction of the "Rautengläser" (Diamond Brand glasses), Wagenfeld's quality-sector initiative, puts the enterprise on a sound financial basis. Notably its "low-priced pressed glass" is converted to quality utility ware, and a wide-ranging line of new models and forms developed. International awards and tributes (1937, gold medal at the Paris World Fair for Jenaer and Lausitzer glass; bronze medal at the Milan Triennale; 1940, Grand Prix of the Milan Triennale)
Wagenfeld helps artists and publicists in financial straits for political reasons (e.g. Ludwig Gies, Alexander Kanoldt, Theodor Heuss) by giving them commissions.

6 Wagenfeld at the VLG/ Weisswasser, 1936

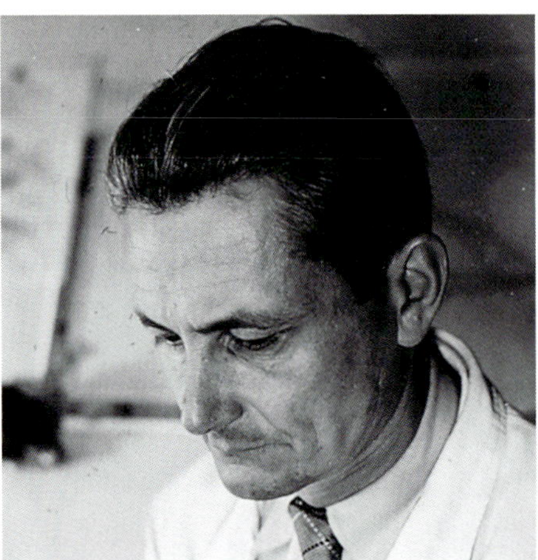

7 The Wagenfeld family in their Berlin flat, 1947/48

1938
The Drawing Academy at Hanau offers Wagenfeld the post of principal. Wagenfeld declines.

1939
Exhibition at Neue Sammlung, Munich.

1940
Exhibition at Museum Kaisertrutz, Görlitz, travelling to Museum Bautzen and Schlossmuseum Breslau. Following an exhibition at the Berlin Kunstdienst, Wagenfeld is pressurised by the SS to conclude a contract with the Bohemia porcelain factory at Neurohlau near Karlsbad/Karlovy Vary (single commission, not carried out).

1941
Exhibition at Kunsthalle Mannheim; Museum für Kunst und Gewerbe, Hamburg.

1942
Marries Erika Paulus.
Called up for war service, sent to serve in Strasbourg and Lüben, Silesia; in Potsdam as wireless operator ("Fine Artists' Detachment").

1943
Released from war service upon a complaint lodged by the glass industry. Resumes work at the VLG. Terminates the contract with Bohemia because they employ concentration camp prisoners (his notice accepted, 1944). The Wagenfelds' daughter, Meike, is born.

1944
Contract with Hutschenreuther china factory, Hohenberg an der Eger (single commission). Having refused to join the NSDAP, Wagenfeld is sent to the Eastern Front (air corps) as a "political parasite"

1945
War ends; Wagenfeld, in Herrmannstadt near Königgrätz, Czechoslovakia, is imprisoned, first by the American, then the Soviet powers (in the Ukraine). Return to Weisswasser, September.

1946
Participates in reconstructing the Oberlausitzer Glaswerke in Weisswasser. Collaborates in the founding of the Werkakademie at Dresden; when this initiative of Will Grohmann and Stephan Hirzel fails, Wagenfeld moves to Berlin. Ambitious plans for an "Industrie-Institut" as a link between teaching and production sites. Invited by Günther von Pechmann to take the post of principal at the Glasfachschule (school of glassmaking) at Zwiesel, Selb, but declines.

1947
Architect Hans Scharoun (like Wagenfeld, from Bremen) calls him to the Architectural Institute of the German Academy of Sciences in Berlin, where he takes charge of the Department of Norms and Standardisation.

1947–1949
Chair for Industrial Design at the Hochschule für Bildende Künste, Berlin, under its principal, Karl Hofer. Elaborates his plan for an industrial institute to be affiliated to the Academy and fundamentally change the relevant training. In the years that follow, numerous invitations to academies and universities (among them, Essen, Hanau [1947]; Saarbrücken [1948]; Karlsruhe, Pforzheim, [1949]; Hamburg, Mannheim, Wuppertal [1951]; Berlin, Bremen, Darmstadt, Krefeld and Lüneburg [1952]). The French Resistance invites Wagenfeld to Paris.

1948
Collection of essays, *Wesen und Gestalt der Dinge um uns (Nature and Form of*

Objects Around Us) published by Verlag Eduard Stichnote, Potsdam. Continuing, extensive journalism; Wagenfeld becomes the most influential theorist in industrial product design in Germany, and appeals out of conviction for a "culture of use", a cultivated way of life in everyday terms in social and societal responsibility.

1949
Wagenfeld moves to Stuttgart. Concludes contract with Württembergische Metallwarenfabrik in Geislingen, making him artistic director of a future quality sector (metal and glass); at the same time, assumes post as head of the industrial design section at the Land of Württemberg's Office of Trade (LGA) in Stuttgart. Consultant to individual firms such as Pott, Solingen. Continues developing his plans for a *Deutsches Institut für Industrielle Standardform* (published under this title in 1950) to be attached to the LGA. The plan fails, and Wagenfeld resigns his post there (1950).

From 1950
Exclusive collaboration in factories for utility goods.

1952
Consultancy agreement with Peill & Putzler for the development of a range of lighting appliances extended (to 1958). Appointed to the Education and Training committee of the Rat für Formgebung (Council for Design). Launches the first "Industry Consultation" between the Werkbund and Philipp Rosenthal, Selb.

1953
Consultancy agreement with Rosenthal Porzellan AG, Selb, for porcelain and glass; own designs until 1953. Consultancy agreement with Peill & Putzler, Düren, for goblet. Gold medal at the Milan Triennale for the WMF glass designs. Appointed to the Rat für Formgebung. Member of working group for industrial design in the Federation of German Industry/Bundesverband der Deutschen Industrie (BDI).

1954
Sets up own workshop in Stuttgart, the "Wagenfeld Workshop, Experimental workshop for industrial models", which also operates as a school. First contacts with Braun AG of Frankfurt am Main. Wagenfeld advises the firm on an official and unofficial basis over the subsequent years; friendship with the brothers Arthur and Erwin Braun and with Fritz Eichler.

1955
Collaboration with Lindner, Bamberg, begins. Development of a range of ceiling, mirror and wall lamps (until 1970). Designs the first cabin service of plastic for Deutsche Lufthansa; household objects for Plasticwerk Johannes Buchsteiner, Gingen (until 1958). Range of light metal mountings for Otto Grosssteinbeck, Velbert (until 1966). Stoves for Vosswerke, Sarstedt (until 1957). Invitations – the only ones to a designer living in Germany – to the International Design Conference in Aspen, Colorado (topic: light). Member of the Industrieform association, Essen. Quits the Deutscher Werkbund because of its retrograde tendencies.

8 Wagenfeld at work, about 1952

1957
Grand Prix at the Milan Triennale for his life's work. Co-editor of the journal, *form. Internationale Revue.* Exhibits at Kunsthalle Mannheim.

1959
Invitation to 1960 World Design Conference in Tokyo. Member of van de Velde Society.

9 Wagenfeld and the American importer, Gordon Fraser at WMF/Geislingen, 1952

1961–1965
Member of advisory panel for the Kaufmann International Design Award, New York.

1962
Honorary member of the Staatliche Akademie der Bildenden Künste, Stuttgart.

1964
Honorary member of senate at Technische Universität Stuttgart. Takes part at "documenta" III in Kassel.

1965
Member of the Akademie der Künste, Berlin.

10 "Bauhäuslers'" get-together: at Tut Schlemmer's (Wilhelm, front, 1st from l., and Erika Wagenfeld, 2nd row, 1st from l.), Stuttgart, 1958

Exhibition at Landesgewerbeamt (Office of Trade) of Baden-Württemberg, Stuttgart; then shown at Deutsches Goldschmiedehaus, Hanau (1966). Exhibition at Landesmuseum, Oldenburg; Kunstkreis Hameln. Certificate of honour for WMF designs at "Industrial Design" Biennale, Ljubljana.

11 Adjudicating at Ludwigshafen (Luran competition tendered by BASF); l. to r.; Willy Rotzler, Alfred Thuma, Wilhelm Wagenfeld, 1964

12 Opening the exhibition at the Landesgewerbeamt (Office of Trade), Stuttgart, 1965

1960
Exhibition at Kunstgewerbemuseum, Zurich, travelling to Stedelijk Museum, Amsterdam (1961); Neue Sammlung, Munich (1961); Akademie der Künste, Berlin (1962).

1966
Contract with WMF/Geislingen terminated.

1968
Berliner Kunstpreis, Heinrich-Tessenow-Medaille of Technische Universität

Hannover, Guest of Honour at Villa Massimo in Rome, honorary member of Deutscher Werkbund, Berlin (after Gropius, Scharoun and Mies van der Rohe).

1969
Federal "Gute Form" award for *Greif* set of drinking glasses.

1970
New contract concluded with WMF/ Geislingen.

1972
Collaboration with the Fürstenberg fine

1978
The Wagenfeld Workshop closes.

1980
Agreement with Tecnolumen, Bremen, revival of the Bauhaus Lamp of 1924, adapted to modern standards by Wagenfeld. Exhibition at Württembergisches Landesmuseum Stuttgart.

1981
Honorary Doctorate of Engineering bestowed by University of Stuttgart.

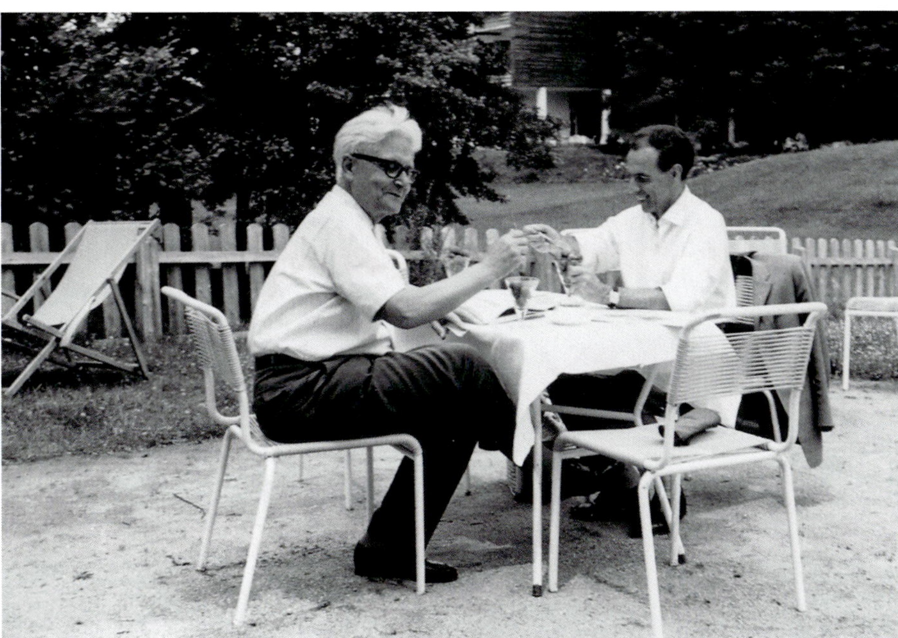

15 Wagenfeld with Viennese sculptor Fred Gillesberger, Island of Faak, Carinthia, Austria, 1975

china works, Weser (until 1974).

1973
Retrospective "wilhelm wagenfeld. 50 jahre mitarbeit in fabriken" at Kunstgewerbemuseum, Cologne, subsequently Hessisches Landesmuseum Darmstadt; Kestner-Museum, Hannover; Neue Sammlung, Munich (1974); Musée des Arts Décoratifs, Paris (1975). The Israel Museum in Jerusalem opens its design department with numerous Wagenfeld designs, which it acquires for its permanent collection.

1982
Federal "Gute Form"-Prize for the Bauhaus Lamp.

13 Receiving the Heinrich-Tessenow-Medaille at the Technische Universität Hannover, 1968

14 In conversation with Kurt Lindner, Bamberg, 1971

1987
Full retrospective of Wilhelm Wagenfeld's œuvre at the Focke-Museum, Landesmuseum für Kunst- und Kulturgeschichte, Bremen; subsequently at Zentralstelle des Deutschen Werkbundes, Frankfurt, Bauhaus-Archiv, Berlin (1988); Design Center Stuttgart (1988).

1988
Wilhelm Wagenfeld offers his home town, Bremen, his estate, on condition that his fundamental considerations and convictions about a responsible industrial culture be placed in relationship to current design. The city senate enters negotiations and considers a change of use for cultural purposes, of the prison at the Ostertor.

1990
Exhibition at Palazzo Serra Gerace, Genoa (in collaboration with the Goethe Institute)

28 May 1990
Wilhelm Wagenfeld dies in Stuttgart.

1991
Exhibition at Securitas Galerie, Bremen; subsequently shown at Porzellanmuseum Fürstenberg/Weser (1992); Offices of the Land of Bremen in Bonn (1992).

1992
The Bremen Senate resolves to reassign the Ostertor police premises as the Wilhelm Wagenfeld Haus/Zentrum für Produktgestaltung (Wilhelm Wagenfeld House/Centre for Product Design).

1993
Wilhelm Wagenfeld Stiftung founded in Bremen. Exhibition at Museum Schloss Philippsruhe, Hanau.

1995
Exhibition at "Göhre" City Museum, Jena, travelling to Grassimuseum, Leipzig (1996), Museum Kaisertrutz, Görlitz (1996), Glasmuseum, Weisswasser (1996).

1996
Exhibition at Barkenhoff, Worpswede.

1997
Exhibition at Deutsche Bundesstiftung Umwelt/German Environment Foundation, Osnabrück.

1998
Wilhelm Wagenfeld Haus opened with the exhibition, "Wilhelm Wagenfeld – Wegbereiter der Moderne" ("W. W., Pioneer of Modernism")

16 Wagenfeld in his flat in Stuttgart, about 1985

Wilhelm Wagenfeld Chronology of Works (1923–1980)

Kathrin Hager

This chronology of works aims to highlight the diversity and complexity of what were frequently simultaneously received design commissions in Wilhelm Wagenfeld's œuvre, and to elucidate the chronological points of concentration in it.

This is not a list of each individual design, but rather of the important products or groups of products which were made in collaboration with his corporate business partners. In contrast to the catalogue raisonné, designs have also been listed where they were developed to a state that would have allowed serial production, but which were nonetheless and for different reasons not adopted for manufacture.

The dates given refer not to the year in which a design was completed, but, as far as this is known, to the first year of production. Only where considerable time passed between the two is the year of a design also listed.

This survey draws on the following sources:

- Œuvre catalogue, in: *Täglich in der Hand. Industrieformen von Wilhelm Wagenfeld aus sechs Jahrzehnten,* ed. Beate Manske and Gudrun Scholz, 4th ed., Bremen 1998.
- Revised catalogue raisonné of the WMF designs, in: *Zeitgemäss und zeitbeständig. Industrieformen von Wilhelm Wagenfeld,* ed. Carlo Burschel and Beate Manske, Bremen 1997, p. 50 ff.
- *Katalog der Entwürfe Wagenfelds für Jenaer Haushaltsglas 1931–1937,* compiled by Helmut Hannes, manuscript, 1999 (preparation in progress for forthcoming publication by the Wilhelm Wagenfeld Stiftung).
- Researches in the archives of the Wilhelm Wagenfeld Stiftung, Bremen.

In the survey below, the first instance of Wagenfeld's collaboration with a firm is emphasised by larger, bold type for the name of the firm; subsequent mentions of the same firm are shown in smaller type and with a preceding dash. Lists of products are given in normal type; subdivisions within groups of products are shown by centred points.

1923–1925

Staatliches Bauhaus Weimar, metal workshop
Mocha machine, fat/lean sauce boats (including the prentice piece), Bauhaus Lamps (glass and metal version), tea scoop, tea caddy, coffee and tea service

1926–1930

Staatliche Bauhochschule Weimar, Hochschule für Handwerk und Baukunst, metal workshop; from 1929, collaboration with industry
Development of models and manufacture of lamps and metal implements
One-off items/small production runs: jar, small bowl, teapot, tray

From 1929 co-operation with
S. A. Loevy/Berlin
Wardrobe wall fixtures, door handle, window latch

Otto Seyffart/Altenburg
Furniture mountings, handle

Walther & Wagner/Schleiz
(in collaboration with the **Sales department** established at the Bauhochschule in 1928)
Hanging and table lamps
Bowls, double bowls, tea caddy, fat/lean sauce boat, coaster for bottles, coaster for glasses

1930

Independent designs for
Architekturbedarf GmbH/Dresden
Renewed production of (reworked) Bauhaus lamp (glass and metal versions)

Thuringian Forest Cottage industry, advisory work on behalf of Thuringian Ministry of the Economy

Weimar Bau- und Wohnungskunst GmbH/Weimar, new establishment out of the former sales organisation of the Bauhochschule (until circa 1933)
– **Walther & Wagner:** double dishes, kettle, tea warmer, lamps for the table, wall and ceiling
– **Jenaer Glaswerk Schott & Gen.:** wall and ceiling lamps (also through the firm's own sales department)

Ottmar Zieher/Schwäbisch Gmünd (until 1932)
Jewellery designs

1931

Jenaer Glaswerk Schott & Gen./Jena, contract for new and further development of household glass (until 1935)
Tea service (teapot, cream jug, sugar bowl, teacup, cake plate), tea warmer, coffee and cocoa cup, tray, milk jug with lid, handle with spring ring for *Sintrax*-coffee machine, dinner and soup plates, stand, vegetable dish
Ceiling and hanging lamps

1932/33

– **Cottage industry, Thuringian Forest:** vases, tumbler, rum decanter, Christmas-tree ball with glass loop
– **Jenaer Glaswerk Schott & Gen.:** tray, cup filter, cocoa jug, egg coddler (for one egg), sauce boat • Advertising leaflets
Ceiling and hanging lamps
– **Ottmar Zieher** (until 1932): jewellery • Publicity (logo, sales catalogue)

1934

Porzellanmanufaktur Fürstenberg/Fürstenberg an der Weser
Service *639* (coffee, tea and dinner service)

– **Jenaer Glaswerk Schott & Gen.:** ice-cream bowl, compote dish, punch jug, egg coddler (for two to three eggs)

1935

Vereinigte Lausitzer Glaswerke (VLG)/Weisswasser, artistic director (until 1949)
Design of catalogues, advertising leaflets and logos (1936–1941)
Services, e. g. *Oberweimar* (also available with decoration), *Bremen, Hochstadt; Kobold* liqueur set, *Oberweimar, Warmbrunn* jugs; vases, flower bowls (also with ornamentation by Charles Crodel), sets of bowls, plates, beakers

– **Jenaer Glaswerk Schott & Gen.:** baking dishes, individual mould (bowl and lid), sauce boat

1936

– **VLG:** (selection) flower bowls and vases with deep cutting, *Paris* floor vase, *Oberweimar* and *Bremen* punch services, hyacinth glasses, *Zölibat* and *Eremit* liqueur decanters, *Zisterne* liqueur set, catering glasses, *Bremen* and *Regensburg* jugs, biscuit jars, preserve jar, bowls • Pressed glass: flower bowls, vase • Pressed household glass: *Stralsund* pudding service, biscuit jars

1937

– **Jenaer Glaswerk Schott & Gen.** (individual commissions): mocha cup, tea/coffee-cup, grog glasses, soup cup, hot-water jug, ragout fin dishes, bowl with lid (vegetable dish)
– **VLG:** (selection) flower bowls and vases with deep-cut patterns, *Munich* and *Berlin* floor vases, *Lobenstein* and *Tiefurt* services, rum decanter, wine measure, *Hermsdorf* jug, plates, biscuit jars, bowls, fruit and flower bowls • Pressed household glass: preserve jars, lemon presses, *Corona* ashtray, flower-pot stands, trays

1938

Rosenthal-Porzellan AG/Selb
Daphne coffee, tea and dinner service (Plössberg works)

– **VLG:** (selection) thick-walled vases (with cut decoration), *Wien* floor vase, *Tiefenbronn* service, catering glasses, cream set, biscuit jar, bowls, fruit and flower bowls with cut decoration
Pressed glass: *Münster* vase • Pressed household glass: *Kubus* storage set, wine cooler, *Erbach* service, preserves jar, *Ceres* and *Zechlin* fruit plates and bowls, egg-cup, stands, *Faktotum* ashtray
Sonderauftrag für **Günther Wagner/**Hannover
Pelikan ink bottles, "Knickflasche" ("Kinked bottle")

1939

– **VLG:** (selection) iced-coffee glass, ice-cream bowl, red wine glass, grog glass, *Basel* tumbler-top decanter; vases • Pressed household glass: apple grater, *Greifswald and Heilbronn* cream service and bowls

1940

Bohemia/Neurohlau, Karlsbad (agreement terminated by Wagenfeld 1943)
Projecting of a coffee, tea and dinner service, the *Neu-Rohlau*

– **VLG:** (selection) *Reichenhall, Hallstadt, Weingarten* services • Pressed household glass: *Mamsell* butter dish, *Ceres* bowl, trays for *Kubus* container set, pattern for coat hook

1944

C. M. Hutschenreuther AG/Hohenberg an der Eger
Further work on the *Neu-Rohlau* service (left incomplete owing to conscription to war service)
Development of a service of heat-resistant porcelain (completed: oven-to-table dishes, in production from 1950)

1947

– **Oberlausitzer Glaswerke Weisswasser,** previously **VLG** (collaboration until 1949)
Beakers, small wine or spirits glass, bowls, cut pattern variations for jugs, glasses and bowls

1948

Hochschule für bildende Künste/Berlin, class for industrial design (to 1949)
Model for a café service developed with students for Staatliche Porzellanmanufaktur Berlin/Kaiserliche Porzellanmanufaktur (not executed)

1949

Sendlinger Optische Glaswerke GmbH/Berlin
Design for a pressed glass service, *Berlin;* further work on *Corona* ashtray; production of *Kubus* containers resumed

Württembergische Metallwarenfabrik (WMF)/Geislingen (to 1977), consulting agreement, artistic management of the quality sector
Models for vases, juice glass, wine glasses (not adopted for serial production)
Metal: first model studies for *Form* 3600 cutlery service

1950

Carl Hugo Pott/Solingen, adviser in his capacity as expert staff at the Office of Trade and Industry at Stuttgart from 1949 to 1950
Cutlery 783/83 (development from the initial drafts of Hermann Gretsch)

Sicherer'sche Apotheke/Heilbronn
Commission to design pharmacy flasks, in collaboration with Heinz Löffelhardt, produced by Gral-Glas, Göppingen, 1955

– **WMF:** glass: vases, biscuit jars

1951

– **WMF:** glass: vases, ashtray, stackable ashtrays in metal rack

1952

Peill & Putzler Glashüttenwerke GmbH/Düren, consulting agreement for the lighting glass sector (until 1958)

Rosenthal-Porzellan AG/Selb, consulting agreement (to 1955)

– **WMF:** glass: vases • Metal: *Form* 3600 cutlery

1953

– **Peill & Putzler** (consultancy agreement extended to the goblet sector): *Prisma, Greif, Staffelstein* drinking glass sets
Wall and hanging lamps
– **Rosenthal:** *Gloriana* coffee, tea and dinner service (Thomas/Marktredwitz) • Bowls with relief decoration, ashtray, table lamps (in co-operation with WMF), vases (one-off pieces)
– **WMF:** glass: drinking glass sets, *Camillo* and *Claudia*, *Mario* and *Margherita;* wine decanter, punch bowls and cups, bowls, cake plates, oil and vinegar flasks • Metal: bowl, cream set with tray, confectionery jars, trays, tea caddy, candelabra

1954

Foundation of the **Wagenfeld Workshop – Werkstatt Wagenfeld, Versuchs- und Entwicklungswerkstatt für Industriemodelle ("Experimental and Development Workshop for Industrial Models")**/Stuttgart

Max Braun AG/Frankfurt (to 1956)

– **Peill & Putzler:** *Ascona* drinking glass set
Wall, ceiling and hanging lamps
– **Rosenthal:** *Patricia* drinking glass set
– **WMF:** glass: vases • Metal: *Max + Moritz* salt/pepper pots ("Junior Twins"), pepper mill, meat serving dishes, preserves jar, stackable egg-cup, sauce boat, double vegetable dishes, bowl, cream set with tray, tray, cake and serving tongs, child's mug, ashtrays, candelabra

1955

Johannes Buchsteiner GmbH u. Co. KG Plasticwerk/Gingen an der Fils (to 1958)
Lufthansa cabin ware, child's bath, bread tray, butter dish, salad servers, punch ladle

Koch's Adler Nähmaschinenwerke AG/Bielefeld
abc portable typewriter and case; sowing machine case of plastic

Lindner GmbH/Bamberg (to 1970)
Lamps for outdoor and interior installation: ceiling, wall, corner and mirror lamps

Otto Grosssteinbeck GmbH (OGRO)/Velbert (to 1966)
First work on door handles and door hand-bars
Developmental studies for door-catch mountings (in co-operation with BKS GmbH/Velbert)

Vosswerke AG/Sarstedt (to 1957)
Sheet-clad stove, tiled stove type

– **Braun:** *combi* combined radio-record player; detail work on: *SK 2* radio, *SK 4* wireless-record player combination, *PC 3* and *G 12* record players, mixer glass, models for electric shavers
– **WMF:** glass: ashtray • Metal: *Atlanta* 4200 cutlery, cigarette box

1956

– **Braun:** *Smoothy* ladies' makeup set (for the American market)
– **Buchsteiner:** colander, egg spoon, egg cup, cake slice, laundry sprinkler, coffee flask, salt/pepper pots, watering can, child's chamber pot, model for a milk can (not executed)
– **Vosswerke:** cast-iron stove (one-off)
– **Werkstatt Wagenfeld:** altar chalice, one-off piece for the chapel of the district hospital in Überlingen (gift)
– **WMF:** glass: jug for iced water (short series, not adopted for production) • Metal: butter dish, napkin ring, salt stick beaker, sugar tongs, wine cooler (one-off)

1957

Gebr. Baumann/Amberg (single commission)
Model studies for an oven-to-table dish, enamel

Dietsche KG/Todtnau
Model studies for handbrushes and toothbrushes

– **Lindner:** wall, corner, ceiling and cellar lighting units, garden lamp
– **OGRO:** hand bars, door handles
– **WMF:** metal: butter or cheese dish, side dish, soup cup, bowl • Hotel silver: sauce boat, sugar bowl, cream jug, trays

1958

– **Buchsteiner:** jam pot with stand
– **Lindner:** mirror lamps
– **Peill & Putzler:** hanging lamps
– **WMF:** glass: vases • Metal: serving forks, tray • Hotel silver: sugar bowl, meat serving dish, vegetable bowl
– **OGRO:** door hand bars

1959

Hengstenberg/Esslingen (single commission for design of packaging glass)

– **Baumann:** oven-to-table dish
– **Lindner:** exterior wall-lamp, ceiling lamp, deco-light bulbs
– **WMF:** glass: trio of vases, candleholder • Metal: small all-purpose bowl, sugar caster, escargot tongs, cocktail shaker • Hotel silver: individual coffee and teapot, sauce boat, soup tureen

1960

Alpina Büromaschinen Werk GmbH/Kaufbeuren (single commission)
Model studies for *Silma* syllabic typewriter (not executed)

Koninklijke Sphinx-Céramique/Maastricht, Holland (single commission)
Model studies for a coffee and tea set. Pattern for a coffeepot and cup (not executed)

– **Lindner:** mirror lamp, safety catch
– **Werkstatt Wagenfeld:** small silver bowl (one-offs and small batches)
– **WMF:** metal: iced coffee cup, vegetable bowl, sauce boat, meat dishes, ashtrays

1961

– **Hengstenberg:** mustard pot with cap and plastic spoon
– **Lindner:** wall, mirror and corner lamps
– **WMF:** glass: 9-part vase series including a floor vase
• Metal: cheese cruet, preserve container

1962

Oskar Schwenk GmbH/Stuttgart (single commission)
Model studies for a meter (not manufactured serially)

Zentra-Apparatebau/Schönaich, Württemberg (single commission)
Model studies for a thermostat (not manufactured serially)

– **Lindner:** lamps for indoor and outdoor installation: wall and ceiling lamps
– **WMF:** glass: double glass, double confectionery bowl, ashtray

1963

– **Lindner:** outside wall lamps, house number lamps, mirror lamps, safety catch
– **WMF:** glass: *Doria, Diana* and *Daphne* drinking glass sets • Metal: iced coffee cup

1964

– **Lindner:** wall lamps
– **Werkstatt Wagenfeld:** silver bowls, fruit bowl (one-offs)
– **WMF:** glass: vase types (not manufactured serially) • Metal: punch bowl with inset and bowl-type stand, double vegetable bowl, partitioned dish, salt stand, mustard pot

1965

– **Lindner:** wall lamps
– **Lindner/Brunnquell GmbH/**Ingolstadt: mirror lamps with reflector
– **Werkstatt Wagenfeld:** silver bowls, double bowls (one-offs)
– **WMF:** metal: side dishes, cheese platter, margarine dish, soup tureen, escargot pans, double vegetable bowl, tipping ashtray, bowls

1966

– **OGRO:** door hand-bars, front door handles, door handles
– **WMF:** metal: cruet stand (oil and vinegar)

1967/68

Bado-Weinbrennerei/Säckingen (single commission)
Designs for spirits bottles/packaging glass

– **WMF** (contractual relationship suspended): metal: preserve jars, cream set with tray (one-off)

1969

– **Werkstatt Wagenfeld:** development models for WMF

1970

– **Lindner:** *Systral* porcelain lamp range
– **Werkstatt Wagenfeld:** 7 altar candlesticks, gift for Johannes-Kirche, Bochum (one-offs)
– **WMF** (new contract, to 1977): further model designs, including model for cutlery (model state ready for serial production, not executed)

1972–1974

Porzellanmanufaktur Fürstenberg/Fürstenberg an der Weser
Stackable ashtrays, double bowl, vases, tea warmer, candelabra

1977

– **WMF:** metal: sausage tongs

1978

Werkstatt Wagenfeld closes

1980

TECNOLUMEN/Bremen
Revival of Wagenfeld's re-worked Bauhaus Lamp of 1924; subsequently, faithful re-editions of Bauhaus and Bauhochschule designs

Bibliography

Aav, Marianne, and Nina Stritzler-Levine (eds.), *Finnish Modern Design. Utopian Ideals and Everyday Realities 1930–1997,* exh. cat. The Bard Graduate Center for Studies in the Decorative Arts New York, New Haven and London 1998.

Abschlussbericht der Enquete-Kommission "Schutz des Menschen und der Umwelt" des 13. Bundestages: Konzept Nachhaltigkeit. Vom Leitbild zur Umsetzung (Zur Sache, 98, 4), Bonn 1998.

Allgemeine Elektrizitäts-Gesellschaft, *AEG Lichttechnik, Leuchtenliste 1954,* Berlin 1954.

Allgemeine Elektrizitäts-Gesellschaft, *Leuchten für HQ-, Na- und Glühlampen,* Berlin 1958.

D'Avossa, Antonio, and Francesca Picchi, *Enzo Mari: il lavoro al centro,* Milan 1999 (Documenti di architettura, 122).

Baumgardt, Rudolf, *Das silberne Band,* Darmstadt 1953.

Benjamin, Walter, *Das Kunstwerk im Zeitalter seiner technischen Reproduzierbarkeit. Drei Studien zur Kunstsoziologie,* Frankfurt am Main 1972.

Beyer, Hans Joachim, and Beatrix Freifrau Wolff Metternich, *Kannenformen der Porzellanmanufaktur Fürstenberg. Stilgeschichtliche Beispiele aus drei Jahrhunderten,* Braunschweig 1983 (Arbeitsberichte aus dem Städtischen Museum Braunschweig, 44).

Blossfeldt, Karl, *Urformen der Natur,* Berlin 1928.

Braun-Feldweg, Wilhelm, *Metall. Werkformen und Arbeitsweisen,* Ravensburg 1950.

Bronzewarenfabrik S. A. Loevy, cat. no. 6, Berlin, undated [1930].

Buddensieg, Tilmann, "Am Ende ein neues Geschirr," in: *Arbeiten in Berlin, lavorare a Berlino, working in Berlin. Ausstellung eines Porzellanservices, entworfen für die KPM von Enzo Mari*, exh. cat. Schloss Charlottenburg, Berlin, et al., Milan 1996, pp. 36 ff.

Buddensieg, Tilmann, and Henning Rogge, *Industriekultur: Peter Behrens und die AEG, 1907–1914,* Berlin 1979.

Burckhardt, François, Juli Capella and Francesca Picchi, *Perché un libro su Enzo Mari – Why write a book on Enzo Mari,* Milan 1997.

Burkhardt, Arthur, "Über die Verkäuflichkeit des Guten," in: Carlo Burschel and Beate Manske (eds.), *Zeitgemäss und zeitbeständig,* Bremen 1997, pp. 48 f.

Burschel, Carlo, "Serielle Handwerkskunst aus der Fabrik – zu den Vasenentwürfen 'WMF 61' von Wilhelm Wagenfeld," in: *Design + Design,* 1999, no. 45, pp. 12–14.

Burschel, Carlo, and Beate Manske (eds.), *Zeitgemäss und zeitbeständig,* Bremen 1997.

Cremer-Thursby, Marc, *Design der dreissiger und vierziger Jahre in Deutschland – Hermann Gretsch: Architekt und Designer (1895–1950),* Frankfurt on Main et al. 1996 (Europäische Hochschulschriften, series 27, vol. 226).

Denhardt, Annette, *Das Metallwarendesign der Württembergischen Metallwarenfabrik (WMF) zwischen 1900 und 1930: Historismus, Jugendstil, Art Deco,* Hamburg 1993 (Form & Interesse, 41).

Dexel, Wilhelm, *Unbekanntes Handwerksgut. Gebrauchsgerät in Metall, Glas und Ton aus acht Jahrhunderten deutscher Vergangenheit,* Berlin 1935 (Schriften zur deutschen Handwerkskunst).

Deutsche Warenkunde, publ. Kunstdienst – Berlin, Berlin 1938; 1939.

Droste, Magdalena, *Die Bauhaus-Leuchte von Carl Jacob Jucker und Wilhelm Wagenfeld,* Frankfurt on Main 1997 (Design Klassiker, 8).

Eichler, Fritz, "Realisationen am Beispiel: Braun AG," in: Hans Wichmann (ed.), *System-Design. Bahnbrecher: Hans Gugelot 1920–1965,* Munich 1984, p. 22 (Industrial design – graphic design, 3).

Die Form. Zeitschrift für gestaltende Arbeit, vol. 5, 1930, nos. 11/12; vol. 6, 1931, no. 10.

Fritz, Bernd, *Die Porzellangeschirre des Rosenthal Konzerns 1891–1979,* Stuttgart 1989.

"Fürstenberg alt und neu," in: *Die Schaulade. Europa-Journal für Porzellan, Keramik, Glas, Hausrat,* issue B, vol. 10, 1934, no. 10, pp. 465–467.

Die Gabel. WMF-Mitteilungen für den Fachhandel.

Gassner, Hubertus, "Zwischen den Stühlen sitzend sich im Kreise drehen," in: H. Gassner (ed.), *Wechselwirkungen. Ungarische Avantgarde in der Weimarer Republik,* exh. cat. Neue Galerie, Kassel, and Museum Bochum; Marburg 1986, pp. 313 f.

Geformtes Metall Gestaltetes Glas. Ein Buch zum Entstehen modernen Hausgeräts. [Festschrift zum 100jährigen Bestehen der WMF], Geislingen an der Steige 1953.

Georgeadis, Sokratis, *Sigfried Giedion. Eine intellektuelle Biographie,* Zurich 1989.

Giedion, Sigfried, *Raum, Zeit, Architektur – Die Entstehung einer neuen Tradition,* Ravensburg 1965.

Glastechnische Berichte. Zeitschrift für Glaskunde, vol. 13, 1935, no. 1.

[Goffitzer, Fritz], *Vom Adel der Form zum reinen Raum. Wolfgang Wersin zum 80. Geburtstag,* publ. Österreichischer Werkbund, selected and compiled by Fritz Goffitzer, Linz an der Donau 1962.

Gronert, Siegfried, *Türdrücker der Moderne. Eine Designgeschichte,* Cologne 1991.

Gronert, Siegfried (ed.), *Form und Industrie. Wilhelm Braun-Feldweg,* Frankfurt am Main 1998.

Gropius, Walter, "Grundsätze der Bauhaus-produktion," in: *Neue Arbeiten der Bauhaus-Werkstätten,* Munich, undated [1925], pp. 5–8 (Bauhausbücher, 7).

Gropius, Walter, *Die neue Architektur und das Bauhaus – Grundzüge und Entwicklung einer Konzeption,* Mainz 1965.

Gründig, Rita, "Keramik und Gefässdesign," in: *Burg Giebichenstein. Die hallesche Kunstschule von den Anfängen bis zur Gegenwart,* exh. cat. Staatliche Galerie Moritzburg Halle and Badisches Landesmuseum Karlsruhe, Halle 1993, pp. 245–282.

Gugelot, Hans, "[speech at the Slade School of Fine Arts, London]," in: Hans Wichmann (ed.), *System-Design. Bahnbrecher: Hans Gugelot 1920–1965,* Munich 1984, pp. 51 f.

Hartlaub, Gustav Friedrich (ed.), *Handwerkskunst im Zeitalter der Maschine. Führer durch die Ausstellung mit einer Rundfrage zum Problem des ewigen Handwerks,* Städtische Kunsthalle Mannheim, Mannheim 1928.

Hecht, Volker, *Die Württembergische Metallwarenfabrik Geislingen/Steige 1853–1945. Geschäftspolitik und Unternehmensentwicklung,* St. Katharinen 1995.

Hegel, Georg Friedrich Wilhelm, *Vorlesungen über die Ästhetik,* ed. Rüdiger Bubner, Stuttgart 1971.

"Heinrich König an Dr. Erich Schott zu dessen 70. Geburtstag," in: *Schott. Jenaer Glaswerk Schott & Gen. Mainz. Werkzeitschrift,* 2, 1961, p. 4.

Hellwag, Fritz E., *Wilhelm Wagenfeld. Formgebung der Industrieware,* publ. Kunstdienst – Berlin, Berlin 1940.

Heyden, Thomas, *Die Bauhaus-Lampe,* publ. Museumspädagogischer Dienst Berlin for Bauhaus-Archiv, Berlin 1992.

Hockemeyer, Lisa, "Hässlichkeit verkauft sich schlecht," in: Carlo Burschel and Beate Manske (eds.), *Zeitgemäss und zeitbeständig,* Bremen 1997, pp. 22–29.

Huber, Gabriele, *Die Porzellan-Manufaktur Allach-München GmbH, eine "Wirtschaftsunternehmung" der SS zum Schutz der "deutschen Seele,"* Marburg 1992.

Hüter, Karl-Heinz, *Das Bauhaus in Weimar,* 2nd ed. Berlin 1976.

Jakobson, Hans-Peter, *Otto Lindig – der Töpfer: 1895–1966,* exh. cat. Museen der Stadt Gera et al., Gera 1990.

Jenaische Zeitung, 14 January 1931.

Kaj Franck. Muotoilija, Formgivare, Designer, Finnish/English, exh. cat. Industrial Museum of Art Helsinki, Porvoo et al. 1992.

Kleine, Peter M., and Klaus Struve (eds.), *Idee: Christian Dell. Einfache, zweckmässige Arbeitsleuchten aus Neheim,* exh. cat. Sparkasse Arnsberg-Sundern, Arnsberg 1995.

Krohn, Gerhard, and Fritz Hierl, *Formschöne Lampen und Beleuchtungsanlagen,* Munich 1952.

Künstler in der Industrie. Vorbildliche Gestaltung industrieller Erzeugnisse, exh. cat. Städtische Kunsthalle Mannheim, Mannheim 1941.

Die Kunst in Industrie und Handel, Jena 1913 (Jahrbuch des Deutschen Werkbundes, 1913).

Kunstschulreform 1900–1933, ed. Hans M. Wingler, Berlin 1977.

Leben und Arbeiten im Industriezeitalter. Eine Ausstellung zur Wirtschafts- und Sozialgeschichte Bayerns seit 1850, publ. Germanisches Nationalmuseum Nürnberg, Stuttgart 1985.

Lehmann, Klaus, "Wie der Edelstahl in die Küche kam," in: Michael Andritzky (ed.), *Oikos. Von der Feuerstelle zur Mikrowelle. Hausrat und Wohnen im Wandel,* exh. cat. Design Center Stuttgart and Museum für Gestaltung, Zurich, Giessen 1992, pp. 166–169.

Lehmann, Klaus, "Was ich Wilhelm Wagenfeld hätte sagen wollen," in: Carlo Burschel and Beate Manske (eds.), *Zeitgemäss und zeitbeständig,* Bremen 1997, pp. 8–11.

Lindner-Eldeco-Lampen 1966, *Glühlampen Elroyal, Elcorona, Elregent und Eldea,* Bamberg 1966.

Lindner GmbH, *Hauptkatalog* for Lindner's sixteen domestic distributor organisations, Bamberg 1960.

Lindner-Leuchten 1956, [sales catalogue], Bamberg 1956.

Lindner-Leuchten 1958, *Porzellan-Leuchten entworfen von Prof. W. Wagenfeld,* Bamberg 1958.

Lindner-Leuchten 1959, *Farbige Lindner-Leuchten für Bad und Küche,* Bamberg 1959.

Lindner-Leuchten 1963, *NWL-Leuchten, entworfen von Wilhelm Wagenfeld,* Bamberg 1963.

Lindner-Leuchten 1971, [concertina leaflet with *Systral* lighting system], Bamberg 1971.

Löffelhardt, Heinz (ed.), *Hermann Gretsch,* publ. Landesgewerbeamt Baden-Württemberg, Stuttgart 1953 (Schriften zur Formgebung, 2).

Lotz, Wilhelm, *Gold und Silber. Deutsche Goldschmiedearbeiten der Gegenwart,* Berlin 1926 (Bücher der Form, 3).

Lotz, Wilhelm, et al. (ed.), *Licht und Beleuchtung. Lichttechnische Fragen unter Berücksichtigung der Bedürfnisse der Architektur,* Berlin 1928 (Bücher der Form, 6).

Lotz, Wilhelm, *Wie richte ich meine Wohnung ein? Modern, gut, mit welchen Kosten?,* Berlin 1930.

Lotz, Wilhelm, *Reise zu den Glasbläsern. Beschauliches und Lehrhaftes von der Glasmacherei,* noted by Wilhelm Lotz, illustrated by Joachim Lutz, Zwickau 1938.

Lütken, Per, *Glas ist Leben,* Kopenhagen 1986.

Manske, Beate, "Zwei Lampen sind nie gleich. Wilhelm Wagenfeld in der Metallwerkstatt des Staatlichen Bauhauses Weimar," in: Klaus Weber (ed.), *Die Metallwerkstatt am Bauhaus,* Berlin 1992, pp. 79–91.

Manske, Beate, "Biografie Wilhelm Wagenfeld," in: *Wilhelm Wagenfeld: gestern, heute, morgen. Lebenskultur im Alltag,* publ. Wilhelm Wagenfeld Stiftung, Bremen 1995, pp. 10–37.

Manske, Beate, "'Fünfzehn Jahre waren nicht vergeblich'. Wilhelm Wagenfelds Mitarbeit in der WMF," in: Carlo Burschel and Beate Manske (eds.), *Zeitgemäss und zeitbeständig,* Bremen 1997, pp. 36–47.

Manske, Beate (ed.), *Original und Serienprodukt,* exh. cat. Wilhelm Wagenfeld Haus Bremen, Bremen 1999.

Manske, Beate, "Die Bauhaus-Leuchte von Wilhelm Wagenfeld," in: B. Manske (ed.), *Original und Serienprodukt,* Bremen 1999, pp. 34–55.

Manske, Beate, and Gudrun Scholz (eds.), *Täglich in der Hand. Industrieformen von Wilhelm Wagenfeld aus sechs Jahrzehnten,* Bremen 1987, 4th ed. 1998.

Marquart, Christian, *Industriekultur – Industriedesign. Ein Stück deutscher Wirtschafts- und Designgeschichte:*

Die Gründung des Verbands Deutscher Industriedesigner, Berlin 1993.

Mauder, Bruno, *Glaserzeugung und Glasveredelung,* Berlin 1942 (Werkstattbericht des Kunstdienstes, 11).

Meisterjahn, Michael, "Produktions- und firmengeschichtliche Aspekte der idell-Fertigung von Kaiser-Leuchten in den letzten Kriegsjahren," in: Peter M. Kleine and Klaus Struve (eds.), *Idee: Christian Dell. Einfache, zweckmässige Arbeitsleuchten aus Neheim,* Arnsberg 1995, pp. 50–61.

"Die Mitarbeit des Künstlers am industriellen Erzeugnis," in: *Die Form. Zeitschrift für gestaltende Arbeit,* vol. 5, 1930, no. 8, pp. 197–221.

Moholy-Nagy, László, "Metallwerkstatt. Vom Weinkrug zur Leuchte," in: Herbert Bayer, Walter Gropius and Ise Gropius (eds.), *Bauhaus 1919–1928* [Exh. cat. The Museum of Modern Art, New York 1938], 3rd ed. Stuttgart 1955, pp. 134–139.

Mumford, Lewis, "'Modern' als Handelsware," in: *Die Form. Zeitschrift für gestaltende Arbeit,* vol. 5, 1930, no. 8, p. 223.

Mundt, Barbara, Susanne Netzer and Ines Hettler, *Interieur + Design 1945–1960 in Deutschland,* Berlin 1993 (Bestandskatalog des Kunstgewerbemuseums, 19).

"[Obituary on Arthur Mehner]," in: *Die Schaulade. Europa-Journal für Porzellan, Keramik, Glas, Hausrat,* vol. 10, 1934, no. 1, p. 35.

Nemitz, Kurt, "Grusswort," in: Carlo Burschel and Beate Manske (eds.), *Zeitgemäss und zeitbeständig,* Bremen 1997, p. 7.

Neue Arbeiten der Bauhaus-Werkstätten, Munich 1925 (Bauhausbücher, 7).

"New Table Glass in Europe and America," in: *The Studio. A bibliography,* vol. 115, 1938, p. 196.

Nicolaisen, Dörte (ed.), *Das andere Bauhaus. Otto Bartning und die Staatliche Bauhochschule Weimar 1926–1930,* exh. cat. Bauhaus-Archiv Berlin and Kunstsammlungen zu Weimar, Berlin 1996.

Nicolaisen, Dörte, "Otto Bartning und die Staatliche Bauhochschule in Weimar 1926–1930," in: D. Nicolaisen (ed.), *Das andere Bauhaus. Otto Bartning und die Staatliche Bauhochschule Weimar 1926–1930,* Berlin 1996, pp. 16–23.

Nietzsche, Friedrich, *Sämtliche Werke. Kritische Studienausgabe,* 15 vols., eds. Giorgio Colli et al., Munich et al. 1980.

Opper, Dieter, "Lehrjahre und graphische Arbeiten," in: Beate Manske and Gudrun Scholz (eds.), *Täglich in der Hand. Industrieformen von Wilhelm Wagenfeld aus sechs Jahrzehnten,* Bremen 1987, 4th ed. 1998, pp. 206–211.

Pap, Gyula, "Zeit des Suchens und Experimentierens" [1978], in: *form + zweck*, vol. 11, 1979, no. 3, p. 57 (2. Bauhausheft).

Passarge, Walter, "Einleitung," in: *Wilhelm Wagenfeld. Ein Künstler in der Industrie,* exh. cat. Kunsthalle Mannheim, Mannheim 1957, unpaged.

Pese, Claus, "Serielle Massenproduktion," in: *Germanisches Nationalmuseum,* Munich 1985, pp. 579–585.

Pese, Claus, "Technik und Ästhetik," in: *Germanisches Nationalmuseum,* Munich 1985, pp. 617–620.

Petsch, Joachim, in cooperation with Wiltrud Petsch-Bahr, *Eigenheim und gute Stube. Zur Geschichte des bürgerlichen Wohnens. Städtebau – Architektur – Einrichtungsstile,* Cologne 1989.

Pfaender, Heinz G., "Die Werkstatt Wagenfeld aus der Sicht eines Dabeigewesenen," in: Beate Manske and Gudrun Scholz (eds.), *Täglich in der Hand. Industrieformen von Wilhelm Wagenfeld aus sechs Jahrzehnten,* Bremen 1987, 4th ed. 1998, pp. 250–254.

Pfaender, Heinz G., *Meine Zeit in der Werkstatt Wagenfeld. Tagebuch 1954–1957,* Hamburg 1998.

Ristow, Imke, *Artur Henning (1880–1959). Das gestalterische Werk und die Lehrtätigkeit an der Staatlichen Keramischen Fachschule Bunzlau,* Weimar 1999.

Die Schaulade. Europa-Journal für Porzellan, Keramik, Glas, Hausrat, vol. 10, 1934, no. 1; vol. 25, 1950, no. 1, no. 6.

Scheiffele, Walter, *Wilhelm Wagenfeld und die moderne Glasindustrie,* Stuttgart 1994.

Schmitt, Peter, *In memoriam Heinrich Löffelhardt (1901–1979). Design für die Glas- und Porzellan-Industrie,* leaflet of Badisches Landesmuseum Karlsruhe, Karlsruhe 1980.

Schmitt, Peter, "Braun-Feldwegs Beitrag zum Glasdesign der fünfziger und sechziger Jahre," in: Siegfried Gronert (ed.), *Form und Industrie. Wilhelm Braun-Feldweg,* Frankfurt 1998, pp. 26–47.

Schneider, Katja, *Burg Giebichenstein. Die Kunstgewerbeschule unter Leitung von Paul Thiersch und Gerhard Marcks 1915 bis 1933,* 2 vols., dissertation, Bonn 1988, Weinheim 1992.

"Schön, neu und zweckmässig. Zur Bauhaus-Ausstellung in Weimar im August 1923," in: *Fachblatt für Holzarbeiter,* 1923, November/December, p. 163.

Schreiber, Hermann, et al., *Die Rosenthal Story: Menschen, Kultur, Wirtschaft,* Düsseldorf and Vienna 1980.

Schwandt, Jörg, *WMF. Glas, Keramik, Metall 1925–1950,* Berlin 1980.

Siemens-Schuckert Werke, *Leuchten für Glühlampen und Mischlichtlampen,* catalogue and price list *inter alia* for interior, porcelain-glass and compression-moulded lamps, Berlin 1956.

Staatliche Bauhochschule Weimar 1929, Weimar 1929.

Struve, Klaus, "Licht – Beleuchtung – Arbeit. Sozial-, Kultur- und technikgeschichtliche Bedeutungen der Beleuchtung von Arbeit mit Hilfe des elektrischen Lichts," in: Jörn Christiansen (ed.), *Bremen wird hell: Hundert Jahre Leben und Arbeiten mit Elektrizität,* exh. cat. Bremer Landesmuseum für Kunst und Kulturgeschichte/Focke-Museum, Bremen 1993, pp. 290–299.

Struve, Klaus, "Leuchten und Licht im Arbeits- und Lebenszusammenhang – Anfänge einer Kultur der Beleuchtung mit elektrischem Licht," in: Peter M. Kleine and Klaus Struve (eds.), *Idee: Christian Dell. Einfache, zweckmässige Arbeitsleuchten aus Neheim,* Arnsberg 1995, pp. 26–37.

Struve, Klaus, and Peter Gohl, "Gutes Licht durch künstliche Beleuchtung," in: *arbeiten + lernen/Technik,* vol. 27, 1997, 3rd quarter, pp. 4–11.

Thormann, Olaf, "Die Leipziger Grassimessen," in: *Wilhelm Wagenfeld: gestern, heute, morgen. Lebenskultur im Alltag,* publ. Wilhelm Wagenfeld Stiftung, Bremen 1995.

Volkwein, Peter (ed.), *Walter Dexel. Design 1935–1946. Typographie 1923–1971,* Ingolstadt 2000.

Wagenfeld, Wilhelm, "Zu den Arbeiten der Metallwerkstatt. Service und Tischlampe," in: *Junge Menschen. Monatshefte für Politik, Kunst, Literatur und Leben aus dem Geiste der jungen Generation,* vol. 5, 1924, no. 8, p. 187 (special issue Bauhaus Weimar).

Wagenfeld, Wilhelm, "Die Beleuchtung von Wohnbauten in unserer Zeit," in: *Spiegellicht Blätter,* May 1931, no. 8, pp. 112–116 (Sonderheft der Zeiss Ikon Werke A.-G. Goerz-Werk, Berlin-Zehlendorf, zur Deutschen Bauausstellung in Berlin 1931).

Wagenfeld, Wilhelm, "Jenaer Glas," in: *Die Form. Zeitschrift für gestaltende Arbeit,* vol. 6, 1931, pp. 461–464.

Wagenfeld, Wilhelm, "Raum und Lichtträger," in: *Die Schaulade. Europa-Journal für Porzellan, Keramik, Glas, Hausrat,* vol. 8, 1932, no. 15, pp. 645 f.

Wagenfeld, Wilhelm, "Glasfachsimpeleien" [1937], in: W. Wagenfeld, *Wesen und*

Gestalt der Dinge um uns, Potsdam 1948, pp. 59–64.

Wagenfeld, Wilhelm, "Berliner Porzellan" [1938], in: Wagenfeld, *Wesen und Gestalt der Dinge um uns,* Potsdam 1948, pp. 44–50.

Wagenfeld, Wilhelm, "Kleine Betrachtungen" [1938], in: Wagenfeld, *Wesen und Gestalt der Dinge um uns,* Potsdam 1948, pp. 26–34.

Wagenfeld, Wilhelm, "Drei Jahre Aufbau und Entwicklung einer Entwurfswerkstatt in der Glasindustrie," in: *Glastechnische Berichte. Zeitschrift für Glaskunde,* vol. 17, 1939, no. 8, p. 247.

Wagenfeld, Wilhelm, "An den Rand geschrieben" [1940], in: Wagenfeld, *Wesen und Gestalt der Dinge um uns,* Potsdam 1948, pp. 24 f.

Wagenfeld, Wilhelm, "Künstlerische Formprobleme der Industrie" [1941], in: Wagenfeld, *Wesen und Gestalt der Dinge um uns,* Potsdam 1948, pp. 77–86.

Wagenfeld, Wilhelm, "'Formschön, Anständig und Gut'. Nachdenkliches über die Gestaltung unseres Hausrates," in: *Echo,* universal edition 1944, pp. 21–30.

Wagenfeld, Wilhelm, "Die Gegenwart in Architektur und Hausrat" [1946], in: Wagenfeld, *Wesen und Gestalt der Dinge um uns,* Potsdam 1948, pp. 87–121.

Wagenfeld, Wilhelm, "Von alltäglichen Dingen" [1947], in: Wagenfeld, *Wesen und Gestalt der Dinge um uns,* Potsdam 1948, pp. 35–43.

Wagenfeld, Wilhelm, *Wesen und Gestalt der Dinge um uns,* Potsdam 1948, unchanged reprint Worpsweder Verlag 1990.

[Wagenfeld, Wilhelm], *Deutsches Institut für industrielle Standardform,* proposed and commented by Wilhelm Wagenfeld, Stuttgart 1950.

Wagenfeld, Wilhelm, "Neues Hausgerät in USA. Rezension zur Stuttgarter Ausstellung: Industrie und Handwerk schaffen neues Hausgerät in USA, 1951," in: *Baukunst und Werkform. Monatsschrift für alle Gebiete der Gestaltung,* vol. 4, 1951, no. 5.

[Wagenfeld, Wilhelm], *leuchten aus putzler glas. Entworfen von Wagenfeld,* Düren, undated [1953].

Wagenfeld, Wilhelm, "Das Gebrauchsgerät und seine industrielle Formgebung," in: *Werk. Schweizer Monatsschrift für Architektur, Kunst und künstlerisches Gewerbe,* vol. 40, 1953, no. 12, p. 412.

[Wagenfeld, Wilhelm], "Prof. Wagenfeld über die Industrielle Formgebung," in: *Innendekoration/Architektur und Wohnform,* vol. 63, 1954/55, Fachliche Mitteilungen, no. 1, pp. 18–20.

Wagenfeld, Wilhelm, "Zweck und Sinn der künstlerischen Mitarbeit in Fabriken" [1957], in: *Wilhelm Wagenfeld. Vom Bauhaus in die Industrie. Ein Querschnitt durch vier Jahrzehnte künstlerischer Mitarbeit in der Industrie,* Stuttgart 1965.

Wagenfeld, Wilhelm, "Industriemesse contra Museum," in: *Wilhelm Wagenfeld. Ein Künstler in der Industrie,* exh. cat. Kunsthalle Mannheim, Mannheim, 1957, unpaged.

Wagenfeld, Wilhelm, "Industrieerzeugnisse gestalten ist keine Hüllenmacherei," in: *Schweizerische Handelszeitung,* 24 November 1960.

Wagenfeld, Wilhelm, "Das Staatliche Bauhaus – die Jahre in Weimar," in: *form. Zeitschrift für Gestaltung,* no. 37, 1967, pp. 17–19.

Wagenfeld, Wilhelm, *Notizen: Künstlerischer Leiter der Vereinigten Lausitzer Glaswerke AG,* typescript, 1977.

Wagenfeld, Wilhelm, "Die Geschichte meiner Bauhaus-Lampe," in: *Bauhaus-Lampe 1924,* brochure of Tecnolumen company, Bremen 1980, unpaged.

Wagenfeld, Wilhelm, "Bauhochschule Weimar. Beginn meiner Industriearbeit," in: Beate Manske and Gudrun Scholz (eds.), *Täglich in der Hand. Industrieformen von Wilhelm Wagenfeld aus sechs Jahrzehnten,* Bremen 1987, 4th ed. 1998, pp. 28–30.

Wagenfeld, Wilhelm, "Notizen. Eine Chronologie nicht realisierter Entwürfe," in: Carlo Burschel and Beate Manske (eds.), *Zeitgemäss und zeitbeständig,* Bremen 1997, pp. 30–35.

Weber, Klaus, "'Wir alle müssen zum Handwerk zurück!' Die keramische Werkstatt des Bauhauses in Dornburg (1920–1925)," in: K. Weber (ed.), *Keramik und Bauhaus. Geschichte und Wirkungen der keramischen Werkstatt des Bauhauses,* exh. cat. Bauhaus-Archiv Berlin, Berlin 1989, pp. 10–29.

Weber, Klaus (ed.), *Die Metallwerkstatt am Bauhaus,* exh. cat. Bauhaus-Archiv Berlin, Berlin 1992.

Weber, Klaus, "Sachliche Bauart. Höchste Qualitätsarbeit. Christian Dell als Lehrer, Silberschmied und Gestalter," in: K. Weber (ed.), *Die Metallwerkstatt am Bauhaus,* Berlin 1992, pp. 9–41.

Weber, Klaus, "'Dienende Geräte'. Die Metallwerkstatt der Bauhochschule," in: Dörte Nicolaisen (ed.), *Das andere Bauhaus. Otto Bartning und die Staatliche Bauhochschule Weimar 1926–1930,* Berlin 1996, pp. 105–121.

Weimar Bau- und Wohnungskunst GmbH, catalogues on lamps and metal appliances for the period 1929 – about 1933.

Wilhelm Wagenfeld, exh. cat. Neue Sammlung des Bayerischen Nationalmuseums, Munich 1939.

Wilhelm Wagenfeld. Ein Künstler in der Industrie, exh. cat. Kunsthalle Mannheim, Mannheim 1957.

Wilhelm Wagenfeld. 30 jahre künstlerische mitarbeit in der industrie, exh. cat. Munich 1961.

Wilhelm Wagenfeld. Vom Bauhaus in die Industrie. Ein Querschnitt durch vier Jahrzehnte künstlerischer Mitarbeit in der Industrie, exh. cat. Landesgewerbeamt Baden-Württemberg, Stuttgart 1965.

Wilhelm Wagenfeld. 50 Jahre Mitarbeit in Fabriken, exh. cat. Kunstgewerbemuseum Köln, Cologne 1973.

Wilhelm Wagenfeld: Handzeichnungen und Druckgraphik, exh. cat. Barkenhoff Worpswede, Bremen 1996.

Winter, Bruno, *Wilhelm Wagenfelds Leuchtenentwürfe,* dissertation, department of Industrial Design, Hochschule für bildende Künste, Hamburg 1992.

WMF-Geschäftsbericht, Geislingen on Steige, 25 July 1947; 9 November 1949; 1950–1953; 1978.

WMF-Mitteilungen. Zeitschrift der Württembergischen Metallwarenfabrik für den Fachhandel, 1953, no. 3/4; 1954, no. 2/3; 1956, nos. 2/3.

WMF-Nachrichten.

WMF-Spiegel.

Wolsdorff, Christian, "Die Bauhaus-Lampe. Versuch einer Rekonstruktion ihrer Entstehungsgeschichte," in: *Design – Formgebung für jedermann, Typen und Prototypen,* exh. cat. Kunstgewerbemuseum Zürich, Zurich 1983, pp. 48–55.

Wolsdorff, Christian, "Designer im Widerspruch," in: *m. d. Möbel interior design,* 1984, no. 4, pp. 27–30.

Württembergische Metallwarenfabrik, *Sortimentskataloge,* Geislingen an der Steige.

Zeitschrift für gewerblichen Rechtsschutz und Urheberrecht (GRUR) 1999, nos. 8/9.

["Zwischenbericht der Metallwerkstatt vom 18. August 1923, Thüringisches Staatsarchiv, Staatliches Bauhaus 1976"], in: *Bauhaus 3,* cat. 9 of Galerie am Sachsenplatz Leipzig, Leipzig 1978, pp. 15 f.

639. Das Fürstenberger Service, sales brochure, Fürstenberg, undated [1934].

Photo Credits

Front cover
Joachim Fliegner, Bremen

Back cover
Wilhelm Wagenfeld Stiftung, Bremen

Front end paper
Wilhelm Wagenfeld Stiftung, Bremen

Frontispiece, p. 4
Ulrich Mack, Hamburg

Back end paper
Wilhelm Wagenfeld Stiftung, Bremen

Siegfried Gronert, pp. 12–23
1, 6 Bauhaus-Universität Weimar
2, 3, 7, 11, 15, 17 Wilhelm Wagenfeld Stiftung, Bremen
4, 5, 13, 14 *Staatliche Bauhochschule Weimar 1929,* Weimar 1929
8, 10 Germanisches Nationalmuseum, Nuremberg
9, 12 Kunstsammlungen zu Weimar
16 Badisches Landesmuseum Karlsruhe
18 Staatliche Kunstsammlungen Dresden, Kunstgewerbemuseum
19, 21 Deutsches Schloss- und Beschläge-museum Velbert
20 *Die Form,* vol. 6, 1931
22, 23 Bauhaus-Archiv Berlin

Beate Manske, pp. 24–37
1, 3, 8, 9 Wilhelm Wagenfeld Stiftung, Bremen, photograph: Joachim Fliegner, Bremen
2 Private collection
4 Kunstsammlungen zu Weimar, photograph: Klaus G. Beyer, Weimar
5–7 Galerie Ulrich Fiedler, Cologne
10, 11 "Licht und Beleuchtung" collection, Klaus Struve, Oldenburg, photographs: Joachim Fliegner, Bremen
12, 13 Bauhaus-Universität, Weimar
14 Deutsche Post AG

Walter Scheiffele, pp. 38–45
1, 7–10, 12, 13 Company archives of the Jenaer Glassworks, Jena
2 *Tschechische Kunst der 20er + 30er Jahre. Avantgarde und Tradition,* exh. cat. Mathildenhöhe Darmstadt, 2 vols, Darmstadt 1988/89, vol. 1, p. 413
3 *Die Form,* vol. 7, no. 1, 1932, p. 25
4, 11 Wilhelm Wagenfeld Stiftung, Bremen
5, 6 Company archives of the Jenaer Glass-works, Mainz, © 2000 bei VG Bild-Kunst, Bonn

Walter Scheiffele, pp. 46–65
1–4, 6–8, 11, 16, 18–22, 25 Wilhelm Wagenfeld Stiftung, Bremen
5 Collection of Luiza and Walter Vitt, Cologne
9 Grassimuseum, Leipzig
10 Works archives of Iittala, Finland
12 Museum Boijmans Van Beuningen, Rotterdam
13 *Czechoslovakian Glass (1359–1980),* New York 1981, unpaged
14 Glass archives of Alfons Hannes
15 Property of Margarete Süssmuth
17, 23 Property of Walter Scheiffele
24 Ernst Neufert, *Industriebauten,* Wiesbaden and Berlin 1973, p. 16
26 Property of Karl Mey Jr.

Klaus Struve, pp. 66–85
1, 3–14, 17–21 Wilhelm Wagenfeld Stiftung, Bremen
2 "Licht und Beleuchtung" collection, Klaus Struve, Oldenburg, photograph: Stoll
15 Property of Walter Scheiffele
16 "Licht und Beleuchtung" collection, Klaus Struve, Oldenburg, photograph: Fliegner

Peter Schmitt, pp. 86–101
1 Die Neue Sammlung, Staatliches Museum für angewandte Kunst, Munich
2 Angermuseum, Erfurt, photograph: Rein-hard Hentze, Halle
3, 5, 7, 8, 11–13, 16–18, 20 Wilhelm Wagen-feld Stiftung, Bremen
4 Arzberg porcelain factory, photograph: Willi Moegle, Stuttgart
6 Kunstsammlungen zu Weimar, photograph: Dressler
9 Bröhan-Museum, Landesmuseum für Jugendstil, Art deco und Funktionalismus, Berlin, photograph: Martin Adam
10 *Deutsche Warenkunde,* Berlin 1939, reproduction photograph: Staatsbibliothek zu Berlin, Preussischer Kulturbesitz
14, 15 *Die Schaulade,* vol. 25, no. 1, 1950, reproduction photograph: Badisches Landesmuseum Karlsruhe
19 Rosenthal Archiv, Selb

Bernd Altenstein, pp. 102–104
1–3 Wilhelm Wagenfeld Stiftung, Bremen

Colour plates pp. 105–120
Joachim Fliegner, Bremen

Rüdiger Joppien, pp. 122–149
1–6, 9, 10, 12, 16, 18, 22, 24, 26–30, 34, 35 Wilhelm Wagenfeld Stiftung, Bremen
7 Archiv Wilhelm Wagenfeld, Stuttgart
8, 11, 20, 32 Museum für Angewandte Kunst, Cologne, photographs: Rheinisches Bildarchiv
13, 15, 19, 25 Museum für Kunst und Gewerbe, Hamburg, photographs: Maria Thrun
14 Finnish Glass Museum, Riihimäki
17, 21, 33 Kunstgewerbemuseum Berlin, photographs: Saturia Linke
23 Marianne Aav and Nina Stritzler-Levine (eds.), *Finnish Modern Design. Utopian Ideals and Everyday Realities 1930–1997,* The Bard Graduate Center for Studies in the Decorative Arts, New Haven and London, 1998
31 Badisches Landesmuseum, Karlsruhe

Carlo Burschel/Heinz Scheiffele, pp. 150–175
1–8, 10–15, 17, 19–22, 26, 28–30 WMF/Geislingen an der Steige
9, 16, 18, 23–25, 27 Wilhelm Wagenfeld Stiftung, Bremen

Volker Albus, pp. 176–185
1–9 Wilhelm Wagenfeld Stiftung, Bremen
10 Wilhelm Wagenfeld Stiftung, Bremen, photograph: Franz Lazi, Stuttgart
11, 12, 15 Works photographs
13 Volker Albus
14 Stefan Rother

Biografie Wagenfeld pp. 186–193
1–16 Wilhelm Wagenfeld Stiftung, Bremen

Prof. Volker Albus (1949)
Graduated as an architect; also furniture/interior designs since 1982. Professor for product design at Staatliche Hochschule für Gestaltung, Karlsruhe, since 1994. Active as a publicist, exhibition planner and designer. Co-editor of the journal *formdiskurs – Zeitschrift für Design und Theorie;* regular contributor to *Design Report.*

Prof. Bernd Altenstein (1943)
Studied sculpture, art education and art history. Academic assistant at Technische Universität Braunschweig, 1970 to 1975. Appointed professor at Hochschule für Künste Bremen, 1975. Member of Deutscher Werkbund, Darmstadt Secession and Künstlersonderbund Deutschland. Numerous exhibitions and works in public collections.

Prof. Dr. Tilmann Buddensieg (1928)
Studied art history and archaeology. Professor of art history at the Freie Universität in Berlin, 1968 to 1976; in Bonn, 1976 to 1993; associate lecturer at Humboldt-Universität Berlin since1995. Publications on early medieval art, on the model of Greek and Roman antiquity in the Renaissance, and since 1970 chiefly on the architecture of Berlin and industrial culture in the 19th and 20th centuries.

Dr. Carlo Burschel (1962)
Diploma in business studies; graduated as a sociologist. Head of environment management at the German environmental foundation, Deutsche Bundesstiftung Umwelt, Osnabrück, 1995 to early 2000. Deputy director, German competence centre for sustainable management/Deutsches Kompetenzzentrum für Nachhaltiges Wirtschaften (Private Universität Witten/ Herdecke). Publisher of *Lehr- und Handbücher zur Ökologischen Unternehmensführung und Umweltökonomie*, Munich and Vienna. Publications on "environment managament" and on the works of Wilhelm Wagenfeld for WMF AG.

Prof. Dr. Siegfried Gronert (1946)
Studied art history, philosophy and media sciences. Professor for the history and theory of design at the faculty of design, Bauhaus-Universität Weimar. Publications on the history of German design in the 20th century.

Kathrin Hager M. A. (1967)
Graduated in applied cultural studies. Involvement in exhibition projects in Lüneburg, Bremen and Hamburg. Member of staff at the Wilhelm Wagenfeld Stiftung, Bremen, since 1999.

Dr. Rüdiger Joppien (1946)
Studied art history, theatre studies and English. From 1977 to 1986, member of staff at the Museum of Arts and Crafts/ Kunstgewerbemuseum in Cologne. Curator at the Museum für Kunst und Gewerbe Hamburg, in the Jugendstil and Modern Department, since 1986. Publications on arts and crafts, design and photography.

Beate Manske M. A. (1946)
Studied art history, archaeology and history before working freelance on exhibitions and publications on 19th and 20th century art and design. Managing director of the Wilhelm Wagenfeld Stiftung, Bremen, since 1993.

Heinz Scheiffele (1942)
Designer at WMF's own studio, having worked in WMF's product development department since 1960. Responsible for the WMF archive since 1990 (covering production from 1870 to the present).

Dr. Walter Scheiffele (1946)
Studied cultural history and graphic design. Lectureships at schools of art and colleges – Hochschule der Künste Berlin, Burg Giebichenstein Halle and the Fachhochschule Anhalt/Dessau. Publications on design and cultural history.

Peter Schmitt M. A. (1939)
Studied literature and education. Text book editor for art education, design and architecture at Otto Maier Verlag, Ravensburg. From 1974, director of the office for the augmentation of teaching design in schools at the Badisches Landesmuseum Karlsruhe; deputy director of the Badisches Landesmuseum Karlsruhe, since 1990, with responsibility for collections and exhibitions in the field of arts and crafts and design. Publications especially on modern glassmaking, stained glass and ceramics.

Prof. Dr. Klaus Struve (1942)
Trained as a stonemason; structural engineer; studied education for vocational schools; tutor for vocational training, vocational education and vocational rehabilitation of handicapped and disadvantaged young people and adults at the Carl von Ossietzky Universität Oldenburg. Professor for Vocational Education at University of Hamburg since 1999, with emphasis on the didactics of civil engineering, wood and plastics technology, colour and paint technology and interior design.

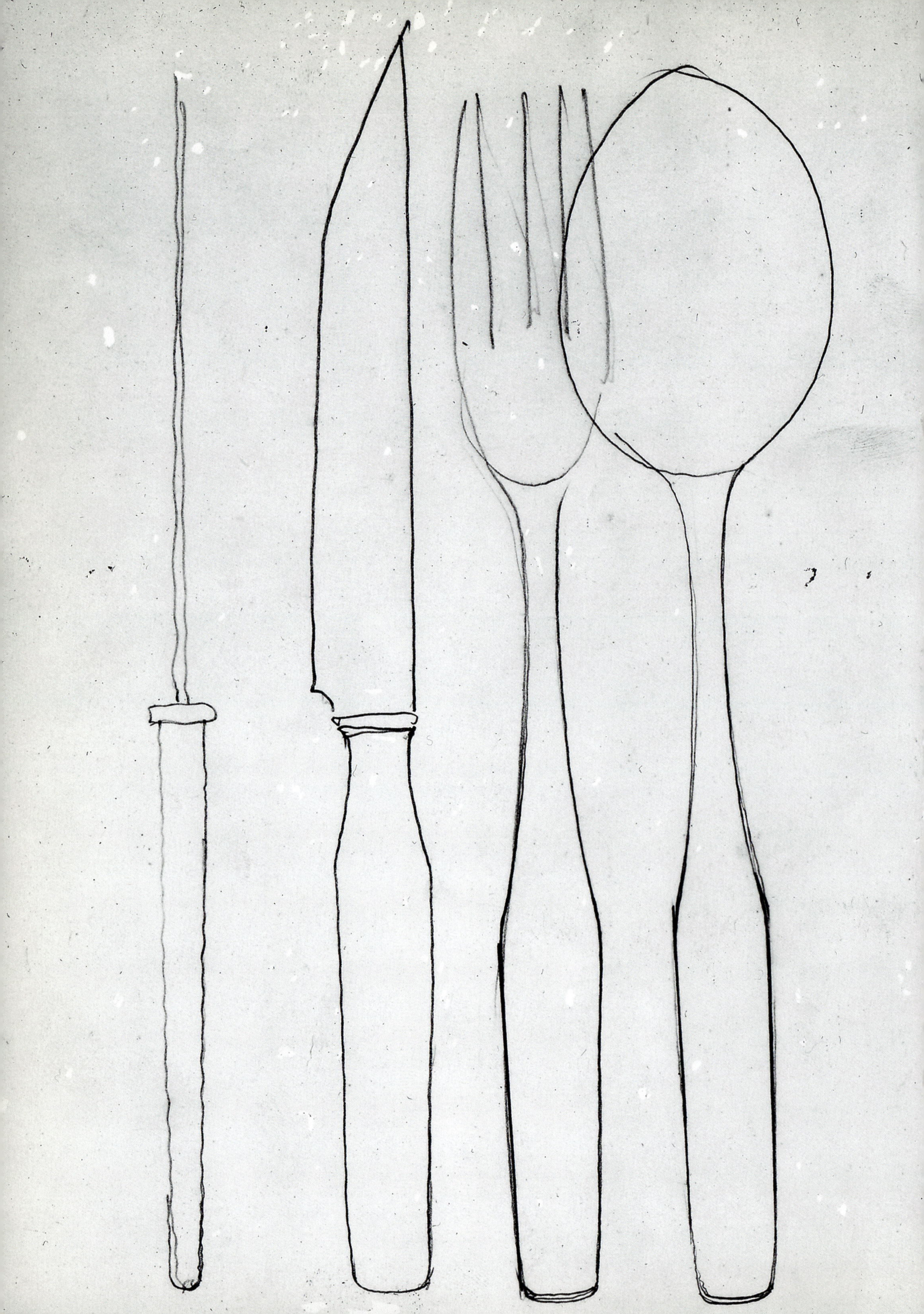

WITHDRAWN

DATE DUE
DATE DUE

3 0380 00010679 9